Through
Wolf's Eyes

Through Wolf's Eyes

To Shearye,

Best Wishes!

Enjoy this Book.

Wayne R. Wolford Sr.

May 12, 2013

Wayne R. Wolford Sr

To order additional copies of this book, contact:
Xlibris Corporation
1-888-795-4274
www.Xlibris.com
Orders@Xlibris.com
93250

Contents

Chapter 1

Warren County History

Blacks were brought into the McMinnville area from all over the world in the 1800's as slaves, approximately 1807, but tracing the roots of one's past is almost impossible.

After viewing the Smithsonian Institute in Washington, D.C. in the year 2001, my attention was drawn, by my wife, to the status of slaves and frees Blacks on display in the mid-state of Tennessee in the 1800's. There was quite a difference between freed Blacks and their slave brothers. The ratio was 1 to 500. Each lighter dot on the display represented 2,000 freed Blacks, compared to the darker shaded dots that had the same value. There was only 1 light dot in the 4 surrounding counties. Looking at the entire state, Tennessee was definitely a slave state. The display was covered with darker shaded dots.

Going back before the Civil War, Plantation owners enjoyed the luxury of buying and selling human beings at the livestock sales, much like a pimp does using women in the same way. Records show that Blacks were sold for as much as $400 and $500 each at the local slave/livestock sales.

After the Civil War in 1863, the Emancipation Proclamation was signed. Many Blacks fled to the North in order to get away from some of the rough treatment and grief they had learned to endure in the Southern states, more so than the Northern states.

Much like today with our job situation, we just don't or won't attempt to take a chance and reach for our dreams and goals. Education plays a major role now and back then.

The Northern states seemed to promise a better life, and a fairer treatment. The families that received their freedom soon ran into hard times, because they did not know how to provide for the livelihood of their families. They had to learn how to be on their own, much like a child leaving home for the very first time, and if they couldn't read nor write, that was a terrible misfortune.

Warren County had to start again after a bloody four-year Civil War among family members.

There are some today that want this war to live on. When family problems arise, families should settle them and put them aside as a learning experience, not to dwell on the problems continuously, but to learn cultures and explore life.

This beautiful county was stripped of almost everything during the conflict here, so with basically nothing to work with, Warren County put it together and worked hand in hand with the skills of brotherhood.

Education was limited because Blacks had very few teachers in the area at this time. The 1870's was a time for one room school houses, wood burning stoves, water from the well or the creek, outhouses, oil lamps to see by, all grades in the same room, take your lunch to school, and get there the best way you can.

Everybody was related in some form or fashion, Blacks, Whites, Indians, and other nationalities, even though none of the groups wanted to claim the other, It's a fact! We are all family.

Last names were common among slaves and owners. If slaves were owned, they would be renamed after the purchase. Women can relate to that once they get married, they take the man's last name and lose their own in most cases.

Later Blacks gained their freedom married under 'Common Law' and legalized their marriages by getting licenses through a minister, or the justice of the peace, so that they could get their real married names.

In the late 1800's Blacks would start moving to and developing small communities in Warren County such as: Leesburg, Bolden Green, Martin Charge, Hiawassee, Viola, Brown Town, Mud Creek, Rock Island, Corinth, Allisonia, Cummings Chapel, Pleasant Hill, the East and North sides of McMinnville, and several others.

It is interesting, while many Blacks had skills of some kind, there were not enough good jobs to be found, so many people that had exceptional skills and a good education decided to leave the area to get a fair chance in society. Those who chose to stay here were forced to work in the regular routine. There were minimal jobs for Blacks such as: house work, washing clothes, yard work, lumberyard, janitorial, nursery, and mule skinning (teamsters).

After the railroad was completed, through McMinnville around 1886, many Blacks turned to the lumberyards and farming after working on the railroad.

Among the less glamorous jobs of Blacks, some are taken for granted. The distilling and bootlegging of alcoholic beverages are examples of this. This was just another way of providing for the family. Times were rough, and funds were short.

The loaning of money was a hard thing in the Black community. Going to the bank was almost an impossible task, once more talking to someone about a loan. Blacks just didn't receive loans from the banks. Storeowners, Bootleggers, Restaurants, and Pool Hall owners gave most loans.

Chapter 2

Warren County Slave
Sales and Owners

1814 Warranty Deeds
Book (pg.90) . . . . (A)

Bill of sale from Lockhart to Harris $475.00
Negro Man; (Luke) Age: 30 yrs. old.

Luke was sold from Thomas K. Harris to Berry Lockhart on February 8, 1810 in Warren County.

Pg. 99 . . . . William Martin 'Will' 15 yrs. old $400.00
Valentine over to William Martin on June 1809.

1824 Warranty Deeds (E)
(Pg. 5) . . . . (2) slaves 'Ginny' 28 yrs. and youngest child 'Hannah' 5 months old . . . . $475.00.

Sandy Owen from George W. Lyles.
(Copy made) . . . . January 14, 1924.

Book (A) 1814 Warranty Deeds
Pg. 104 . . . 'Jo' (slave) 22 yrs. old $500.00
Richard Burge to Frank Burge . . . . December 12, 1809.

Pg. 104 . . . Sale: (1) Man 23 yrs. old 'Pete' $500.00
Richard Burge to Frank Burge . . . . December 12, 1809.

Pg. 105 . . . . (Slave) 'Lyolsa' . . . . 45 yrs. old . . . $200.00
Richard Burge to Frank Burge . . . . December 12, 1809.

Warren County . . . Warranty Book (A) 1814
Pg. 105 (Slave) 'Bob' . . . . 15 yrs. old $400.00
Richard Burge to Frank Burge . . . December 12, 1809.

Pg. 106 (Slave) 'Sand' . . . . 22 yrs. old $500.00
Richard Burge to Frank Burge . . . December 12, 1809.

Pg. 106. (Slave) . . . Girl . . . 'Buckie' . . . . 9 yrs. old . . . $400.00
Richard Burge to Frank Burge . . . . Dec 12, 1809.

Pg. 421 . . . (Slave) 'Judy' 35 yrs. old $250.00
George Nelson to James Clendenen . . . July 1813.

Warren County Deeds . . . Book 'B' . . . 1814
Pg. 27 (1) (Slave) 'Nan' (Woman) $242.00
John Hammon to Leroy Harmon . . . . October 22 1812.

Pg. 28 . . . (3 Slaves) . . . 'Pete,' . . . 'Hannah' . . . & 'Nan'
John Hammon to Leroy Harmon . . . October 22, 1812

Pg. 66 (Slave) "Givens' . . . 11 yrs. old $500.00
John Armstrong to William Smartt . . . . May 20, 1813.

Pg. 64 (Slave) 'Larry' (Man) 21 yrs. old $372.41
John Armstrong to William C. Smartt . . . March 22, 1813.

Pg. 88 . . . (3 Slaves) . . . Phillie 24 yrs. old (Mom);
                                  Allick 4 yrs. old (Son);
                                  Charlotie 2 yrs. old Daughter) $533.33

John Armstrong to William C. Smartt . . . November 17, 1813.

Pg. 89 (2 slaves) . . . 'Mollie' & child 'Ayes' $500.00
John Hammon Sr. to John Hammon Jr. on December 5, 1813.

Pg. 113 (1) (Slave man); 'Dick' . . . 20 yrs. old
Owner; Thomas Wilcher . . . . March 2, 1815

Pg. 214 (1 Woman)
Owner . . . . Joseph Colvelle . . . October 13, 1815.

Pg. 228. Sale of Mullato girl. 'Hannah' 4 yrs. old . . . $100.00
'Morning White' to Charles Hunter . . . . December 18, 1815.

Pg. 228 . . . Arron Higginbotham sold slave named
Higginbotham . . . .
July 11, 1816.

Pg. 351 . . . Sold and delivered to George Hammons from Molly
Jinkins . . . (1) Slave woman . . . 'Phillis' 55 yrs. old . . . $300.00 . . .
September 2, 1818.

Slavery

In order to fully grasp the magnitude of our current problems, we must reopen the books on the events of slavery. Our objective should be to cry stale tears for the past, nor rekindle old hatreds for past injustices. Instead, we should seek to enlighten our path of today by better understanding where and how the lights were turned out yesterday. We've got to understand that slavery should be viewed as a starting point for understanding the Black American psyche, and not as an end point.

The Africans were made indentured servants (giving service for a stated length of time, usually seven years) to the planters or farmers who had traded for them.

There were also White and Native American indentured servants in Warren County, and like the Africans, they received no wages. They were bound to their owners just as slaves were to masters.

Indentured servants grew to hate their lives and began to run away. The Native American indentured servants knew the countryside. They would vanish within the forests and find their way back to their own communities, often taking the former Africans and the White servants with them.

A child born of a slave mother inherited her status. If the mother had bought her freedom, the child was born free.

It is difficult to believe, but throughout the plantation period there were free blacks as well as slaves in the county. Their position was always unstable and dangerous, for at any time they could be sold back into bondage. Some white slave owners hated and feared freed blacks, who they believed set a bad example for their slaves.

Work

Slavery was forced labor; the work of a slave was "from day clear to first dark." The day's toil would begin just before sunrise and would end at dusk. Except for certain chores, Sunday work was uncommon but not unheard of if the crops required it. On Saturdays slaves were often permitted to quit the fields at noon. They were also given holidays, most commonly at Christmas and after crops were laid by. Work was a daily chore, beginning in early childhood and continuing until death or total disability. The slave was forced to work under the threat of abuse or even death, but the work was not for the purpose of providing for his or her needs. The work was for the slave master. The slave would neither profit from his or her labor nor enjoy the benefits of their labor. A good crop did not improve the life a slave, nor their family or the slave community. Instead, it improved the life and the community of the slave master. Work came to be despised as any punishment is despised. Work became hated, as does any activity which accomplishes no reward for the doer. Work became identified with slavery. Even today, Black American uses a slang expression which refers to a job as a "slave" communicates this painful connection. Many Blacks became over dependent on welfare as a way of life. This too can be related to the historical root of associating work with slavery. Black slang, songs, jokes, and attitudes, transmitted from one generation to the next, preserve these reactions as if they were acquired yesterday.

Property

The slave was permitted to own nothing or very little. Certainly, property and the finer material objects such as clothes, jewelry etc., were reserved for the slave master. Slaves wore shabby and insufficient apparel made from some variety of cheap "Negro cloth."

The slave master's fine house, beautiful landscaping; exquisite clothes and objects were associated with his power and status. In the same way that the slave looked upon his master with hatred and resentment, he also resented and envied the masters passions because those possessions were associated with freedom and power to direct one's life, family and community.

Slavery produced an unnatural attraction to material objects. The cast off hat or dress passed down from the "Big House" to the cabin, became a symbol of pride and status. By wearing "Massah's" old hat or "Missis" old dress, one could play at being Massah or Missis for a few moments.

Leadership

Probably one of the most destructive influences, which have grown out of slavery, is the disrespect of Black American leadership. The allegory is seen throughtout nature that the most certain way to destroy life is to cut off the head. This is especially true as a social principle. One of the things that was systematically done during slavery was the elimination of control of any emerging head or leader. Such heads were identified as "uppity or arrogant," and were branded as the kind of troublemakers who were destined to bring trouble to the slave community. The entire slave community was often required to carry an extra burden, or deprived of some small privilege, because of such "uppity slaves."

The Clown

Another serious handicap which slaves inherited from slavery is the African American clown. One of the primary forms of remaining in favor with the slave master by the slave was to provide entertainment for the master and his household. The slave owner prided himself in his superiority by being entertained by the slave. The jester, the clown, or the fool, as the inferior one who was responsible for making his superior laugh. Clowning became one of the primary ways that the violent and abusive slave master could be controlled and manipulated.

Personal Inferiority

A systematic process of creating a sense of inferiority in the proud African was necessary in order to maintain them as slaves. This was done by humiliating and dehumanizing acts such as public beatings, parading them on slave blocks unclothed, and inspecting them as thought they were cattle or horses. They were forbidden to communicate with other slaves which would have been a basis for maintaining some self-respect. Young children were separated from their mothers because the mother's love might cultivate some self-respect in the child.

Cleanliness and personal effectiveness are fairly essential in the maintenance of self-respect. The slaves were kept filthy and the very nature of physical restraints over long periods of time began to develop in the people a sense of their helplessness. The loss of the ability to even clean one's body and to shield oneself from a blow began to teach the slave that he should have no self-respect.

These things, combined with the insults, the loss of cultural traditions, rituals, family life, religion, and even names, served to cement the loss of self-respect. As the slave master exalted himself and enforced respect of him-self, he was increasingly viewed as superior to the slaves. The slave was forced to bow and bend to the slave owner and treat him as a god. With the image of a Caucasian man as God, and with all kinds of images of Africans as dirty and only half human, it was inevitable that a sense of inferiority would grow into the African-American personality.

Community Division

One of the most serious disturbances of community development from the slavery period is "community division." The age-old pattern of divide-and-conquer was utilized with so many other tricks in order to destroy the black American community life.

All kinds of devices were utilized in order to make sure that the slaves would not be able to come together. There were major social divisions constructed by the master. The house workers and the field workers constituted the major separation among the slaves. The house slaves were permitted to wear better clothes, eat slightly better foods and, most importantly, they were permitted to take care of the personal needs of the master and his household.

The slaves who were the illegitimate off spring of the master were usually given greater privileges. Along with other house slaves, they were delegated authority over the field hands of the master.

The most piteous device for seeking status in the slave community was that of boasting about the white ancestors or talking pride in a light complexion. In the eyes of the whites, the "Mulatto" was tainted as much as the "pure" Negro, and as hopelessly tied to the inferior caste.

The slaves with certain skills such as ironworkers, blacksmiths or carpenters, were separated from the common field hands and made to believe that they were something quite special.

The Family

The family is the very foundation of healthy, constructive, and personal and community life. The destruction or damage to the African American was accomplished by destroying marriage, fatherhood and motherhood. Slaveholders believed the institution of marriage was that the slave has no rights; of course, he or she cannot have the rights of a husband, a wife. The slave is a chattel (an item of moveable personal property) does not marry. The slave is not ranked among sentient beings, but among things, and things are not married.

The African American man was evaluated by his ability to endure strenuous work and to produce children. He was viewed by the slave master as a stud and a workhorse. The stronger and more children he sired, the greater the expansion of the master's slave-holdings and the greater was his financial worth.

The African American woman was valued primarily as a breeder or sexual receptacle to show the capacity to have healthy children.

Émancipation Proclamation

The Emancipation Proclamation was drafted in 1862 and put into effect on January 1, 1863. It freed about a million slaves in the states and parts that had seceded from the Union and were in rebellion. It exempted Tennessee and parishes around New Orleans because they were then considered under federal government control.*

*Some 3 million slaves in states bordering on the North and not in rebellion (Missouri, Kentucky, and counties of western Virginia, Maryland, and Delaware) were not affected by the Proclamation and were not yet free.

Afterword

With the ratification of the Thirteenth Amendment to the Constitution on December 18, 1865, there was freedom, finally, for all of the 4 million African Americans. There would be no more bondage, no more running away. Slavery was abolished in Warren County and America. And never had humankind seen freedom given at once to so many.

What do you do with freedom? The free people wondered, but when they had time of their own to think about it, they knew. Some Warren Countians thought they would own the land of their former so-called masters. Many of the great mansions now stood deserted. The slave quarter cabins were largely empty as well.

The Blacks knew they would have to learn to defend themselves. They were free to have rain soak them day and night as they lay unsheltered. Nothing had ever come easy for them. And liberty would not come without hardship. If they ran now, it was only from disease and starvation, and from the race haters.

In 1866, the Civil Rights Acts were passed, giving African Americans citizenship and protecting them from oppressive laws and codes.

After the Civil War, African Americans were able to find the best in life. They were free to seek education and to found their own universities. They were free to find jobs, to live together in families, to own land, to farm, to make homes, to cook and clean for themselves, to raise babies that were their own, to paint, to write, to sing, to read. And they were free to defend themselves as, increasing; attempts were made to reenslave them.

They did all of these things almost as soon as the war was over. For 200 and some odd years some have continued to do so.

Chapter 3

Huddleston—Jennings Post 208

Part 1

Huddleston—Jennings
American Legion Post #208
Of the
American Legion Department of Tennessee

Founded in 1943. The American Legion Post 208 was erected in 1945, by Roy Spencer. His first cousins sold him the land (Ellick and Ethel Grayson) in the Leesburg Community for $175.00. The Trustees for Post 208 at this time were: Lawson Gwynn, Fred Nowlin and Thomas Irvin. The First National Bank has been handling the Posts funds for as long as anyone can remember. The remains of the old post home still stand, in a run down lot in the Leesburg community. Post 208 started its operation in 1945, as far as a permanent location for functions. Meetings, dances, fellowship, gatherings all took place at this historic location. After the war the club came into full swing. On any given Saturday night the "Hall" was accommodating anywhere from 150 to 200 people, whether it is spring, summer, winter or fall.

The American legion post 208 was run under bylaws that met at least once every three months. There was an "Executive Committee" of at least four members. Elections were done annually at the June meeting. The government and management were entrusted to the 'Executive Committee'. This committee hired employees to help run the club, later post members were selected to run the operation in order to save money. Such members as; Franklin Womack, Charles 'Muggin' Martin, and Elmer Martin Sr. (to name a few.)

Much of the past history of Post 208 is long gone. The Post Commanders, vice Commanders, Post Adjutants, Finance officers, Post Historians, and post Chaplains, and Sergeant-at-Arms are few in numbers today. Accounts of this post had been packed away, are thrown away. Only a few accounts were saved by members and the State of Tennessee office in Nashville, Tennessee.

This Post was known for its involvement throughout the Black community. Americanism, ceremonials, children and youth programs, veteran affairs, and last but not least the American Legion Auxiliary. These ladies served their country and community well.

The Post inspired patriotism and good citizenship, and always having activities for community and civic betterment. When a loved one had left this earth the post was concerned and presented burial rituals. Laboring for the betterment of the Veterans child, to act as intermediary for a needy child of a war veteran.

The fulfillment of the Legion's pledge that "no child of a war veteran shall be in need of the necessities of life, and a square deal for every child".

Memberships have never been a serious problem, until recent years (1980's-1990's), fewer veterans got involved with activities. Only a few good people were able, are had time to indulge in functions.

The Auxiliary was in charge of the visiting and comforting of members and their familiars when sick or bereaved, and visiting ex-servicemen and women in nearby hospitals such as the Nashville and Murfreesboro Veterans hospitals. There were times when the Auxiliary invited Veterans from Nashville and Murfreesboro to come to McMinnville to enjoy dinner on Christmas. They would come by the busloads. The meals and programs were held at the 208 Post.

Because taking a picture was almost forbidden many memories are long gone. People did not want their pictures taken, and those who did were out of luck, because of the number of cameras available.

This is a rare photo of American Legion Post 208 members in the 1960's: Mrs. Emerson Savage: was a past President of (Aux.), William Hayes Miller: was Commander, (Legion) Lillian Higginbotham: present (Auxiliary) Mrs. Frances Bonner: past President (Auxiliary), Eunice Johnson: past Commander (Legion), Fred Nowlin: past Commander (Legion), Mrs. Mabel Ford: past President (Auxiliary), Mr. Jonah Patterson past Commander (Legion).

Legion Hosts Auxiliary

Members of American Legion Post 208 were hosts to the post's Ladies' Auxiliary recently as the 43rd birthday of the veterans organization was being marked. Present and past officers of the post attending the banquet are pictured above at the speaker's table. At front are Mrs. Emerson Savage, past president; William H. Miller, commander; and Lillian Higginbotham, president. Standing, Mrs. Frances Bonner, past president; Eunice Johnson, past commander; Fred Nowlin, past commander; and Mrs. Mabel Ford, past president.

In November 1946, Girl Scout troop number five was organized and sponsored by the American Legion Post Auxiliary 208. In 1947 the girls were seventeen strong.

In 1946 of October, the Boy Scout troop number 175 was organized and sponsored by American Legion Post 208. In 1947 the boys were 34 strong.

Part 2

Black War Veterans

Black War Veterans:

Adcock, Horace	WWI
Baker, Mike	**Vet**
Bains, Samuel	**WW1**
Barnhill, William Dwight	**Vietnam-NAVY**
Barns, John	**WW1**
Bartley, Robert D.	**WW1**
Bates, Benjamin	**Pearl Harbor**
Bates, Earnest Wade	**WW1**
Bates, Harrison	**WI**
Bates, Jewel Thomas	**Korean**
Bates, Joseph Brown	WW2
Bates, Paul W.	**WW2**
Bates, Willie Randolph	WW2
Biles, Bobby	Korean
Biles, Fred	Korean
Biles, Harrison	**WW1**
Biles, Harrison E. Jr.	**Vet**
Biles, Harrison E. Sr.	Korean
Blue, Clarence	**WW2**
Blue, John Burr	**WW2**
Bolden, Clarence Delton	Korean
Bonner, Buford Franklin	**Korean**
Bonner, Edward	**WW2**
Bonner, Frank H.	**Vet**
Bonner, Frank T.	**Vet**
Bonner, Thomas Harrison	**Vietnam**
Bonner, Thomas N.	**Vet**

Borum, Richard Allen Jr.	Vietnam
Boyd, Charles Emery Sr.	Vietnam
Bradford, Harrison	WW1
Brown, Doak A.	WW1
Brown, Elcain	Korean
Brown, Gillie	WWI
Brown, Harding	WW2
Brown, James	WW2
Brown, James E.	WW2
Brown, James O.	WW1
Brown, Marvin L.	WW2
Brown, R. C.	Korean
Brown, Richmond	WW2
Brown, Robert Charles	WW2
Brown, Rose	WW1
Carr, Jessie Lee	WW2
Carr, Jessie Ray	Vietnam
Coonrod, Billy	Vietnam
Coonrod, Earley	WW1
Coonrod, George	WW1
Cope, Hardy Jr.	WW2
Cope, Jerry Joe Louis	Korean
Crabtree, Charles Dillard Sr.	WW2
Crabtree, Dillard Cardon	WW2
Crisp, Donald	Vet
Crisp, Thurman William	Vet
Curtis, Clarence Roy	Vietnam
Curtis, L. V.	WW2
Davis, Rayford	WW2
Dillard, Herman Lee	Vet
Dillard, William Kenneth	Vet
Donaldson, David A.	WW2
Dotsen, Maxey H.	WW1

Dotson, Remis	WW1
Durley, James A.	WW1
Edge, Jim	WWI
English, London	Vet
Etter, Leroy Ted Louis	Korean
Evans, Gary	Desert Storm
Evans, James	Vet
Evans, Robert Harold	WW2
Faulkner, Harvey Lee	WW1
Faulkner, James Oliver	WW1
Finger, Columbus	WW1
Finger, Seba	WW1
Finger, Winford	WW1
Ford, Frank	WW1
Foster, Walter	WW1
France, Homer	WW1
France, Oliver	WW1
Gibson, Ernest Sr.	Desert Storm
Gipson, Waymon N.	WW1
Grayson, Charles Aaron	Vet.
Grayson, Eddie Jr. Desert	Storm
Grayson, Eddie Sr.	Vet
Grayson, George L.	WW2
Grayson, Hugh	WW1
Grayson, James E.	Korean
Grayson, Thomas	WW2
Green, Arbury	Korean
Gribble, Alton	Vet
Gribble, Charles R.	WW1
Gribble, Joe	WW1
Gribble, Murphy	WW1
Guerard, Augustus Jr.	Vet
Guerard, Victor	Vet

Gwynn, Charles Edmond	Vet
Gwynn, James Stanley	WW1
Gwynn, Lawson	WW1
Gwynn, Leonard	WW1
Gwynn, Roy	WW1
Gwynn, Will	WW1
Gwynn, William	WW1
Hammons, John	WW1
Harris, Jimmie	WW2
Henegar, Walter	WW2
Henny, Howard Sr.	WW2
Higginbotham, Marcus Rubin	WW1
Hill, Charles	WW1
Holland, Will	WW1
Hopkins, Virgil	WW1
Huddleston, Asbury ***	WW1
Hudgins, Edward Lee	Korean
Huggins, George E.	WW2
Huggins, Kenneth	Korean
Huggins, Ray R.	Korean, Vietnam
Huggins, William A.	WW2
Hunter, Buford 'Razz'	WW2
Hunter, Thomas	WW1
Irvin, Thomas W.	WW2
Jennings, Otis Falls ***	WW1
Johnson, Eunice Jefferson	Korean
Johnson, Eunice L.	Vet
Johnson, Nelson	WW1
Johnson, Paul W.	WW2
Jones, James Albert	WW1
Jones, Virgil	Vet
Keel, Robert Harold	Korean
King, Jerry W.	Marines-Nat. Guard

Knight, Fred Allen Jr.	WW2
Knox, Lee	WW1
Lee, Edd David	WW1
Leftrict, Charles Franklin Jr.	Korean
Leftrict, Donald Ray	Vietnam
Leftrict, Edd	WW2
Locke, Fred Jr.	Vietnam-Desert Storm
Locke, Fred Sr.	WW2
Locke, Hugh	Korean
Locke, Johnny Clarence	Vet
Locke, John R.	WW2
Locke, Larry Randolph	Desert storm-Vietnam
Locust, Richard	WW2
Lusk, Charles M.	Vietnam
Lusk, Harold	WW2
Lusk, James Elridge	Vietnam
Lusk, Marschel Brady	Vietnam
Lusk, Marvin Taylor Jr.	Vietnam
Lusk, Marvin Taylor Sr.	WW2
Lusk, Robert Kewen	Vietnam
Lusk, Will 'Rusty'	WW1
Lusk, William	WW1
Main, Morris Monroe	WW1
Malone, Clifton	WW1
Malone, Orvil K.	WW1
Marbury, Ivy Willis	WW2
Marbury, James	Vietnam
Martin, Almond C. ***	WW1 died in France of pneumonia Sept. 28 1918
Martin, Bud	WW2
Martin, Charles Lester	Vet
Martin, Charles 'Muggins'	Vet
Martin, Clarence C. Jr.	Desert Storm

Martin, Clarence C. Sr.	Korean &Vietnam
Martin, Clarence Cornelius	Korean
Martin, Clarence Edward	Korean
Martin, Clinton	WW2
Martin, Donald	Desert Storm
Martin, Edward	WW2
Martin, Elmer	WW2
Martin, Elmer C. Sr.	WW1
Martin, Eulous	WW2
Martin, Everett	WW1
Martin, French	WW1
Martin, Henry A.	WW2
Martin, Herman	WW2
Martin, Hobert T.	WW2
Martin, Howard Thomas Jr.	Vietnam
Martin, Howard T.	Vet
Martin, James Edward	Korean
Martin, James Dillard	WW1
Martin, Jerry Edward	Vietnam
Martin, Jim E.	WW2
Martin, Lawrence William Jr.	Korean
Martin, Michael	Desert Storm
Martin, Morris Monroe	WW1
Martin, Raymond	WW2
Martin, Sanford J.	WW2
Martin, Tarlton H.	WW2
Martin, Theron	WW2
Martin, Thomas Eugene Leonard	WW1
Martin, Thomas Ollie	WW2
Martin, Vance	WW2
McGee, Charles Lee	Korean
McGee, Donald D.	Vet

McGee, Fred	WW1
McReynolds, George Augusta	WW1
McReynolds, Jack	Vet
McReynolds, Jerry Wayne	Vet
McReynolds, Nathaniel	WW1
McReynolds, Robert Jr.	Vietnam
McReynolds, Roy Calvin Sr.	Korean
McReynolds, Tommy Ray	Vietnam
McReynolds, Wallace	WW2
McReynolds, Willie N.	WW2
Miller, William Hayes	Korean
Morford, Hoyt	WW1
Mount, Ollie	WW2
Mount, Ollie Randolph	Vet
Northcutt, David H.	WW2
Northcutt, Frank	WW1
Northcutt, Lester	WW1
Northcutt, Thomas Edward	WW2
Northcutt, Wayman E.	WW1
Nowlin, Fred L.	WW2
Nowlin, Steve	Desert Storm
Nowlin, William 'Bill'	Vietnam
Officer, Charles	Vietnam
Officer, Horace	WW1
Officer, Paul H.	WW2
Paige, Thomas G. Jr.	WW2
Patterson, Jonah	WW2
Peppers, Charles Eugene	Korean
Peppers, Rollie	WW1
Prater, Benjamin	WW1
Pryor, Henry C.	WW1
Quinn, Jerry Wayne	Vietnam
Ramsey, Alex Wade	Panama

Ramsey, Alfred Donald	Vet
Ramsey, Bill	Vet
Ramsey, Carl William	Vietnam
Ramsey, Clarence	WW1
Ramsey, Clyde William	WW2
Ramsey, Douglas Wayne	Vet
Ramsey, Ernest	WW2
Ramsey, James	WW1
Ramsey, James Clarence	Korean
Ramsey, James Jr.	Vet
Ramsey, James Louis	Vet
Ramsey, James Michael Sr.	Korean
Ramsey, James Monroe	WW2
Ramsey, Jimmy	Desert Storm Vet
Ramsey, Joe Thomas	WW2
Ramsey, John	WW1
Ramsey, Karl William	Vietnam
Ramsey, Leroy ***	Korean
Ramsey, Leroy Stokes	Vet
Ramsey, Paul Herbert	Vet
Ramsey, William	WW2
Redman, Thurman	WW1
Reedy, Terry	Vet
Rhodes, James	Vet
Rice, Henry	Vet
Rivers, Fermon	WW2
Robertson, James	Desert Storm
Rowan, Carl Thomas	Korean
Rowan, Charles Edward	Korean
Rowan, Leroy	Korean
Rowan, Thos or Thomas	WW1
Rowan, Robert	WW2
Rowan, William McKinley	WW1

Savage, Dallas Lee	Korean
Savage, Emerson	WW2
Savage, Fred Donald	Vet
Savage, George	WW1
Savage, Haskell	WW2
Savage, Henry B.	WW2
Savage, Hillis Jr.	WW2
Savage, Lucian	WW1
Savage, Wesley Lee	WW2
Scott, Eugene M.	WW2
Scott, Erby	WW2
Shell, Clarence	WW2
Shelton, Herman	WW2
Shockley, Herman L.	WW2
Shockley, Herman Lee	Korean
Shockley, Horace Edwin	Vet
Shockley, Jim Emery	WW1
Smith, Billie	WW2
Smith, Frank Jr.	WW2
Smith, Frank Jr.	Vietnam & Des. Storm
Smith, James Lester	Vietnam
Smith, Louis	Vet. Medical
Smith, Phillip Jr.	Korean
Smith, Phillip Sr.	WW1
Solomon, Floyd	WW1
Solomon, Jake	Korean
Solomon, Richard E.	WW2
Spencer, Everett Lee	WW2
Spencer, Eunous Dillon	WW2
Spencer, Fermon Reams	Korean
Spencer, Harrison L	WW2
Spencer, Roy S.	WW2
Spurlock, Bob	WW1

Spurlock, Charles Nathaniel	WW1
Spurlock, George	WW2
Spurlock, William Richard	WW1
Strode, Benton	Vietnam
Strode, Curtis L.	Desert Storm
Strode, Estie Jack	Korean
Strode, Fred	WW2
Strode, James Clinton	Korean
Strode, Ralph	Desert Storm
Talley, Beauford	WW2
Taylor, James Howard	Vietnam
Terry, Homer Louis	Vietnam
Terry, John	Desert storm
Terry, John W.	WW2
Terry, Nathaniel	WW2
Terry, Walter	WW2
Thacker, Ramey	WW1
Thomas, Howard	Panama
Thomas, William	Vet
Toney, Norman	WW2
Vaughn, Elzie Louis	Vet
Vaughn, John	WW1
Walling, Marcus Willis	Korean
Walling, Raymond H.	WW2
Webb, Robert	WW1
Webb, Willis M.	WW2
White, Charles Jr.	Korean
White, Richard	Vet
Wiley, Gregory	Vet
Winton, Charles J.	WW2
Winton, H. B.	WW2
Wolford, Wayne R. Sr.	Desert Storm
Womack, Ernest Sr.	WW1

Womack, Frank	WW1
Womack, James M.	WW2
Wood, Eden	WW1
Wood, Eugene Franklin	Korean
Wood, James Edwin	WW1
Wood, Malcolm Raleigh	WW1
Wood, Thomas	Vietnam
Wood, Thomas Lee	Vietnam
Wood, William T.	WW2
Woodlee, Daniel Frank	WW1
Woodlee, Franklin J.	Korean
Woodlee, Jess Edward	WW1
Woodlee, Jessie	WW1
Woods, Charles	WW1
Woods, Lee	WW1
Woods, James Sr.	WW2
Woods, Marles	WW1
Woods, William T.	WW2
York, Jim ***	WW1
Young, Alfred Bernard	Vietnam
Young, Harold	Korean

(***) Means died on active duty.

Part 3

Photo's of Veterans

then, widespread prejudice in the North had kept blacks from serving. "I have had the question put to me often," said General William T. Sherman, "'Is not a Negro as good as a white man to stop a bullet?' Yes! and a sand-bag is better; but can a Negro do our skirmishing and picket duty? Can they improvise

These soldiers are pictured at Camp William Penn in Pennsylvania. Each black regiment had all white officers. "The officers and men are both carefully picked," wrote Governor John Andrews concerning the formation of the 54th Massachusetts. "We

Civil War Black Soldiers

IN LINE FOR REVIEW.
Members of the 15th Infantry being reviewed. A sturdy and determined line of fighting men.

15th Infantry WWI

A QUARTETTE WHICH GAVE GOOD ENTERTAINMENT.
These colored members of the 301st Stevedore Regiment were attached to the 23rd Engineers in France.

301st Soldiers WWI

PHOTOGRAPHED IN A VILLAGE IN GERMANY.
A member of the 369th (old 15th N. Y.) brought this picture back with him. He is wearing the smile which tells the story. The war is over.

369th Soldier WWI

UNITED STATES COLORED LABOR TROOPS BOARDING A TRANSPORT.
An American Negro battalion entering a pier ready to board a transport. These husky doughboys perform their tasks with a vim and a will.

Black Labor Troops WWI

Edd McReynolds 1924

Charlie Hill, WWI medic.

1995 American Legion Members
L-R J. Patterson, R. Davis, E. Johnson, F. Locke Sr., A. Green,
W. Wolford Sr., F. Locke Jr., J. Solomon, & R. Hudgins

Arbury Green

Benjamin Bates

'L. JAMES... MABS-24, MAG-24, ...

Air ...

Captain William Ramsey
Captain Joella Ramsey

SMSGT Alfred Ramsey
Reinlistment

BILLIE SMITH

Brewster Bonner

Brown Williams

Carl Thomas Rowan

Charles Peppers

Charlie Lusk
2007

Clarence 'Bill' Martin Sr.

Clarence 'Bill' Martin Jr.

Clarence Blue

Clarence C. Martin 1947

Dave Ramsey

Donald Martin 1975

Dwight Barnhill

Edward Savage

Eugene London

Eugene Wood

Eulous Martin

Eunice Johnson 1996

Fred Locke Sr.

Harold Lusk

Part 4

American Legion 'The Hall'

There's much history to be said about American Legion Post 208. Soldiers have gone off to war, and returned home, and discussed certain values, friendships, loneliness, and joys of visiting other sites and countries. The Post was a place to party on Saturday nights. Sometimes there would be a D. J., and other times bands would come in to play for the crowd. There were some very good vocal groups, and bands around this area. The Jukebox was always available when all else felled. Ice-cold beer and soda pop were sold. Birthday parties were given. Baby showers were given. There's no record of weddings being given there, but I'm sure there were a few.

When there was a Rocket baseball game in town the visiting team would be invited to stay and have a good time at the club. Sometimes the players wouldn't shower or change clothes before coming. (I refer to Post 208 as the 'Club', because that is what some people called it).

The name most recognized when mentioning Post 208 was "The Hall".

In the 1940's through the 1970's, there weren't many places for blacks to go and party. Even though the American Legion Post 208 acquired a lot of financial funds, they always seem to share with the community, Funds were always provided for the needy. Anytime anyone needed help, Post 208 was always there.

There are many stories out there, some we will never know, and some we will never hear, there were good ones and bad ones. American Legion Post 208 was an outstanding Post and did a lot for the community.

American Legion Post 208 is still a thriving organization. A last count was approximately 34 members.

The meetings are at various places, but the tradition still continues on.

Richmond Brown

Robert Edward Bonner

Robert Kewen Lusk

Roy Calvin McReynolds

Staff Sargent James Ramsey

Tarlton H. Martin

Thomas Lee Woods

Thurman Benton Strode 1962

Tommy McReynolds

Anthony 'Tony' Martin

William "Bill" Jones
Air Force   1945 - 46

Part 5

Huddleston-Jennings

Post 208's temporary charter was granted on August 31, 1945. The original charter had eighteen (18) charter members, which formed the Post in 1945.

Samuel Bain was the first Post Commander and Fred L. Nowlin was the first Adjutant. The first address given was: RR1 Box 160, McMinnville, TN. 38006. Copies of reference cards show the Post Commanders and Post Adjutants since 1945. Post 208's permanent charter was granted on November 9, 1953.

Year	Members	Positions	Names
1946	43	Cmd.	Samuel Bain
		Adj.	Fred Nowlin
1947	37	Cmd.	Roy Spencer
		Adj.	Fred Nowlin
1948	27	Cmd.	Franklin Woodlee
		Adj.	Fred Nowlin
1949	21	Cmd.	Lawson Gwynn
		Adj.	Fred Nowlin
1950	12	Cmd.	Fred Nowlin
		Adj.	Franklin Woodlee
1951	37	Cmd.	Roy Spencer
		Adj.	Franklin Woodlee
1952	26	Cmd.	Roy Spencer
		Adj.	Buford Hunter
1953	22	Cmd.	Jonah Patterson
		Adj.	Franklin Woodlee
1954	10	Cmd.	Fred Nowlin
		Adj.	Franklin Woodlee
1955	21	Cmd.	Fred Nowlin
		Adj.	Franklin Woodlee

1956	25	Cmd.	Franklin Woodlee
		Adj.	Fred Nowlin
1957	36	Cmd.	Clarence E. Martin
		Adj.	Fred Nowlin
1958	50	Cmd.	Clarence E. Martin
		Adj.	Fred Nowlin
1959	32	Cmd.	Roy Spencer
		Adj.	Franklin Woodlee
1960	30	Cmd.	Eunice Johnson
		Adj.	Franklin Woodlee
1961	40	Cmd.	William Hayes Miller
		Adj.	Charles Martin
1962	43	Cmd.	Jonah Patterson
		Adj.	Charles Martin
1963	37	Cmd.	Harvey League
		Adj.	Charles Martin
1964	56	Cmd.	Harvey League
		Adj.	Charles Martin
1965	53	Cmd.	Harvey League
		Adj.	Charles Martin
1966	50	Cmd.	Harvey League
		Adj.	Charles Martin
1967	45	Cmd.	Harrison E. Biles Jr.
		Adj.	Charles Martin
1968	48	Cmd.	Jonah Patterson
		Adj.	Harrison E. Biles Jr.
1969	34	Cmd.	Jonah Patterson
		Adj.	Harrison E. Biles Jr.
1970	20	Cmd.	Nathaniel Terry
		Adj.	Harrison E. Biles Jr.
1971	15	Cmd.	Marschel Lusk
		Adj.	Harrison E. Biles Jr.

1972	15	Cmd.	Fred Nowlin
		Adj.	Harrison E. Biles Jr.
1973	15	Cmd.	William H. Miller
		Adj.	Harrison E. Biles
1974	22	Cmd.	William H. Miller
		Adj.	Frank Smith Jr.
1975	21	Cmd.	Carl W. Ramsey
		Adj.	Frank Smith Jr.
1976	15	Cmd.	Harrison E. Biles Jr.
		Adj.	Fred Nowlin
1977	26	Cmd.	Harrison E. Biles Jr.
		Adj.	Fred Nowlin
1978	22	Cmd.	Alfred Ramsey
		Adj.	Fred Nowlin
1979	31	Cmd.	Alfred Ramsey
		Adj.	Fred Nowlin
1980	24	Cmd.	Alfred Ramsey
		Adj.	Fred Nowlin
1981	17	Cmd.	Alfred Ramsey
		Adj.	Fred Nowlin
1982	23	Cmd.	Herman Shockley
		Adj.	Fred Nowlin
1983	16	Cmd.	Herman Shockley
		Adj.	Fred Nowlin
1984	38	Cmd.	Herman Shockley
		Adj.	Fred L. Nowlin
1985	34	Cmd.	Herman Shockley
		Adj.	Fred L. Nowlin
1986	35	Cmd.	Herman Shockley
		Adj.	Fred L. Nowlin
1987	38	Cmd.	Herman Shockley
		Adj.	Fred L. Nowlin

1988	24	Cmd.	James E. Martin
		Adj.	Eulous Martin
1989	29	Cmd.	James E. Martin
		Adj.	Eulous Martin
1990	19	Cmd.	James E. Martin
		Adj.	Eulous Martin
1991	21	Cmd.	James E. Martin
		Adj.	Eulous Martin
1992	20	Cmd.	James E. Martin
		Adj.	Eulous Martin
1993	32	Cmd.	Jerry King
		Adj.	Eunice Johnson
1994	39	Cmd.	Harold Young
		Adj.	Eunice Johnson
1995	34	Cmd.	Fred Locke Jr.
		Adj.	Ray R. Huggins
1996	37	Cmd.	Wayne R. Wolford Sr.
		Adj.	Ray R. Huggins
1997	34	Cmd.	Wayne R. Wolford Sr.
		Adj.	Ray R. Huggins
1998	36	Cmd.	Wayne R. Wolford Sr.
		Adj.	Ray R. Huggins
1999	33	Cmd.	Wayne R. Wolford Sr.
		Adj.	Ray R. Huggins
2000	31	Cmd.	Wayne R. Wolford Sr.
		Adj.	Ray R. Huggins
2001	30	Cmd.	Wayne R. Wolford Sr.
		Adj.	Ray R. Huggins
2002	31	Cmd.	Wayne R. Wolford Sr.
		Adj.	Ray R. Huggins
2003	30	Cmd.	Wayne R. Wolford Sr.
		Adj.	Ray R. Huggins

2004	30	Cmd.	Wayne R. Wolford Sr.
		Adj.	Ray R. Huggins
2005	32	Cmd.	Wayne R. Wolford Sr.
		Adj.	Ray Huggins
2006	31	Cmd.	Wayne R. Wolford Sr.
		Adj.	Ray Huggins
2007	33	Cmd.	Wayne R. Wolford Sr.
		Adj.	Ray Huggins
2008	30	Cmd.	Wayne R. Wolford Sr.
		Adj.	Ray Huggins
2009	25	Cmd.	Wayne R. Wolford Sr.
		Adj.	Ray Huggins
2010	24	Cmd.	Wayne R. Wolford Sr.
		Adj.	Ray Huggins
2011	20	Cmd.	Wayne R. Wolford Sr.
		Adj.	Fred Locke Jr.
2012	20	Cmd.	Wayne R. Wolford Sr.
		Adj.	Fred Locke Jr.

Wayne R. Wolford Sr.

Jerry King

Joe Thomas Ramsey

Johnny Locke

Kenneth Huggins

Larry Locke

Ray Huggins

Leroy Ramsey died in Korean War

Mack Hunt Young
Air Force   1959 - 60

Marvin T. Lusk Sr.

Paul H. Ramsey

**Rayford Davis 63 year member of
American Legion Posts #173 & #208**

Buford 'Razz' Hunter

Richard A. Borum

Richard Allen Borum Sr. WWII

Part 6

Original Members of American Legion Post 208

The American Legion Post for Blacks was located on Congo Street before the property and administration was done to complete a Post in the Leesburg community outside of McMinnville's city limits.

The original members that started the American Post # 208, Huddleston-Jennings were:

Thos Rowan	110 Edgefield
Tom Hunter	City
Frank Ford	Faulkner Street
Harvey Faulkner	Faulkner Street
Fred L. Nowlin	104 Edgefield
Roley Peppers	217 East End Drive
Haskell Savage	P. O. Box 17
Phillip Smith	115 East End Drive
Markus Higginbotham	17 East End Drive
Herman L. Shockley	East Main Street
Charlie Hill	64 Lane Street
William M. Rowan	RR6
Nathaniel McReynolds	120 Murphy Street
Hugh Grayson	RR6
Samuel Bain	City
William Ramsey	120 Edgefield Street
Edd David Lee	City
Franklin J. Woodlee	P.O. Box 123

They all were residents of Warren County.

There were no air-conditioning units, no heat pumps, only windows open during the hot summer months and a wood & coal burning stove to heat those chilly winter days. Even though "The

Hall" was small in size, the capacity crowd could hold approximately two hundred people.

At one time during its existence the Post had an "Honor Guard." If a Veteran were laid to rest, the "Honor Guard" would preside over the funeral.

In 1994 American Legion Post consisted of:

Commander:	**Harold Young**
Vice Commander:	**Fred Locke Jr.**
Finance Officer:	**Marvin T. Lusk Jr.**
Chaplin:	**Benjamin Bates**
Adjutant:	**Eunice Johnson**
Sergeant-of-Arms:	**Jake Solomon**

Hillis Savage Jr.

Howard Henny Sr.

Jake Solomon

James Franklin Settles

James Grayson

James M. Womack

James Ramsey

James Rhodes

Part 7

Facts of World War II

1. The War started in 1941 and ended in 1945.
2. The pay for Black enlisted Sailors, started at $21.00 a month, but the White service members received $9.00 more after basic training, where as the Black service member didn't.
3. Some Black service members never went to Basic Training Camp, so wherever there was a job, they were put there.
4. Food; Blacks ate in all Black Mess halls, the food was the same, but the whites ate in an all white Mess hall.
5. White Officers would belittle Black service members, because they were considered inferior. Most Blacks were thought to be 'Uncle Toms', or ignorant.
6. Rank; only had its privileges when speaking to another Black service member, not to their White counterpart.
7. Liberty; which is also called a 'Pass', was done on the same basis as the current policy, but the service members couldn't go to the same places, nor do the same things together. That's just the way it was.
8. Jobs on ships: out of a possible 125 crew-members, only 4 Sailors were Black aboard ship. They were called 'Mess men', or 'Mess Attendants'. In their words they were "Flunkies."
9. Jobs after the War; these were labor jobs, and not many of them to go around.
10. In various places in the world: other nationalities had heard that Blacks had tails tucked away in their trousers, and that the color of their dark complected skin would come off with a good rub. Young children would come up to a person of color after they decided that they weren't going to be eaten, and touched the skin and hair the good Lord gave Blacks.
11. Jobs for ground troops; truck drivers, infantrymen, supply, medics, food service, road builders, quartermasters, company clerks, airfields and bridges builders.

12. Medal of Honor; 469 of these medals were given out, but none to a Black Officer, or enlisted troop.
13. Distinguished Service Cross; was the highest, 273 awards were given. Silver Stars, Distinguished Flying Cross, Soldiers Medals, Bronze Stars and Air Medals.
14. Black Division; the 92nd Division lost over three thousand men in the Rome campaign.
15. The War Department shows; 65 Silver Stars, 70 Bronze Stars and 1,300 Purple Hearts.

Out of 369,369 Tennesseans that served in World War II, 5,731 died, two of these service members were black, and lived in Warren County. (Asbury Huddleston and Otis Falls Jennings) American Legion Post 208 was named in Remembrance of these two servicemen.

William Nowlin

Part 8

American Legion meets the Challenge

As we honor those Americans who undauntedly and courageously contributed to the defense of this nation, often overlooked in our remembrances are the valiant efforts of the Black Americans. Throughout the war years they repeatedly had to battle adversaries on two fronts: the enemy overseas and racism at home. Black Americans recognized the paradox of fighting a world war for the "four freedoms" while being subject to prejudicial practices in this United States. Thus as the war unfolded they insisted on the privileges of full citizenship.

Black Americans were ready to work and fight for their country, but at the same time they demanded an end to the discrimination against them.

Over 2.5 million Black American men registered for the draft, and Black women volunteered in large numbers. While serving in the Air Force, Army, Army Air Force, Navy, Marine Corps, and Coast Guard, they experienced continuing discrimination and segregation. Despite these impediments, many Black men and women met the challenge and persevered. They served with distinction, made valuable contributions to the war effort, and earn well-deserved praise and commendations for their struggles and sacrifices.

Part 9

The Dates of the Wars

April 6, 1917	World War 1	Nov. 11, 1918 (USA)
Dec. 8, 1941	World War 2	Sept. 2, 1945 (USA)
June 25, 1950	Korean War	July 27, 1953
March 1965	Vietnam War	April 29, 1975
Dec. 20, 1989	Panama	Jan.31, 1990
Feb. 24, 1991	Operation Desert Storm	Feb. 28, 1991
Oct. 7, 2001	Afghanistan War	Present 2011
March 17, 2006	Iraq War	Aug. 31, 2010

Part 10

Military Awards and Medals Information

F018 Bronze Star Medal (Est. 1944)

Criteria: Heroic or meritorious achievement or service not involving participation in aerial flight.
Attachments: Bronze Oak Leaf Device, Silver Oak Leaf Device, Bronze Letter "V" Device

Notes: Awarded to World War II holders of Army Combat Infantryman Badge or Combat Medical Badge.

F029 Purple Heart Medal (Est. 1932)

Criteria: Awarded to any member of the U.S. Armed Forces killed or wounded in an armed conflict.
Attachments: Bronze Oak Leaf Device, Silver Oak Leaf Device

Notes: Wound Ribbon appeared circa 1917-18 but was never officially authorized. (Army used Wound Chevrons during World War I.)

F023 Army Commendation Medal (Est. 1945)

Dates: (retro to 1941)
Criteria: Heroism, meritorious achievement, or service.
Attachments: Bronze Oak Leaf Device, Silver Oak Leaf Device, Bronze Letter "V" Device

Notes: Originally a ribbon-only award then designated "Army Commendation Ribbon with Pendant". Redesignated: "Army Commendation Medal" in 1960.

F033 Army Good Conduct Medal (Est. 1941)

Criteria: Exemplary conduct, efficiency and fidelity during three years of active enlisted service with the U.S. Army (1 Year during wartime).
Attachments: Bronze Good Conduct Knot Device, Silver Good Conduct Knot Device

F047 American Defense Service Medal WWII (Est. 1941)

Dates: 1939-41
Criteria: Army: 12 months of active duty service during 1939-41
Attachments: Bronze Star Device

F049 American Campaign Medal—WWII (Est 1942)

Dates: 1941-46
Criteria: Service outside the U.S. in the American theater for 30 days or within the continental US for one year.
Attachments: Bronze Star Device, Silver Star Device

F050 Asiatic Pacific Campaign Medal—WWII (Est 1942)

Dates: 1941-46

Criteria: Service in the Asiatic-Pacific theater for 30 days or receipt of any combat decoration.

Attachments: Silver Star Device, Bronze Star Device, Bronze Arrowhead Device—Mounted

F051 European—African—Middle Eastern Campaign Medal (Est 1942)

Dates: 1941-45

Criteria: Service in the European—African—Middle Eastern theater for 30 days or receipt of any combat decoration.

Attachments: Silver Star Device, Bronze Star Device, Bronze Arrowhead Device—Mounted

F052 World War II (WWII) Victory Medal (Est 1945)

Dates: 1941-46

Criteria: Awarded for service in US Armed Forces between 1941 and 1946.

F053 WWII Army of Occupation Medal (Est 1946)

Dates: 1945-55 (Berlin: 1945-90)

Criteria: 30 consecutive days of service in occupied territories of former enemies during above periods.

Attachments: Berlin Airplane Device—Mounted, Japan Bar Device, Germany Bar Device

Notes: Army Air Force personnel also eligible. For service in Berlin until the early 90s. Japan and Germany bars are not auth for wear on ribbons.

F057 National Defense Service Medal—NDSM (Est 1953)

Dates: 1950-54, 1961-74, 1990-95
Criteria: Any honorable active duty service during any of the above periods.
Attachments: Bronze Star Device

Notes: Re-instituted in 1966 and 1991 for Vietnam and Southwest Asia (Gulf War) actions respectively.

F079 Philippine Defense Medal—World War II (Est 1945)

Criteria: Service in defense of the Philippines between 8 December 1941 and 15 June 1942
Attachments: Bronze Star Device

Notes: Only the ribbon may be worn on the US military uniform.

F080 Philippine Liberation Medal—World War II (Est 1945)

Criteria: Service in the liberation of the Philippines between 17 October 1944 and 3 September 1945.
Attachments: Bronze Star Device

Notes: Only the ribbon may be worn on the US military uniform.

F238 Overseas Service Commemorative Medal Boxed With Ribbon

Criteria: Struck to honor all Soldiers, Sailors, Marines and Airmen who served in an overseas theater or expeditionary operation outside the United States for 30 days or more.

F239 Combat Service Commemorative Medal Boxed With Ribbon

Criteria: Struck to honor all Soldiers, Sailors, Marines and Airmen who served in an overseas combat theater or expeditionary combat operation.

F230 World War II Victory Commemorative Medal Boxed With Ribbon (Est 1995)

Dates: 1941-1946
Criteria: Struck to honor all who served in the United States Armed Forces During WWII and those who worked in war industry.

F229 Asiatic Pacific Victory Commemorative Medal Boxed With Ribbon (Est 1995)

Dates: 1941-1946
Criteria: Struck to honor all soldiers, sailors, marines and airmen who served in or supported the Pacific Theater.

F228 Victory in Europe Commemorative
Medal Boxed With Ribbon (Est 1995)

Dates: 1941-1946
Criteria: Struck to honor all soldiers, sailors, marines and airmen who served in the European, African and Middle Eastern Theaters During WWII.

F245 Armed Forces Retired Commemorative Medal (Est 2001)

Dates: 1775-Present
Criteria: Designed to honor the devotion, loyalty and achievement of all who retired from a military career in the service of their nation.

Chapter 4

The Game of Baseball

Baseball is one of the oldest and most popular spectator's sports. It is often called the national pastime in the United States. Because of a strong tradition and great popularity, it is assumed that people go to the park mostly to drink beer and swell up on pizzas and hotdogs nowadays. Many people see baseball as a way to make a lot of money, most not realizing that it's really a fun game.

Before the modern day era, ball players didn't know anything about a pitching machines, Astro Turf, video games and batting cages. It was a good feeling just to get to an open field with a few rocks, and bushes and freshly cut grass. Stickball was popular in some areas. This game consisted of a mop or broomstick handle and tennis ball, if you can afford one. Rubber balls were the most inexpensive, but by the time you hit the rubber ball three or four times it tore in half. Sometimes we were so poor and we had to play with half of a ball in order to finish the game. (That was fun!) The exciting part of playing with a rubber ball or tennis ball was you could make it do all sorts of movements.

The ballpark at Rocket field consists of 5 acres: infield, outfield, and foul territory. A pitcher's mound slightly rose from the ground: 66

in. from home plate to accommodate each team: visitor's and home. Just before each game a few of the organizations would get some lye and mark home box and foul lines. Two circles were marked off just in front of the dugouts and coaches lines. There is still a reminder of the old ballpark standing in deep center field of this ballpark. It is the flagpole. The old flagpole was moved because kids climb up and broke the staff, so the manager Joe Edward had this raised.

There is still no fence in which you can knock a ball over. The ball either sails to the river or you can reach as many bases that you can on a hit.

The Rockets were pretty well equipped in the 1960's and the 1970's. Everyone had a complete uniform, glove, spikes (metal) and batting helmets. The catcher wore special protective gear including a helmet, a chest protector and shin guards. The metal bats weren't used in those days, only the good old wooden Louisville Slugger.

Amateur baseball is the old the form of organized baseball. The first professional teams began as amateur clubs.

There is evidence that people played games involving a stick and a ball since the early days of civilization. Ancient cultures such as Persia, Egypt, and Greece played stick and ball games for recreation and as part of certain ceremonies. Europeans brought stick and ball games to the American colonies as early as the 1600's.

By 1800 stick and ball became popular in North America. By the 1850's landowners were regularly maintaining baseball parks to rent to baseball teams. Baseball teams customarily collected donations from fans to cover cost.

The first professional baseball team, Cincinnati Red Stockings, begin play in 1869. They traveled the country in that year, playing before thousands of fans in winnings 60 games without a loss.

From the mid 1800's until the mid 1940's Black players were not allowed to compete in the major leagues. Instead they enjoyed teams made up entirely of Black players and many of these teams formed leagues that were known collectively as the Negro leagues and Semi-pro leagues.

The great depression disrupted play in the Negro Leagues during the early 1930's. Outstanding players in the Negro Leagues included: Josh Gipson, pitcher Satchel Paige and outfielder James Bell who used to be nick named 'Cool Papa.' Many of the best Black players integrated into the majors thus showing a decline in attendance on the ball fields during the 1950's.

Baseball suffered during World War II (1939-1945), as most of the baseball players were called to military service. Teams and fans also endured travel restrictions and limits on supplies. After the war, baseball began to grow again.

McMinnville Rockets
Semi-Pro Baseball Team 1962 (Photo)

L-R; Top; JOE EDWARD RAMSEY 'COOPE'
LORETTA STRODE
MARCELLUS
SUTTON : UMPIRE
JOHN STRODE
BOBBY COPE (BALL BOY)
FRANKLIN 'BUBA' WOMACK
JAMES 'MOODY' EVANS
JAMES RUSSELL RAMSEY
J0HN L. 'ABE' THOMAS: COACH/MANAGER
ELMER JR. MARTIN
TOMMY WOODARD: (BAT BOY)
ULLYSSE CULLEY
WILLIE 'BAMA' SMITH: GEN. MANAGER

Front Row L-R; J. C. WILLIAMS
ROBERT 'MOJO' HARRIS
HARVEY 'HAND JIVE' LEAGUE
LARRY 'DOBY' BROWN
JACK STRODE: PLAYER/COACH
E. B. MALONE
HAROLD 'LEFTY' THOMAS, Gerald 'PEPPER': (BAT BOY)

1978

JERRY 'EGGHEAD' MARTIN JR.
GREGORY MARTIN
LARRY 'DOBY' BROWN
ROBERT MARTIN
CHRIS BILES
ELMER 'JR' MARTIN
STEVE THOMAS
DANNY MARTIN
LESTER STRODE
JEFFERY 'CHICK' MARTIN
RICKY TERRY
THOMAS 'RED EYE' MARTIN

McMinnville 'Rockets' & Viola 'Clowns'
Managers/Coaches

Willie 'Bama' Smith

Harold 'Lefty' Thomas

Harold 'Lefty' Thomas

Born July 2, 1937, Harold pitched his way into all of the hearts of the sluggers that faced him. Number '8' was probably the best pitcher the Viola Clowns or the McMinnville has ever seen. He pitched from 1952 until1973. Dazzling you with a sharp breaking curve ball, then a very quick fastball and don't forget the change up. "When we started playing baseball in Viola Tenn. (Clowns), everyone called us little boys, but we beat almost every team we played", says Harold. "When Jack Strode was the manager of the Rockets, about six players had stayed out all night long and he wouldn't let us play," Jack said, "that if I can win with you, I can lose without you." "I will never forget that," says Harold. He put the second string in, and sent us home.

The stars that were worn on the front of the uniforms represented homeruns, per Thomas.

"Jack Strode, then manager/coach would tell you to do something one time, and that was that".

Fred 'Mousey' Winton was watching his girlfriend in the stands when she said, "come on Fred, hit the ball." "He was so busy watching her while he was at the plate that when he turned around the baseball popped him dead up side the head, and knocked him out." He came too sometime later, but we laughed until we cried afterwards. "Mousy was ok after awhile. Just a small knot on his head."

JERRY 'EGG HEAD' MARTIN
JERRY 'BEETLE' KING
ROBERT 'MOJO' HARRIS
ROBERT 'MAC' McREYNOLDS JR.
DANNY MARTIN
GREGORY MARTIN
MICHEAL 'JOHN' MARTIN
ROBERT 'HEAD MONSTER' MARTIN
HOWARD 'DOONY' HENNY JR.
DWIGHT 'SUG' BARNHILL
RONNIE 'GHOST' BLEVINS
THOMAS 'RED EYE' MARTIN

THE
McMINNVILLE ROCKETS
SEMI-PRO
BASEBALL TEAM

Only the two baseball fields and a monument are reminders of the glory days of Semi-Pro, as we knew it. This is an era when things finally started to change and teams, government, work places, clubs, organizations integrated, allowing the entire United States to enjoy living together. Things changed almost too fast for independent, and community baseball teams.

The Viola Clowns (Viola Tenn.) and McMinnville Rockets, two independent Semi-Pro baseball teams that delighted local crowds long before Willie Mays, are Jackie Robinson broke the race barrier in the majors.

The McMinnville Rockets started as far back as the 1930's before The Great War (WWI). The Viola team started in the 1940's until the 1950's. Viola Clowns later merged with the Rockets, which played during segregation that continued on into integration.

One of the first written documents of the Rockets was titled 'Maynard Hurls Rockets To Win.' This was dated the 21st of May 1948. With Fred Maynard on the mound, the McMinnville Rockets, local (then referred to as colored) baseball club scored their first win of the season over Murfreesboro Tenn. All-stars last Sunday by a two run margin. The final score was 11-9. In a slump near the middle of the game, Fred Maynard, (who comes here from Livingston) scored seven strikeouts in a row to give his team a lead they held until the end of the game.

Winchester Tenn. will meet the Rockets in McMinnville Sunday. Game time is listed at 2:30pm at Memorial field (the Old Fair Grounds).

"C. Martin (Clarence E. Martin) Homers to give Rockets victory" Placing three pitchers in the limelight at Memorial Field,

Sunday (June 4, 1948), The McMinnville Rockets raced to their second win of the season with a basketball or football score of 21 to 17.

Winchester furnished the Rockets opposition. The local home run slugger Clarence E. Martin hit the games only homer in the seventh inning with two men on base.

"Rockets Maintain Perfect Record"

June 25, 1948, when the cost of going to the movies was 25cents
The McMinnville Rockets baseball club continued their straight line of wins Sunday when they scored a 10 to 8 victory over Winchester, Tenn. on the opponent's diamond.

Winning three games and tying one, the rockets have a perfect `season's record. Their game with Woodbury, Tenn. was called due to rain when the teams were deadlocked 5 to 5.

Hurling a record game, Bill Clarence Martin Jr., 17 years old pitcher of Rockets, clocked a 3-hit game, scoring 9 strike-outs in 6 innings. Jay Cope, went 5 for 6, was the best hitter. The Rockets will play at home Sunday against the Nashville All-stars, 2:30pm at Memorial Field.

On July 2, 1948 the price of lamb was 35 cents a pound the "Rockets Coast To Fifth Win" the youngster Bill C. Martin hurled for the Rockets to win their fifth straight wins of the season. Bill Martin allowed the Tullahoma ('9') Team 3 hits as his team marched to a 9 to 6 victory at Memorial Field. Randolph Ramsey, 17 years old, formed the other half of the Rocket Battery.

John Walter Terry, in the box for the Rockets, the first three innings allowed the Tullahoma Tenn. players 4 of their 7 hits. The Rockets as they error clocked a total of 14 hits twice.

Best hitters on the Rockets parade were Jay Cope and Franklin J. Woodlee, each with 4 for 5 hits.

The McMinnville Rockets have filed an application to enter the state baseball tournament in Nashville, Tenn. late August, will meet Nashville's H. G. Hill players in a Sunday game starting at 2:30pm.

April 20, 1962, "Rockets To Open Sunday"

The McMinnville Rockets start their season beginning Sunday at Fair Grounds Park at 1:45pm. The Rockets foe will be the H. G. Hill Nashville team. The team has been working out regularly for the past several weeks, and is out fitted with new uniforms donated by the merchants and business people of McMinnville. Although the first game will be played at the Fair Grounds, team officials say that work is underway to refurbish the old Viola baseball park for use as the team's home diamond for the '62' season.

Willie 'Bama' Smith is the Manager of the 'Nine,' George 'Shakey' Haynes is Secretary, and Joe 'Edward' Ramsey is treasurer; Estie 'Jack' Strode is the team's Field Captain.

Other members of the team include; Harvey 'Hand Jive' League, J. C. 'Bo' Williams, Harold 'Lefty' Thomas, James Settles, Elmer Jr. Martin, Robert 'Mojo' Harris, Larry 'Doby' Brown, Franklin J. Woodlee, Jim Martin, Ralph Strode, Fred Morford Thomas, E. B. Malone, Hugh Locke, and John Strode.

April 27, 1962 "Rockets Try for Second"

The McMinnville Rockets will be going for their second victory of this season at Nolensville, Tenn. Sunday at 2pm.

The Rockets, composed of a very athletic group of men, played their first game Sunday at the Fair Grounds. The score was 8 to 7. It was a sweet victory over the H. G. Hill team of Nashville. For local fans who would like to make the trip to Nolensville with the Rockets, a bus will leave Bernard High School at 11am. Bus fare is: (get this, $1.50 for the round trip).

While Nikita Khrushchev was the Russian Communist leader in another part of the world, "The Rockets Rip Milton Here". Dated May 8, 1962, the McMinnville Rocket baseball team with only a lopsided loss to Nolensville marred their record, won their second straight Sunday with a 19 to 11 win over a home game at Fair Grounds Park over the Milton Tenn. 'Braves.'

Shortstop J. C. 'Bo' Williams was the hitting and fielding star for the local outfit, racking up a 4 for 6 at the plate (including a lead-off home run in the first inning), and turning in a pair of fielding gems to nip Milton rallies. The Braves got to McMinnville starter Fred Thomas for four runs in the first inning on three hits, two walks and a hit batter. Fred Thomas settled down and pitched well until he weakened in the fourth inning.

Harold 'Lefty' Thomas, who held the Braves in check the rest of the way, relieved him.

The Rockets (now 2-1) for the season travel to Little Hope Saturday. A Bus will leave from Bernard at noon.

May 18, 1962, you could buy fishing equipment at Western Tire Store, on 112N. Spring Street. "Rockets Win 6 to 5 Behind Thomas Home Run." The

McMinnville Rockets broke even in a pair of baseball games last weekend leaving their season record at 3-2. They lost Saturday to Little Hope 'Red Sox' 19 to 2, then came back Sunday for a 6 to 5 win over the Smithville 'Tigers.'

Both games were played away from home.

The Rockets finally settled down in the last five innings Sunday to pick up the 6 to 5 win over their archrivals, The Smithville 'Tigers', on a grand-slam homerun by Fred Morford Thomas.

Trailing 5 to 2 going into the top half of the ninth inning, the Rockets loaded the bases with two men out, Morford Thomas smashed the second pitch into left field pea patch to give McMinnville the 6 to 5 win.

Pitcher Harold 'Lefty' Thomas went the distance for the Rockets, and picked up the pitching victory.

'Lefty' was in trouble several times, but registered a tough clutch performance by bearing down with two men on base and snuffing out one Smithville threat after another.

Eight big races each Saturday night at the McMinnville Speedway can be seen for $1.00. "Seven More Home Games For Rockets" June 1, 1962. The McMinnville Rockets announced earlier this week they would have a seven game schedule during the remainder of the season, with only one road game scheduled during this time.

The Rockets, now sporting a 3-3 record for the season, will open a five game home stand next Sunday (June 10, 1962) and after a game at Sparta Tenn., will close with two more home games in late July.

The Rockets home games are played on the new baseball diamond located just off Beersheba road in the park adjoining the Warren County Rescue Squad building. The park is now known as Rocket Baseball field. The games start at 2:30pm.

There is a possibility a game will be played at the Rocket's park Sunday afternoon, but team officials said Wednesday that the name of the team was not known at the time. The Rockets will start a left-handed pitcher.

The Rockets suffered their third loss of the season to the Milton 'Braves' 10-7. It evened the season series between the two teams at 1-1, and also squared the Rockets record at 3 and 3.

Here is the remainder of the Rocket's schedule;

June 10—LaVergne Tenn. 'Red Sox' (home)
June 17—Nashville Tenn. 'All-Stars' (home)
June 24—Nashville Tenn. 'H.G. Hill' (home)
July 1—Manchester Tenn. (home)
July 8—Sparta 'Tigers' (home)
July 15—Sparta 'Tigers' (away)
July 22—Winchester 'Tigers' (home)
July 29—Milton 'Braves' Tenn. (home)

By June 8, 1962 the payment for a brand new Rambler automobile per month was $51.22. "Rockets win 3-2; Host Sox Sunday"

The McMinnville Rockets fresh from their fourth win of the season, will seek their fifth Sunday afternoon when they play host to the LaVergne 'Red Sox' at the Beersheba road park. The game will begin at 2:30pm.

The Rockets defeated the Tullahoma 'All-Stars' Sunday 3-2 in a rain-shortened game on a home run by Harvey 'Hand Jive' League. The game was called at the end of 5 1/3 innings.

Meanwhile, Rocket officials said Wednesday that improvements are being made on the new park. A fence and bleachers are being built.

June 15, 1962 "Rockets Rip Sox, Take On Nashville" The McMinnville Rockets will seek their sixth win of the season Sunday at the new Beersheba road park when they take on the Nashville 'All-Stars' at 2:30pm. The Rockets pushed its record to 5-3-1 last Sunday with a 14 to 6 win over the LaVergne 'Red Sox.'

Shortstop Larry 'Doby' Brown blasted a home run in the first inning to put the Rockets ahead, but the game was tied 6 to 6 at the end of five innings of play.

The Rockets scored six runs in the sixth and added two in the seventh.

Ralph Strode started for the Rockets, and was touched for four runs in the first three innings. Harold 'Lefty' Thomas relieved in the fourth and limited the Red Sox to two runs the rest of the game. Thomas blanked LaVergne over the last four innings.

June 19, 1962 "Rockets Zip By Nashville Stars 11 to 5"

After a slow start, The McMinnville Rockets teed off on Nashville pitching in the fifth inning and went on to win 11 to 5 over the Stars and push their season record to 6-3-1.

The 'Rockets' 11 runs came off a 16-hit attack at the plate.

Harold 'Lefty' Thomas pitched, for the local crew, and gave up two runs on four hits. After Nashville got two runs and three hits off Ralph Strode in 2/3 of the seventh, Fred Morford Thomas came on in relief and gave up one run on two hits the last 2 1/3 innings.

The Rockets play the Smithville 'Tigers' at Beersheba Road Park Sunday, June 24, 1962 at 2:30pm.

While the McMinnville Cardinals pounded walnut 7-1 Grove across town,

"Manchester Tests Power of Rockets" June 29, 1962 Harold 'Lefty' Thomas chocked off the Smithville 'Tigers' on eight hits Sunday, and the Rockets blasted their arch-rivals by a 22 to 9 score at Rocket Park.

Thomas, a southpaw now sporting a 4-0 season record himself, went all the way for the home team. He struck out 10 Tigers and walked only three.

The bats for the Rockets were cold at the outset, and the local (colored) outfit trailed the visitors most of the first five innings. Smithville got a pair of runs in the first inning, but the Rockets pecked away with single runs in the first three to finally go ahead 3 to 2. Smithville came right back with another pair of runs off Thomas in the fourth for a 4 to 3 lead. Then McMinnville's bats began to speak—and by the time Smithville scored another duet of runs in the seventh, the Rockets were leading 12 to 4. Every member of the Rockets squad scored at least once as they pounded

Smithville's Buddy McClain and Billy Phillips for 51 hits and the Tigers chipped in with 16 errors. J.C. Williams, Harvey League, Hugh Locke and Harold 'Lefty' Thomas all scored three runs. Robert 'Mojo' Harris, James

'Moody' Evans, Jack E. Strode and Russell Ramsey each registered. A pair and single runs were scored by Fred Morford Thomas and Paul Woods.

McMinnville now has a 7-3-1 record for the season and will face Manchester at Rocket Park, Sunday at 2:30pm. A 4th of July game with Tullahoma has also been added to the Rockets schedule.

By July 13, 1962 "Rockets Try For Third Win In A Role" The McMinnville Rockets (10-4-1) will be on the road Sunday for a game with the Sparta 'Giants' at Sparta Tenn.

The Rockets will carry a two game winning streak into the Sparta game. On June 30, they lost to Lewisburg 12-6 in their first night game of the season, but bounced that back July fourth to blast Tullahoma 15-6 in a game played on Rocket Field. Then Sunday they edged Sparta 15-12 in a home game.

Louis Smith pitched the first three innings Sunday, but was relieved in the fourth by Harold 'Lefty' Thomas who pitched the last 6 innings and got credit for the win. Thomas aided his own superb pitching by hitting home runs in his first two times at bat. James Russell Ramsey also hit two home runs for the Rockets Sunday.

In July 17, 1962 while One Hour Martinizing's special was two ladies dresses to be cleaned for $1.29, The "Rockets Triumph". The 'Rockets' racked five Sparta pitchers for 22 runs Sunday as they bombed the 'Giants' 22-10 at Sparta Tenn. for the 11th victory of the season. They have four losses.

Included in the Rockets 22 run barrage were home runs by; J.C 'Bo' Williams and first baseman Fred M. Thomas.

The Rockets started right-hander George 'Shakey' Haynes on the mound. He pitched the first five innings and gave up four of the 'Giants' 10 runs. He was relieved in the sixth by southpaw Harold 'Lefty' Thomas, who pitched the rest of the way.

The Nashville 'Stars' will be the 'Rockets' next foe in a home game Sunday at 2:30pm on the Rocket field.

July 24, 1962, "Rockets Win Twelfth 7-6". Home runs by J. C. 'Bo' Williams and Harvey 'Hand Jive' League propelled the McMinnville Rockets to a 17-6 win over the Nashville Tenn. 'Stars' here Sunday. It was the Rockets fourth win in a row. The local team used three pitchers-two right-handers and one southpaw against the Nashville team.

The Rockets record is now (12-4-1), with nine game left to play.

August 10, 1962 "Rockets Set Fourth Unbeaten Winchester"

The Rockets fresh from a 9-3 win over Lewisburg that gave them a (13-4-1) record, and their sixth straight win—take on undefeated Winchester at Rocket Park Sunday. The Rockets plan to start a right-hander Sunday as they try to snap the Tigers winning ways. It will be either Strode, George 'Shakey' Haynes, or Louis Smith.

Fred Morford Thomas, also a right-hander pitched the first seven innings of the Rockets win over Lewisburg Tenn. Sunday. He was relieved by 'Lefty' Thomas.

August 31, 1962 "Three Games In Weekend For Rockets"

A full diet of baseball is on tap this weekend for the local team as they seek to improve their (13-5-1) season record with a three game set that includes a Sunday double header.

The Rockets go to Cookeville Friday night to play the Cookeville 'All-Stars,' then return home for a double header Sunday. The first game of the twin bill will see the Rockets host the Murfreesboro 'Tigers' at 1:15pm. The second game will be between the Rockets and Cookeville.

Murfreesboro, The 'Rockets' foe in the first game, stopped the local team's winning streak Sunday with a 5-3 win at Murfreesboro

Tenn. Harold 'Lefty' Thomas went all the way on the mound for McMinnville, and was charged with the loss.

Playing up until September 14, 1962, "Rockets Try For 17-6-1 Mark Sunday". The McMinnville Rockets will try to pick up their 17th win of the season and make it two in a row over the 'Tennessee Stars' Sunday when they tangle with the Cleveland Tenn. team at Rocket Park here. Game time 2:30 pm.

The Rockets out lasted the 'Stars' at Cleveland last Sunday 12-11, as South-paw Harold 'Lefty' Thomas pitched the route. The game ran their record to (17-6-1).

The local (colored) outfit is already assured of a winning season, with only two games left on the schedule. They will wind up the season next Sunday against the Cookeville 'All-Stars'. It will also be a home game. The season ended with the Rockets finishing a 20-6-1 record.

JFG peanut butter was 3 pounds for 89cents and 4 pounds of Lard cost 39 cents, in April 12, 1963. "Rockets Open Sunday" Rockets will open Sunday against the 'Tennessee Stars' at Cleveland Tenn. Rocket officials do not know the remainder of the schedule at present, but indicated that the team will be on the road for the first two games and then will play two or three games at home.

The two road games at the outset of the season are necessary in order to allow time for improvements to the Rocket baseball field located on Beersheba road.

Ernest's Roadside Market was having a 20-week fishing contest during April 26 1963. "Rockets Win" The Rockets won their first victory—a 16-4 conquest of Sparta—under their belts. Harvey 'Hand Jive' League and Thomas B. Tubbs drove in home runs to win the seesaw battle over the Cleveland 'Tennessee All-Stars' at Cleveland Tenn.

The Rockets defeated the 'All-Stars' at Cleveland in the second game of the season 15-14.

Left-hander Ronnie Blevins started on the mound, but gave way to Fred M. Thomas after 1 2/3 innings. Fred pitched through the eighth, and Harold 'Lefty' Thomas relieved and preserved the victory.

The first two games were played on the road, while members of the team worked on the field and made extensive improvements of this summers' play.

The Rockets also played the Columbia in an exhibition game, but lost by 5 to 1 score. Ralph Strode and Harold 'Lefty' Thomas shared the mound chores against Columbia, Tennessee.

The next game will be Sunday in McMinnville against the Nashville 'Stars.'

May 24, 1963 "Rockets Rip Stars: Play Shelbyville". Fresh from a 25 to 1 shellacking, the 'Rockets' downed the Nashville 'All-Stars.' Rockets go to Shelbyville, Tenn.

Sunday seeking revenge for one of the two defeats they suffered in compiling a (4-2) record.

Shelbyville defeated the Rockets two weeks ago in the second game of a double header after the local team had defeated the 'Tennessee Stars' of Cleveland in the first game.

In Sundays runaway, Harold 'Lefty' Thomas pitched the entire five innings for the Rockets, who wrapped up the game with a big 13—run outburst in the fourth inning. The game was called at the end of five.

June 14, 1963 "Rockets Host Lynchburg"

Three pitchers failed to stem the tide Sunday and the Rockets were defeated 11-8 by Lebanon, Tenn.

Harold Thomas pitched the first three innings and had to retire after being spiked. Ralph Strode replaced 'Lefty' Thomas and pitched four innings, then Fred M. Thomas was on the mound the last three.

The Rockets will meet Lynchburg Sunday at 2:30pm, at the Rocket Ball Park.

June 25, 1963 "Rockets Dump Lebanon"

Across town John Hobbs won for the 'Red Sox' pitching a complete 8-1 game, while a route going pitching was performed by

Harold Thomas on this side of town. Extra timely base hits of Charles 'Scooky' Crabtree, Fred M. Thomas, Tubbs, and Harvey 'Hand Jive' League, paced the team to a 7-3 win over Lebanon Sunday.

Crabtree, Tubbs, and League all connected for doubles with the sacks full of Rockets.

The Rockets will be on the road Sunday for a game with the Murfreesboro 'All-Stars.' The Rockets finished with a W-L-T season.

1 8 4 0

April 14, 1964 "Duel Rockets In Friday Night Game"

The 'Cardinals' (across town white team) will tangle with 'Rockets' tonight (Friday) at the Fairgrounds, not Rocket Ball Park, in an exhibition game at 7pm.

David Phifer will be on the mound for the 'Cardinals,' left-hander Harold Thomas is slated to start for the Rockets. The 'Rocket' have won nine games and lost six (9-6).

Cardinal manager David Rhea said, "The players on both teams have been clamoring for an inter-city tilt for several weeks, and tonight's game was scheduled last Sunday following the Rockets' 7-6 win over Murfreesboro."

"We feel that it will be good for the fans," Rhea said, "win or lose, it would really be helpful for us in giving us a chance to shake off the staleness before getting back on the Mountain Valley League circuit Sunday."

May 15, 1964 "Rockets Play Two Sunday"

The McMinnville Rockets make their 1964 home debut Sunday when they host Lebanon and Columbia at Rocket Park, located just off Beersheba highway near the McMinnville Housing project. The first game against Lebanon, will start at 12:30pm. The Rockets were defeated in their season opener last Sunday when they dropped a 12-3 decision at Shelbyville, Tenn.

June 5, 1964 "Northside, Rockets Play Sunday"

The Northside 'Cubs' and the 'Rockets'—two of McMinnville's' top Semi-Pro baseball teams, will tangle in a specially scheduled game Sunday at 1:30pm at the Rocket Baseball field adjacent to the Civil Defense building.

Northside is currently leading the Warren County League with a 3-1 record, while the Rockets, perennially one of the Mid-State Independent units start off with a shakey start with a 2-5 record. "Both teams will send their best pitchers to the mound Sunday." Northside player/coach Jodie Crick said.

Tuesday he wants to use Ronald Rigsby 2-1, and Rocket Coach Willie 'Bama' Smith plans to go with Russell Ramsey a left-hander.

The batting order will be:

> cf—Bruce Boyd
> lf—Doug Grissom
> rf-Tony Boyd
> 3b—Gerald Bounds
> p—Ronald Rigsby
> c—Ross Rains
> ss-Jodie Crick
> 2b—Richie Clark
> 1b—Ronnie Clark

The Rockets line-up includes:

> p—Russell Ramsey
> rf—Bobby Hudgens
> cf—Larry 'Doby' Brown
> 1b—Elmer Jr. Martin
> 3b—Jack Strode
> ss—J.C. 'Bo' Williams
> 2b—Charles 'Scooky' Crabtree
> 1b—Marshall Thomas
> c-Robert 'Mojo' Harris

The Rockets will also play Cookeville, Tenn. immediately following the Northside game.

Northside and the Rockets will split the gate proceeds, and Coach Crick said the 'Cubs' would use their share to pay for new uniforms recently purchased for the team, and buy new catcher's equipment. Admission will be 25 cents for kids, and 50 cents for adults.

June 12, 1964

"Rockets Go To Columbia"

The McMinnville Rockets who broke out of a slump with a vengeance last Sunday by trouncing the cross town (Northside) team 28-12, will go to Columbia, Tenn. Sunday for a game with the Columbia 'Red Sox.'

The Rockets who now carry a 3-5 record, will depart from Bernard High School by bus at 8:30am Sunday, the fans who wish to accompany may ride the bus paying a $2.00 fee.

June 19, 1964, while across town the County League standings were:

Team	Win	Loss
1. Northside	5	1
2. Midway	3	1
3. Caldwell St.	4	3
4. Centertown	1	4
5. Viola	0	4

The local colored team the "Rockets Win; Play Sunday" fresh from their third win the Rockets will play a double header Sunday at the Rocket ball Park on Beersheba road.

They will tangle with Dekota, Tenn. in the first game and then meet Tullahoma in the second. Harold Thomas will be the starting pitcher for the Rockets, with J.C. Williams at shortstop, Jack Strode at third base, Larry 'Doby' Brown in center field, Robert 'Mojo' Harris behind the plate, Elmer Jr. Martin in left field, Russell Ramsey at first base, Charles 'Scooky' Crabtree at second base, and Robert Hudgins in right field.

The Rockets split a twin bill last Sunday with Columbia 'Red Sox.' Columbia won the first game 20 to 0, but the Rockets came back to win the second game 14 to 0.

June 26, 1964

"Warren County Stars, Vie Here Sunday"

The WLC 'All-Stars' will host the McMinnville Rockets in an exhibition game Sunday at 2:30 pm at Fair Grounds Park, Located near the Smithville highway.

Admission to the game will be 25 cents, and 50 cents and 'All-Star' managers, Jodie Crick and Robert Turner say their share of the proceeds will be used for the purchase of trophies for the league champions.

Leading off the 'All-Stars' Sunday will be baseman Gerald Bounds, and following him in the batting order will be:

> 2b Ronald Rigsby
> ss Charles Winston
> 3b Bobby Solomon
> lf James Bennett
> cf Jim McCarty
> rf Bill Montandon
> c Harold Johnson
> p Marshall Solomon

The Rockets Batting order will read:

> 3b Jack Strode
> c Robert 'Mojo' Harris
> rf Elmer Jr. Martin
> ss J.C. 'Bo' Williams

2b Wayne 'Wolf' Wolford
lf Charles 'Scooky' Crabtree
cf Larry 'Doby' Brown
1b Russell Ramsey
p James Clinton Strode

June 30, 1964

"Rockets Tip County Loop Stars 5-4"

Left-hander Harold 'Lefty' Thomas cooled off the bats of The Warren County League 'All-Stars' in a seven-inning relief stint Sunday, and the McMinnville Rockets finally got to Marshall Solomon in the last two innings to pull out a 15-5.

The 'All-Stars' scored three runs in the first three innings and held a 3-1 lead at the end of seven. Before the Rockets touched Solomon for four hits and four runs in the last two innings. The Midway South paw had suffered only one hit.

Three of the five hits off Solomon were for extra bases: Triples by J.C. Williams and Robert 'Mojo' Harris, and a double by Charles 'Scooky' Crabtree. The other Rocket hits were by Jack Strode and Larry 'Doby' Brown.

Charles Winton led the 'All-Stars' with two singles, while Jim McCarty, Solomon, James Bennett and Harold Johnson had a hit apiece. Bennett's hit was a first inning triple that scored two runs.

Harold 'Lefty' Thomas was the winning pitcher, holding the All-Stars to one hit and one run the last seven innings while striking out 13.

July 31, 1964

"Rockets win 7th in a Row"

As Johnson suffered from a torn lip when he collided with teammate Charles Winton near the pitchers mound Saturday night in the County League All-Stars 15-5 loss to the Rockets. Stitches were required to close the wound.

The 'Rockets' now sporting a seven-game win streak, take on Columbia in a double-header at the Rocket Park.

The Rockets won their 7th straight Saturday night as Harold 'Lefty' Thomas hurled them to a 15-5 win over the WCL All-Stars. Charles 'Scooky' Crabtree led the hitting with four hits in five appearances at the plate.

They made it 8 in a row Sunday as they edged the Smithville 'Tigers' 6-5. Fred Morford Thomas, pitching in relief of Harold Thomas got the win. (Player/ Coach) Jack Strode and James Russell Ramsey hit home runs.

August 11, 1964

"Rockets Tip Murfreesboro 7 to 6"

The Rockets defeated the Murfreesboro 'Tigers' 7 to 6 Sunday for their ninth win of the season, behind the fine pitching of James 'Clinton' Strode, and Fred Morford Thomas.

James Clinton Strode started on the mound, and was relieved by Morford Thomas, with Thomas getting credit for the win. Thomas also helped his own cause with a home run, and Robert 'Mojo' Harris had a key double.

The 'Rockets' will play the McMinnville 'Cardinals' at Fair Grounds Park Friday night at 7pm. Then host the Smithville 'Tigers' Sunday 2pm at Rocket Field.

August 18, 1964

"Phifer's Hurling Stops Rockets 8-1"

David Phifer stifled the Rockets on three hits Friday night, and the Cardinals ruptured the Rockets eight game win streak 8-1 in the first inter-city semi-pro baseball clash of the season.

"David was never better in his life," Cardinal manager David Rhea commented after the game. "He over powered the normally heavy-hitting Rockets with his fast ball, and with his unusual sharp control."

The only run off the Cardinals right hander was an unexpected marker in the second inning that gave the Rockets a 1-0 lead. Charles Crabtree was safe on an error by second baseman Don Roberts to start the inning, and then Crabtree stole second and third, and scored on a wild throw to catcher David Hillis.

Harold 'Lefty' Thomas, the starter and loser for the Rockets, and both runners scored as Percy Phifer singled for the 'Cards' ninth hit off Thomas.

Roberts and Duke led the Cardinals with two hits apiece, and James 'Clinton' Strode, Robert 'Mojo' Harris and Harold Thomas had the three hits for the Rockets.

August 18, 1964

"Rockets Face Doyle Nine"

The Rockets will try to get another win streak started Wednesday night when they host Doyle at 7:30pm. The Rockets also have a home game against South Pittsburg Sunday at 2:30 pm. Harold Thomas a lefty is expected to be the starting pitcher against Doyle, while Morford Thomas will probably throw against South Pittsburg.

August 28, 1964

"Rockets to Play Sunday"

Four games are on tap Sunday afternoon at the McMinnville Rocket's diamond.

Meeting the Rockets will be South Pittsburg and Tullahoma. South Pittsburg will also field a girls' team and a little league team against local groups. The girl's game will open at 12:30 p.m.

September 4, 1964 when a 6 pack of beer was $1.39

"The Rockets Host Red Birds"

The Rockets will host the McMinnville 'Cardinals' in their second intra city semi-pro baseball game of the season, Sunday at 2:30 p.m. at Rocket Ball Field.

The Rockets will be trying to break a two game losing streak (they lost 2 games Sunday) and at the time will be out to avenge a 8-1 Cardinal win earlier in the season that ended a eight game Rocket win streak.

The Rockets also have a game scheduled at South Pittsburg Monday, and fans interested in making the trip are asked to contact: Willie 'Bama' Smith, Cowan 'Kind' Roberts or Joe 'Edward' Ramsey.

April 30, 1968

"Rockets lose opener to Fayetteville 3-1"

The Rockets opened their '68 baseball season in Fayetteville and suffered a stinging 3-1 defeat as hitting seemed to be the big problem for the Rockets.

Rockets' coach, Harold 'Lefty' Thomas praised the pitching of his right-hander, Danny Sullivan after returning to McMinnville. Thomas said, "You just couldn't have asked for a better pitched game than the job Sullivan turned in. Our hitting was what beat us." Danny went the distance on the mound, struck out 12 batters and gave up only four hits. He issued only one base on balls for the full nine innings.

Fayetteville took the lead 1-0 in the fifth inning and then increased to 3-0 in the eighth; by the sending two more runs across the plate. The Rockets picked up their only run in the final inning when Russell Ramsey Stroked a double to left for the first hit off the Fayetteville pitching staff, and then a walk to Bobby Cope, later developed into a double steal and an error on the third baseman enabled the Rockets to push across a run.

May 7, 1968

"McMinnville Rockets defeat Cookeville 6-4"

A fine relief job by Danny Sullivan and tripplers socked by Larry 'Doby' Brown and Elmer 'Jr.' Martin proved just to be enough for the local Rockets to overcome a Cookeville lead and capture victory number 1 for the '68 season.

The Rockets picked up a run in the first inning as Dwight 'Sug' Barnhill led off with a walk and Tom Weeden was hit by a pitch, Wayne 'Wolf' Wolford followed by reaching base trying to sacrifice, then with the bases loaded and one out, Ronnie Danhoff lifted a single to drive in a run and give the Rockets a 1-0 lead.

The Rockets picked up a run in the second and third inning to give them a 3-0 lead, but Cookeville scored a run in the bottom of the third after Bobby Cope had retired the first six batters on strikes. With McMinnville leading 3-1, Cookeville's J. Roberts and E. Strode hit back-to-back homers off Cope, so coach Harold Thomas called upon his curve ball artist Danny Sullivan to take over mound duties.

Sullivan came on in the fifth and retired the side on strikes then sat them down in the sixth inning on strikes and added on more to his total in the seventh as he retired the Cookeville batters without issuing a hit.

The Rockets picked up 10 hits Sunday with Bobby Cope, Elmer 'Jr.' Martin and Wayne 'Wolf' Wolford each collecting two. Cookeville was stopped on four hits.

Sullivan relieved Cope in the fifth with the score notched at 3-3, finished and got the credit for the win. Sullivan's record now stands at 1-1 with his loss being suffered to Fayetteville.

The local sport fans will have the opportunity to come out and watch the Rockets at home Sunday, May 12, 1968 as they tangle with a tough Murfreesboro out fit. The Rockets' two opening games have been away. Game time will be at 2p.m. on the Rockets' Diamond located behind the new housing projects.

May 9, 1968, while baseball/football coach Pedro Paz was coaching Central high,

"The Rockets were to host Murfreesboro"

The Rockets supporting a 1-1 record for the 68' season will host Murfreesboro Sunday.

Coaches Harold Thomas and Willie Smith have fine pitching with Danny Sullivan and Bobby Cope taking care of all mound duties. Sullivan has worked 12 innings and sent 19 batters back to the bench by strikeouts. Bobby Cope served up the other seven innings with 10 strikeouts to his credit. In the hitting department, Larry 'Doby' Brown, Elmer 'Jr.' Martin, James Russell Ramsey, Robert 'Mojo' Harris, and Wayne 'Wolf' Wolford are supporting them now and later as the season rolls on, Coach Thomas thinks his team will be very tough, and will play some fine ball for the local fans to watch.

May 14, 1968 "As Rockets Romp 8-0"

A strong combination of Danny Sullivan and John Hobbs coupled with the 16 hit attack powered the Rockets to a 8-0 victory over Murfreesboro Sunday in a diamond tilt played at the park.

Sullivan started on the mound for the Rockets and retired the first six batters to face him. Larry 'Doby' Brown opened the first frame for the Rockets by popping to the third baseman, but Wayne 'Wolf' Wolford connected for a triple to left center and scored on a ringing hit up the middle by Bobby Cope. Elmer 'Jr' Martin followed with a hit, but died on the base pass as Ronnie Danhoff and Larry Tate failed to drive him around.

With Danny Sullivan and the Rockets enjoying a 1-0 lead, E.B. Malone reached base off Sullivan when he grounded a ball back to second baseman.

The Rockets were retired in order for the third inning, but after the Rocket hurler sat down the Rutherford County out fit again without a run, Ronnie Danhoff led off the Fourth with a double to left center and scored on a run producing single by Larry Tate. Ronnie Blevins followed with a double to plate Tate home to give the Rockets a 3-0 lead going into the fifth.

Sullivan came back with his big curve ball in the fifth inning and registered three more strike outs and gave away to John Hobbs in the seventh by finishing the sixth inning with a strike out to run his total to 11 for the six innings he worked. The Murfreesboro outfit collected on two hits from him, which was two singles.

Hobbs came in the seventh and sit down three straight batters vie the strike out way. Hobbs finished the tilt yielding only one hit and striking out seven batters running the total to 18 for the pitching of Rocket Hurlers.

McMinnville erupted for three big runs in the sixth inning as Blevins led by reaching base on an error. Gregory Martin pinch hitting for Howard 'Doony' Henny, ripped a double to center, but Ronnie 'Ghost' Blevins was thrown out going into third base. Sullivan delivered a single, his third of the day to put two runners on with one out Larry 'Doby' Brown Stroked a single to plate one run and Wayne 'Wolf' Wolford then delivered a two run double to send the Rockets out to a 7-0 lead.

Leading the Rockets at the plate with his hits was Danny Sullivan, who collected three for the day. Wayne Wolford, Bobby Cope, Elmer 'Jr.' Martin, Ronnie Danhoff and Ronnie Blevins had two hits each. The Rockets are now 2-1 for the season.

The local out fit is scheduled to travel to Murfreesboro next Sunday to battle the Rutherford County Crew.

May 21, 1968

"Little Hope Tips Rockets"

The Rockets traveled to Rutherford County Sunday to battle Little Hope on the diamond and came back an 8-3 loser.

Wayne Sullens started on the mound for the Rockets and received help from John Hobbs. Sullens got credit for thee loss in his first start of the season. This loss to Little Hope puts the Rockets at a 2-2 record.

June 4, 1968

"Twice on Sunday"

The Rockets baseball club jumped out to a 6-0 lead in the first game and watched the visitors knot the score then came back to win 8-6 and again go out 4-2 in the night cap and barely hold on to a 4-3 victory for a double win to run their record to 4-2 for the season.

In the opener Sunday, Larry Brown singled in the first frame with one out, and then Bobby Cope rapped a hit to right and Elmer 'Jr.' Martin followed with a single to drive in Brown and Cope to give the Rockets a 2-0 lead.

The Rockets enjoyed a big four run rally in the second inning with Robert 'Mojo' Harris leading off with a base on balls, Howard 'Doony' Henny was hit by a pitch and John 'Fireball' Hobbs popped to right field for the first out. Wayne Wolford rapped a run producing hit and Cope followed with his second hit to drive in two more big runs and give the local outfit a 6-0 lead.

John Hobbs on the mound for the Rockets held them scoreless for five innings issuing only one hit that in the third inning. Fayetteville came up with two runs off Hobbs in the sixth and another tally in the seventh to cut the lead to 6-3.

The visitors scored three more big runs in the eighth frame on one hit off Hobbs. With one out, coach Harold Thomas called upon Danny Sullivan to relieve Hobbs of the mound duties. Sullivan came in and got the side out and set them down in order in the ninth.

Ronnie Danhoff stepped to the plate in the eighth inning and parked a fastball over the left field fence for a solo round tripper to give the Rockets a 7-6 lead. 'Mojo' Harris reached base on an error and scored on Gregory Martin's hit to run the score at 8-6. Danhoff's blow was a winning factor.

Danny Sullivan started on the mound in the nightcap for the Rockets and issued the visitors a run in the first frame on two hits. The local crew came back in the bottom of the inning and sent two rallies across home plate as Wayne 'Wolf' Wolford led off with a single and John Hobbs drew a base on balls. Russell Ramsey drove a hit up the middle, but Hobbs was out at the plate trying to score behind Wolford. Ramsey scored on a throwing error to give the Rockets a 2-1 lead.

Hits for Elmer 'Jr.' Martin, Ronnie Danhoff and Larry Tate produced two more runs in the third to give the Rockets a 4-1 lead. Fayetteville picked up their second run off Sullivan, so coach Harold Thomas called upon Bobby Cope to aid Sullivan in relief. Cope came on and pitched strong issuing the victors only one hit. The Rockets made a clean sweep for the day with a 4-3 victory in the second game.

The McMinnville Rockets and Viola Clowns

The Rockets were first managed and coached by Remus Terry in the 1930's. The team wore very hot cotton uniforms. The colors were gray with blue trim. The letters M & R were on the left side of the shirts and on the middle of the ball caps.

By the early 1970's the uniforms changed to a cool polyester uniform. White shirts with navy blue sleeves, and stripes, the pants were white with pin stripes. The baseball caps were navy blue with a large white 'R' in the front, and navy blue socks. The Rockets played on numerous baseball fields during their existence, before they owned their own ball field. Earlier years were played on a field found now behind Bobby Ray Elementary school, which is at the present time a football field. The Rockets played at the Old Fair Grounds that is now called 'Magnetec' Corp. on Red road. Another field that was of use was located on Beersheba Street before you get to the on existing bridge. In the 1940's there was a field to be cleared before each game was played, located next to the Garment Factory on Sparta Street. By 1962 the Rockets built a clubhouse with bleaches on a field off of Beersheba (Cope) street, where the water plant now stands. By the early 1970's the home field was permanently established. In order to accommodate more fans the field was moved farther into the left field. Home plate was moved at this time and remains this way today. Eulous Martin and Marcellus Sutton built the clubhouse along with several of the Baseball players. The clubhouse still stands today at 'Rocket' ball field. Willie 'Bama' Smith paid $20.00 for the use of the ball field at Century Electric, now Magnetec, then the Old Fair Grounds.

In 1948 Willie 'Bama' Smith took over the management from Remus Terry, and coached with Jack Estie Strode a well-rounded team to many victories, for years to come.

These two African-American baseball teams integrated in the early sixties. This was another door that opened for the people of Warren County, and a treat for visiting teams. This was the first team to integrate during this era. When opposing teams played us they were amazed of the progress in a small southern town.

These two independent Semi-Pro teams played all throughout the state of Tennessee and Alabama. There wasn't a championship to be won, but the bragging rights were the most important issue. The Rockets would play their cross-town rivals, which were in a league, and played for championships. Every year the Rockets would play the McMinnville 'All-Stars,' or the top team. The 'All-Stars' team consisted of the best players of the six teams. There was only one recording of the Rockets being defeated by the 'All-Stars.'

The history of these two teams Viola 'Clowns' & McMinnville Rockets is as rich as the heritage we stand for. There were good times and bad times. Some of the visitor's ball fields were cow pastures. The opposing team would clear the cows out of the field and clean up the cow droppings just before game time. There were some places such as Milton, Tennessee where for one instant there wouldn't be but ten people sitting around the field, then all of a sudden people would come out of the woods, as many as a couple of hundred fans to watch the game. Before the Rocket Park was completely ours, we had to shovel off cow droppings before we practiced or played any games. Avalon Dairies owned the property before the city gave us the rights. The worst thing in the world is to run after a ball and dive. Guess what the prize is! There was no running water there, unless you went down to the river, which ran along the outfield borders.

The local team paid the umpires, and as a rule they were good. Some of the calls were highly controversial, and you could see the tension in the eyes, not to mention some out burst. The fans of both teams supported their team immensely. In the earlier days, fans would travel to see a game by cars. By the 60's buses were provided to travel to other towns to play baseball. The fans would load up the buses to assure a seat for the treat they were about to receive.

The magnificent nine of Viola, which consisted of nine family members before other players, joined them. This was considered one of the best baseball teams of the fifties. The coach and a few of the 'Clowns' merged with the McMinnville 'Rockets' and formed a super team.

Neither the 'Clowns' nor the 'Rockets' have ever recorded a losing season. Even though they played mostly on Sunday, it was known that about 30 games were played each season. There were many double headers played. Sometimes the Rockets would play three games a day. There was a list of hitters that could really excited the crowed, these hard hitters were known to knock out windows in the near by schools and other buildings. Some of these good hitters could reach down and lift a baseball seemingly straight up in the air, and then finally coasting its way out of the ballpark. Some of the balls were never found. The defense on a good day was unbelievable.

Some of these players would start playing in the organization at a very young age. Fourteen years old and would play until they reached 50 years of age. So many years have gone by since the last baseball games, records are very hard to find. Many newspaper articles and hear say from the older generation is all we have left. Many players have moved in the last 10 to 15 years and discarded any extra load such as uniforms, bats, balls, gloves and scorebooks. Thinking that they would never be used for any particular purpose again. Very few people took cameras to the ballpark, because they were going to have a good time, not take pictures. Most blacks in the 1930's-1960's didn't even own a camera. Even in the local newspapers there just wasn't a need to get a picture because the team did not have the right credentials to be recognized. The color of the skin of the ball player held back their immediate exposure to a large group of people. In the mid sixties when the team integrated, the exposure began to grow and pictures were beginning to pop up in the media.

The Rockets had an abundance of teaching talent. There were times when Willie 'Bama' Smith would yell out instructions. 'Abe' Thomas would show different forms of fielding the ball. Harold Thomas would teach the art of refined pitching. Elmer 'Jr.' Martin, Jack Strode and Michael J. Martin took up the coaching and manage ring task in the late 1970's to the 1980's. They were excellent baseball players in their own right, and time.

I guess you could say that Joe Edward Ramsey was the general manager for a great deal of these years. Joe and I. V. Joe were the main collectors at the gate. I. V. Joe was known for his hamburgers and French fries.

Occasionally you would see a bootleg bottle of moonshine or a bottle of beer. We are still trying to find out where this stuff came from, when we lived in a dry county.

Just to name a few: first baseman James Russell Ramsey could hit a baseball a mile high, and two miles long with one mighty swing. Russell as we called him, was an excellent first baseman, and a powerful clean-up hitter.

The Rockets would go to Nashville and Pikesville to play the prison inmates. There were wild times too. Players James Clinton Strode and Jack Strode rode down the highway going to Decatur, Tenn. In Tom Weeden's '57 Mercury, passing a cigarette lighter from one car to another traveling over one hundred mile per hour. Needless to say they made it to the game in one piece.

Clarence E. Martin

Worked as a porter at the Brown Hotel as a youngster. Ray Roberts gave him his checkbook when he went off to college, not even his wife nor kids had that privilege. Once Clarence asked Ray Roberts if he could borrow $200 to help purchase a new car. Ray said, "I'll give you $200 but I wouldn't loan you the money. Clarence played with the Rocket organization from 1943 to 1948. He was 15 years old when he started playing. He remembers very well the pitch that made him decide a career change, as though it were just yesterday. The pitched baseball hit him as he was in the batters box. He says he was distracted, and before he knew it the ball hit him right in the bridge of the nose. Both eyes were darkened for a few days. He thought it was about time to give up baseball then.

Clarence remembers that a sports writer by the name of Rayford Davis would on occasions interview this young athlete. This was rare for this particular time and era. There were some very positive reviews. As years passed they became good friends. Clarence said, "Whites attended our games in those days, but we never got a chance to play any of their teams, that's just the way it was then in the 1940's."

"We had full uniforms and collected money and donations at the gate." "We traveled to places like South Pittsburgh and Columbia Tennessee. Hitting Homeruns at the age of 15 is a great task."

Clarence remembers Carl T. Rowan playing alongside of him in the infield. Carl was much smaller than Clarence, but he held his own. These guys also played some organized football in their day.

McMINNVILLE ROCKETS—These young men make up the McMinnville Rockets, who hold a 4-2 record after sweeping a doubleheader from Fayetteville Sunday afternoon at the Rocket park. Elmer Martin, Jr., Ronnie Danhof, Bobby Cope and Larry Tate had big hits in producing runs that enabled the Rockets to take both games. Danny Sullivan picked up the victories in both games, but John Hobbs and Bobby Cope pitched fine ball. The Rockets lost once to Fayetteville earlier in the season and once to Little Hope of Rutherford county. They have defeated Cookeville, Little Hope, and Fayetteville twice.

1974 'Rockets'

James Russell Ramsey

Russell as he was called could hit a ball a mile high and two miles long with one mighty left handed swing. He was an excellent 1st baseman and clean up hitter. Pitchers did not like the thought of facing him at the plate. If you put one (baseball) around his ankles he would send it to the river.

Russell was considered a long ball hitter. When in Spencer one hot Sunday July day in 1973 an older white citizen of the town stated that we should leave there before sundown if we won the game. We won! Russell broke out three windows for homeruns himself. The school windows were located across the street from the ballpark. Do you know that nothing was said to us out of the way when we packed up and prepared to go home; later Spencer came to the Rocket Park to play the home team.

Ronnie 'Ghost' Blevins / Robert 'Mac' Mc Reynolds

Ronnie played a mean outfielder, he could shoot you down am a right field is easy as picking berries from a vine. The strong arm of this left-hander was a sight to see. There was no such thing as a looping throw. The throw was like a bullet on a straight line to its destination.

Ronnie had a chance to go to the big leagues, "but girls got in the way" he said. The New York Yankees were taken a good look at him. 'Ghost' as he was sometimes called pitched quite a bit during his career as a Rocket.

Robert 'Mac' McReynolds Jr. remembers when he was called upon in a practice session to bunt the ball. Bobby Cope was pitching at the time knew Robert couldn't bunt when Robert faced the pitch, he literally faced the pitch. The ball filed off the bat into 'Mac's' chest, Bobby said "Somebody said try it again," and 'Mac' did, again squaring around with his whole body of the ball popped off the bat into his chest once again and this time he almost lost his breath.

Ronnie Blevins & 'Mac' Robert Reynolds played in some other sports during their youthful days. Ronnie played football as an eighth grader for the Bernard High School 'Tigers' and the BHS Basketball team later.

Robert 'Mac' Reynolds played basketball for the McMinnville City High School team. He had a scholarship to attend the local University, but because of the times he was denied a chance to be picked up. He still feels that if the right people where in his corner he could have made it to college sports, but a fellow class member was chosen over him because many white students are selected instead of blacks.

Bobby Cope, & Elmer Jr. Martin
R. Danhof, J. Hobbs, D. Sullivan, & Brown

Robert 'Mojo' Harris

'Mojo' started playing baseball at the age of fourteen years old. He played with Viola 'Clowns' and the McMinnville 'Rockets', and McMinnville 'Cardinals.' The ageless wonder played until

he reached the golden age of 51 years old. Bad knees were the only thing the stopped him. 'Mojo' was known for his jive talking behind the plate. There wasn't a man he feared coming into home plate. He was often known to catch a complete inning without wearing his facemask. If you thought about stealing a base of him, you had better think again. 'Mojo' was a natural long ball hitter. Once in a while he would play first base, but mostly Catcher. 'Mojo' was considered the most powerful consistent hitter. 'Mojo' threw out 85% of the base runners that tried to steal on him.

Baseball is still in his blood, after retiring from the State as a Road Supervisor, and he continued to encounter with the baseball system as a youth umpire and the baseball commissioner. He is truly a leader and a role model for all.

Joe Edward Ramsey's Stories

Of the (Donohue, Ancestors) 1940 walking, or mules were the mode of travel, when Joe lived in the Arcade Community.

Rocket Ball Field was cleared in late 1950's. A wooden fence was on one side of the house and bleachers. On the other side Jack Strode and Clinton got lumber for the fence. The City of McMinnville gave the ball field to the Rockets. The players and fans worked on the field until dark every night until they were finished. Urban renewal helped fund the field with $3000.00.

Elcain Brown, Marcellus Sutton and the Team helped to build the present building at the southeast corner of the park.

After the Ramsey's and Fred Hoover built the ball field in Viola, the 'Clowns' would play games occasionally when the 'Red Sox' and 'Cubs' were out of town.

Most of the time the Viola 'Clowns' played on Saturday's because the league games to on Sunday's.

While Viola's league consisted of six white teams, the 'Clowns' played many teams in and around this area.

The 'Rockets' would play at the baseball field behind Central High, in the 1940's, which was a makeshift field. It was part of a cornfield. This is presently called Bobby Ray Memorial Elementary School.

On the Viola baseball field in the 1940's in order to get a drink of water you would have go down to a lone water faucet located a ways down the right field corner.

Players competed for the love of the game and fans were more willing to watch. The Viola 'Clowns' came to join the 'Rockets' in the 1960's. The team was managed by John 'Abe' Thomas. Some of players were Harold, Morford, 'Skin,' Jr. 'Mule,' Jack, Clinton, Harvey, Russell, and Louis Smith.

The 'Rockets' played prison inmates at Pikesville State Farm, in the late 1960's.

The 'Rockets' played on Bobby Ray Elementary School ball field (Central High School) around 1940.

Carpenter Eulous Martin and Marcellus Sutton did missionary work on 'Rocket' Park.

In Milton, Tennessee players had to run the cows off the field in order to play ball. There were numerous rocks on this ball field.

The 'Rockets' played at the Nashville ballpark, which at this time and still is the minor league ballpark.

Bobby Cope, Howard 'Dunny' Henny & Dan Smith

Danny Smith Sr. at
Rocket Ball Park

**L-R top row; J. Martin, J. King, R. Harris,
R. McReynolds, D. Martin & G. Martin
2nd row; M. Martin, R. Martin, H. Henny,
D. Barnhill, R. Blevins,& T. Martin
Front L-R; W. Wolford & L. Brown
1975 McMinnville 'Rockets'**

Wayne R. 'Wolf' Wolford Sr.

I started playing baseball with the McMinnville Rockets at the age of sixteen years old. Jack Strode decided that it was my time to step up and hold the position that he so graciously played, (3rd base).

We wore the cotton uniforms, which were white and blue, until the 1970's. The newer uniforms were blue caps with the white letter 'R' in front. The shirts were white with blue pin stripes and blue letters 'Rockets' across the chest. The pants were also white with blue pin stripes and we had blue and white socks.

At various times in my career, I played third and second base and I also pitched. My contribution to the 'Rockets' were during the years of 1964-1983. Even though I served in the U.S. Army from 1975-1995, I still got to come home and engage in some games. In the early part of my career I batted in the top portion of the line-up. Mainly starting out just being a base hitter, then in the 70's I started to stroke a few balls out of the park. I was considered a very fast base runner. I used my head and thought a play out before the ball was ever hit.

One of my first little league coaches (J.C. Williams) taught me to always be aware when you are on the ball diamond, (and I mean the hard way). While horse playing at practice one hot summer at the age of eleven, I looked up just in time to see a baseball coming straight toward my head. Just so happens I caught it. J.C. was trying to get my attention, and he did. Even to this day, when I walk anywhere near a ball field, I pay attention to where the ball is.

Those were the good old days; when Willie 'Bama' Smith was yelling out instructions, 'Abe' Thomas was showing different forms of fielding, running, and hitting. Joe Ramsey was collecting money at the gate to keep the organization going strong. I.V. Joe Ramsey, cooked hamburgers at the concession stand. Jack Strode kept all of us in line and acting professional at all times. Even though we didn't drink we would see bootleg whiskey, moonshine, and bottled beer in the stands.

Mr. Howard Henny Sr. was always the 'Rocket's' chief fan. He would always put on a good show during the ball game. He really loved baseball. Whether the game was at home or on the road, he was one of the many faithful fans.

Mr. Sutton was primarily the home plate umpire for many years.

The Viola Clowns

John Leonard 'Abe' Thomas

The Viola 'Clowns' started playing baseball in the 1940's, coached by John 'Abe' Thomas Sr. This team was located in Viola, Tennessee in the late forties. There was a baseball field already to play on. Their white counter parts named the Viola 'Red Sox' played on, and owned that field. The black team, the Viola 'Clowns' would pay a small amount of money to use the baseball field when the 'Red Sox' were playing at another field or out of town. The field and some of the lights still remain for big events the town holds.

The Clowns consisted of all family members at the start. The Magnificent Nine of Viola were made of family members before others joined the team. Coach John L. 'Abe' Thomas Sr. was considered the best coach of his time. The Clowns played various teams in the surrounding mid-state.

Their uniforms consisted of a heavy gray sweat pants, and dark blue sweat shirts. They terrorized the entire baseball community locally. The pitching was excellent, hitting and base running was not to be forgotten, not to mention the coaching staff.

Cars were the main source of transportation to and from the games. A small fee of $.50 was collected at the gate. The Viola Ball field still stands today across from the Viola Post Office. Later in the fifties the 'Clowns' merged with the McMinnville 'Rockets.'

Facts

· The Rockets organization had to go to Tullahoma, Tn. To purchase their baseballs. They later found out that the balls were seconds and were unfit to play with. The 'Rockets' always said a prayer before the game started.

The 'Rockets' played on the new fairgrounds in the early 1960's.

Marcellus Sutton did the foundation to the old baseball club house as well as the new the house, Al King Brown along with Eulous Martin did most of the construction work along with some of the other baseball players.

- Riverside, and Little Hope in Murfreesboro Tenn. Ball fields were so bad that that you couldn't wear spikes. (Steel spikes were worn at this time), this was an early 1960's.
- The famous by NFL Quarterback 'Jefferson Street Joe' played for the Nashville All-Stars in the 1950's' while playing the 'Rockets' before he became a Pro.
- The 'Rockets' traveled to State Farm Penitentiary to play game of baseball with the inmates.

'WHERE THEY PLAYED'

ALEXANDRIA, TENN.
ALGOOD, TENN.
BEERSHEBA SPRINGS, TENN.
BELL BUCKLE, TENN.
CARTHAGE, TENN.
CELINA, TENN.
CHAPEL HILL, TENN.
CHARLOTTE, TENN.
CHATTANOOGA, TENN.
CLEVELAND, TENN.
COLUMBIA, TENN.
COOKEVILLE, TENN.
COWAN, TENN.
DECHARD, TENN.
FAYETTEVILLE, TENN.
FRANKLIN, TENN.
HUNTLAND, TENN.
HUNTSVILLE, ALABAMA
JASPER, TENN.
JESSUP, TENN.
La VERGNE, TENN.
LACASS, TENN.
LEBANON, TENN.
LENOIR CITY, TENN.
LITTLE HOPE, TENN.
LYNCHBURG, TENN.
MANCHESTER, TENN.

McMINNVILLE, TENN.
MILTON, TENN.
MT. JULIET, TENN.
MURFREESBORO, TENN.
NASHVILLE, TENN.
NOLANSVILLE, TENN.
PULASKI, TENN.
RIVERSIDE, TENN.
ROCKWOOD, TENN.
SCOTTSBORO, TENN.
SHELBYVILLE, TENN.
SHERWOOD, TENN.
SILVER POINT, TENN.
SMITHVILLE, TENN.
SMYRNA, TENN.
SOUTH PITTSBURG, TENN.
SPARTA, TENN.
SPENCER, TENN.
STEVENSON, TENN.
TULLAHOMA, TENN.
VIOLA, TENN.
WATERTOWN, TENN.
WHITFIELD, TENN.
WINCHESTER, TENN.
WOODBURY, TENN.

'Rocket' Ball Park

'Rocket' Baseball Monument at Leroy Ramsey Park

1940's 'Rocket' Baseball game on Red Road (the old Fairgrounds)

The Rockets & Clowns

After most home games both ball teams and fans would end up at the American Legion Post 208, in Leesburg—better known as the 'Hall.' This was a place to 'cool out' after the game or games, or reminisce with friends about past games. The younger people under drinking age could not enter this establishment when beer was being sold. There were plenty of cold drinks (sodas) fish sandwiches, hamburgers and most of all-music. The jukebox would be thumping to the sounds of Otis Redding, The Temptations, Marvin Gaye, Wilson Pickett, Aretha Franklin, Ray Charles and many more artists of the times.

Sometimes the visiting team didn't leave for home until the wee hours of the morning. Most of the time on Saturdays a band was to play at the 'Hall.'

The dress code was come as you are, and please bring some money. Sometimes the players wouldn't shower or change clothes before going to the 'Hall.' You can imagine the odor.

Players Names

VIOLA CLOWNS & McMINNVILLE ROCKETS

30	RICHARD 'ROCK EYED-SLIM' LOWE; 1B
30	JOHN WALTER 'SNAKE' TERRY; C, 1B
30	JOHN LEONARD 'ABE' THOMAS SR.; V / CLOWNS, SB, CF, MNG. COACH
30	REMUS TERRY; INF, MNG.
30	FRANK LOCKE; OF
30	WILLIE HENNESSEY; INF.
30	BUDDY YOUNG; 1B
30	PAUL 'TOOT' RAMSEY; INF
30	'BUNNY' HENNEGAR; OF
30	MAXWELL 'MACK' PATTERSON; INF.
30	ADGE SHOCKLEY; INF
30	JOHN ED WOODARD; OF
30	MACK 'MAC' YOUNG; C
30	H. C. DONABURY; INF
30	SAM SIMS JR.; INF
30	JAMES RHODES; INF.
30	LAWRENCE BROWN; OF
30	HENRY SAVAGE; OF
30	WILL 'RUSTY' LUSK; INF.
30	LOUIE 'SLICK' RAMSEY; SB
30	BEN HENNEGAR; INF
40	JOE BROWN BATES; OF
40	HAROLD BUFORD ETTER; INF
40	GEORGE NORTHCUTT; V/ CLOWNS, OF
40	HOLLIS NORTHCUTT; V/CLOWNS, 3B
40	ROSSIE NORTHCUTT; V/CLOWNS, INF
40	R. D. 'BUD' NORTHCUTT; V/CLOWNS, SB
40	BOBBY BILES; OF, 1B

40	GEORGE 'BOOTS' THOMAS; V / CLOWNS, 1B
40	WILLIAM 'SON' RAMSEY; UMPIRED ONLY
30	GEORGE MARTIN; P
40	RANDOPH RAMSEY 'HACK'; C.
40	SON GRAYSON; CF
40	HERBERT 'HUB' COPE; P
40	LAWRENCE MARTIN JR.; 1B
40	CLARENCE 'BILL' MARTIN; P
40	ROBERT L. 'BOZO' McREYNOLDS; C
40	WILLIE 'BAMA' SMITH; P, V/CLOWNS, MNG, Coach
40	BILLIE SMITH; P
40	JOHN WALTER 'SNAKE' TERRY; C, 1B
30	WALL C. 'WALTER' HENNEGAR; C
30	FRED MAYNARD; 1B, MNG.
40	FRANKLIN J. WOODLEE; SS
40	JAMES 'MULE' HENNEGAR; OF
40	JOHN LOCKE; C
40	LAWRENCE 'JAY' COPE JR.; INF
40	JAMES 'JIM' MARTIN; OF
30	HERMAN 'BUSTER' MARTIN; 1B
40	CLARENCE E. 'SONNY' MARTIN; CF
40	HARVEY 'HAND JIVE' LEAGUE; CF, OF
40	CHARLES SHOCKLEY; OF, P
40	D. C. SHOCKLEY; OF
40	JIM MARTIN; INF
40	CARL T. ROWAN; 2B
40	HARDY COPE JR.; INF
40	CLYDE RAMSEY; INF
40	ELCAIN BROWN; 2B
40	BUFORD 'RAZZ' HUNTER; OF
40	LOUIS SMITH; P
40	GENE NORTHCUTT; V/CLOWNS, P

40   IRBY SCOTT; OF.

50   TOM 'BOOKER' NORTHCUTT; INF, CF, V/
      CLOWNS 50 THOMAS 'LITTLE TOM'
      NORTHCUTT; INF, CLOWNS 50 FRANK BUFORD
      BONNER; V/CLOWNS, P

50   LEONARD GWYNN; CF, V/CLOWNS

50   FREEMAN 'SKIN' THOMAS; C, V/CLOWNS

50   BOBBY LEE 'SARGE' OFFICER; UMPIRED ONLY

50   BOBBY GWYNN; 1B, V / CLOWNS

50   JOE EDWARD 'COOPE' RAMSEY; CLUB
      ORGANIZER (ROCKETS)

50   H. C. 'MULE' THOMAS; 2B, 3B, V/CLOWNS

50   J. W. THOMAS; P, OF, V/CLOWNS

50   HUGH LOCKE; OF

50   PAUL ALEXANDER; C

50   GEORGE 'SHAKEY' HAYNES; P

50   JAMES 'MOODY' EVANS; 3B

50   JAMES CLINTON STRODE; P, 1B

50   ESTIE JACK STRODE; V/ CLOWNS, 3B, 2B, MNG.
      COACH, (ROCKETS)

50   L. V. THOMAS; V/CLOWNS, SS

50   IVY JOE RAMSEY; ASSIT. CLUB ORGANIZER
      (ROCKETS)

50   HAROLD 'LEFTY' THOMAS; V / CLOWNS, P,
      (ROCKETS) 1B, MNG. COACH

50   FRED 'MOUSEY' WINTON; OF, V/CLOWNS

50   FRED MORFORD THOMAS; P, OF, V/CLOWNS &
      ROCKETS

50   ELZIE VAUGHN ; V/CLOWNS, OF

50   JAMES 'KNOBBIE' GWYNN; OF, 1B

50   JAMES 'J. C.' WILLIAMS; V/CLOWNS, SS INF,
      (ROCKETS)

50   JAMES RUSSELL RAMSEY; P, 1B, V/CLOWNS,
      (ROCKETS)

50	FRANKLIN 'TURTLE' WOMACK; OF
50	GEORGE 'BUCK' JONES; OF
50	ULYSSE CULLY; C
50	CHARLES 'HACK' SETTLES; V/CLOWNS, 1B, CF
60	TOM WEEDEN; C, UTL
60	MARCELLUS SUTTON; UMPIRE ONLY
60	ROLLIE SETTLES; OF
60	MARSCHEL LUSK; OF, SS
60	ROBERT 'MOJO' HARRIS; C, V/CLOWNS, ROCKETS
60	ELMER MARTIN JR.; RF, 2B, 1B, P, MNG, COACH
60	LARRY 'DOBY' BROWN; SS, 2B, OF, UTL
60	BOBBY LEE SHOCKLEY; OF
60	CHARLES 'SCOOKY' CRABTREE; 2B, SS, P
60	ROBERT LOUIS 'BOBBY' COPE SR.; P, 1B
60	MICHAEL 'JOHN' MARTIN; OF, UTL, MNG, COACH (ROCKETS)
60	DAN SMITH SR. OF
60	JERRY 'EGG HEAD' MARTIN; P, OF, UTL
60	WILLIAM 'ZEKE' HARRIS; OF
60	PAUL WOODS; INF
60	ROBERT 'BOBBY' HUDGINS; RF
60	RONNIE DANHOFF; P
60	THOMAS MARSHALL; OF
60	RONNIE 'GHOST' BLEVINS; P, OF
60	DANNY 'SULL' SULLIVAN; P
60	RALPH STRODE; P
60	THOMAS H. BONNER; P
60	JOHN STRODE; OF
60	ZOLLIE SETTLES; 1B, OF
60	JOHN 'PUDGE' HOBBS; P, 3B, INF
60	ANDREW BILES; 1B
60	ROBERT 'MAC' McREYNOLDS JR.; OF

60	RICKY COPE; 3B, OF
60	LOUIS 'TURKEY' BATTLES; OF
60	E. B. MALONE; OF
60	CARLOS GRAY; INF
60	CLARENCE ROY 'PEE WEE' CURTIS; P, OF
60	TOMMY WOODARD; P, OF
70	JIMMY WALKER; P
60	MARSHALL THOMAS; 1B
60	WAYNE R. 'WOLF' WOLFORD SR.; 3B, 2B, P
70	LARRY TATE; C
70	LARRY H. GWYN; INF
70	GREGORY 'ROOSTER' MARTIN; OF
70	WILLIAM DWIGHT 'SUG' BARNHILL; 2B, SS
70	HOWARD 'DOONY' HENNY JR.; OF
70	WILLIAM 'GEEK' MARTIN; OF, UTL
70	THOMAS 'RED EYE' MARTIN; P, INF
70	DANNY MARTIN; C, P, SS
70	DENNIS 'DINK' STRODE; 3B
70	ROBERT 'HEAD MONSTER' MARTIN; 1B, 2B
70	LESTER 'LES' STRODE; P, UTL
70	JEFFERY 'CHICK' MARTIN; CF
70	CHRIS BILES; C
80	RODNEY THOMAS; OF, 3B
70	JERRY 'BEETLE' KING; 2B, OF
70	STEVE THOMAS; P, C, SS, UTL
70	HOWARD THOMAS; C, UTL
70	WILLIAM THOMAS; OF, 3B
70	RAY THOMAS; 2B, P
70	CHARLES 'COACH' DALTON; 1B, OF
70	GARY WAYNE SULLENS; P
80	JEFFERY PINCHEON; SS
70	ERIC BONNER; OF
70	RICKY TERRY; C, 2B

60	THOMAS B. 'MOODY' TUBBS; P
80	JEROME 'ROME' MARTIN; OF
80	GARY COPE; P
80	ROBERT LOUIS 'ROB' COPE JR.; P, IB
80	RANDALL ROBERTSON; OF
80	PAUL SMITH; P, OF
80	DAN SMITH JR.; P
80	ALLEN 'AL' MARTIN; OF, 2B
80	TEDDY MARTIN; OF
80	CLAYTON MARTIN; OF
80	TERRY 'T. C.' COPE; OF
80	STEVE HARVEY; C
80	BILLY 'SNAKE' RAMSEY; OF
80	NELSON O'NEAL; INF, 2B
80	ALEX W. 'TICK' RAMSEY; UTL
80	REGGIE PINCHEON; 3B

*** P-pitcher, 1B-first base, 2B-second base, SS-shortstop, 3B-third base, C-catcher, OF-outfielder, INF-infielder, UTL-utility player, MNG-manager.

Gary Cope
L. A. Dodgers

Jerry Martin
Charlotte Rangers • P

Jerry 'Goobie' Martin

Lester Strode
Bullpen Coach-Chicago Cubs

Chapter 5

Stories

Bates, Benjamin Jr.

World War II Veteran (Hero)

Education: completed High School at Bernard High School. Earned a Bachelors of Science Degree at Tennessee State University.

Enlistment: Navy in 1939.
Participated in the Battle of Peal Harbor.
Invasion of Guadalcanal and Tulagi Harbor in the Solomon Islands.
Credited with the sinking of 2 enemy Destroyers.
Occupation of the Philippines
Invasion of Okinawa
Occupation of Japan.
During World War II, Ben Bates was serving his country alongside Dorrie Miller (another famous black military hero), at Pearl Harbor.

He was awarded the Purple Heart. Ben's Daughter Stear Bates lives in Chessape, Virginia.

Retired as Chief Petty Officer from the United States Navy.

Civilian Work Experience: Retired from the Nashville Postal Service.

Returned to McMinnville to live, until he died.

Bates **Interview 2001**

Reverend Bates built the Bates home after World War II. He built the home within the time frame of 1945 to 1946. Blocks were made with their hands. There was a farm in Martin Charge that they owned so the lumber of the house was gotten there. Trees were taken to the mill for the finished products. Rev. Bates made sure each child could have its own room. He was married to Woodley and they had nine children.

During World War II, Ben Bates was serving his country alongside Dorrie Miller (the famous black military hero), at Pearl Harbor. He was awarded the Purple Heart. Ben's Daughter Stear Bates lives in Chessape, Virginia.

Jewel Bates and Clarence Martin got into a fight down at Sloppy Rock one night. Neither of them remembered what the fight was about. The next morning at 7:00 AM, Jewel got up looking for Clarence Martin and found him. Jewel said, "I want to shake your hand because I couldn't take another beaten like this." We are still friends. That's the worst beating I've ever had. Were about the same size, and in those days you didn't get a gun. If you got whipped, you got whipped."

Paul Bates owned and operated a restaurant on Sloppy Rock until he entered the Army; then his father took it over between the time periods of 1939-1942. Sloppy Rock was located at the foot of Spring Street. Mrs. Ella Fingers owned the place before Paul. Rev. Bates cooked rabbit in the restaurant and called it "speed mule running with gravy."

James Bates published a book for the City-State Library, but did not have a Copyright for it. Jewel worked at the local funeral home.

One day, a teacher asked Paul Bates if he wanted to be like his daddy and he replied, "no, no, not like my daddy. Then the teacher asked why? "Because he died at the age of seventy-three and here I am eighty-one," Paul replied.

Even though Bates father was a preacher, sometimes if you've heard the way he'd talk to their mule named 'Lumber' you wouldn't think so.

Reverend Bates preached at the Church of Christ. As a contractor, Bates built a Church of Christ in McMinnville, Sparta, and Smithville,

Jewel, James and Paul helped Reverend Bates make blocks for East End Drive Church of Christ.

James remembers having fried chicken almost every day, but on Sundays, the visiting preacher would come and eat. The children weren't allowed to eat until the preacher had finished eating.

Fred Nowlin used to live next door to the Bates during the 1940's. Joe and Carl T. Rowan grew up together. Some of the common things to do in McMinnville during the 1930's and 1940's were: go to church, fight, or sit up on the corner at night and listen to Charles Rowan tell lies. The guys would call him Charles Ryan.

James said he thought he read in the Bible somewhere it said, that women should be silent. Jewel said, "Go get the Bible, I am the head of this house!" (Smile) Clarence Martin said, "I don't think my wife Barbara ever read that." Barbara said, "I don't think that is in our Bible."

Paul Bates; "Everybody says they believe in the Bible, but in the Bible they said Methuselah lived to be nine hundred and some years old. If that's true, then someone had to be older than he was to know how old he was." (Smile)

Joe Bates; "Ginny Irvin couldn't read nor write, so Joe used to hold her hand so she could sign her checks. The taxi cab driver, Cunningham, took her to the bank and brought her back home. Four of the Bates brothers went to World War II. Jewel went to Korea. James was still in high school around the 1950's.

Jewel Bates; "Clarence bought a 1948 Chevy after he got discharged from service. He went to Sparta one night, and after coming back to McMinnville the car ran out of oil. They finally got home and Jewel's dad towed the car back the rest of the way. Clarence and Jewel replaced the engine in the car. They tried it out; then they pulled it out on the street and took off but something still wasn't quite right with the car. The local mechanic Ray Roberts said, "I'll tell you what you did wrong, you put the clutch in backwards. So we took it out and put it back together again. So when I went back to Pennsylvania to get discharged from the military, Jewel asked, "what happened to that car?" Clarence replied, well I burned that engine up. I think Eulous sold that car. It was just sitting in the back of the house. He sold it for $25.00. I did get to carry it through three years of college. James Bates asked, how much did you pay for that car? Probably about $600 dollars, then he bought a 1955 Chevy after that.

Jewel: Leroy Ramsey was killed in combat in Korea. Carton Tarlton was wounded in World War II, he still carries the bullet. Herbert Franklin grew up around here and was drafted into the military in Indianapolis, Indiana. Butler Smith was a native of McMinnville and fought in Korea, and moved to Dayton, Ohio to live. During World War Two many blacks could not go into combat. They served at surplus units etc . . . . They complained so much, that when the Korean War came about they were put on the front lines. Black soldiers in Germany would volunteer to go to Korea, a forty-five days delay and route to the states so they could go to Korea. For lot of soldiers it was unthinkable to volunteer to go fight someone they didn't even know. Jewel however did not face combat action.

Clarence; "When I went to El Toro, California, I volunteered to go to Korea. However, the marines sent me to Camp Pendleton instead. I arrived there on New Year's Day, for permanent duty.

Jewel; "While stationed in Bomhom, Germany on Christmas Eve, I walked around an ammunition dump pulling guard duty. The ammunition dump was 5 miles out in the middle of nowhere. Just me and my carbine rifle—all about myself. So the next day some guy told me you should put in for pass, you've got to have a holiday. So I went to the Sergeant and asked for a three day pass because I was on guard duty for so long." The Sergeant said, soldier let me tell you something, you're in the Army 365 days a year, 24 hours a day, seven days a week, ain't no such thing as the holidays in the Army; So get the heck out here!" I'll always remember that. Every day is a work day.

Some interesting facts;

(1) World War One Veterans include; Louis (Louie) Bates, who was the brother of Rev. Bates. Charlie Hill bought a new car every year, and was a disabled veteran. Ben Prater's wife Sidney Prater lived on Edgefield Street.

(2) The following men had cars in 1930's; Matt (Dan) Handley, Charlie Hill, Roy Spencer, and Roy Gwynn.

(3) Ed Cherry worked for Charlie Hill. One day while trying to get up Beersheba Hill with the wagon, the wagon became stuck, so Charlie picked up a limb form a tree, and handed it to Ed. As Ed began pushing the wagon, Charlie said, Pour it to me." That man pulled that wagon. He was a strong and stout man. He wasn't big, but he pulled that wagon all over town.

Jewel Bates; Professor James' son thought that he was car. He would come out of the house and go up the hill and would shift gears. He was always running, so he changed from a car to a truck, and ran down off the hill and got stuck. The old man (Reverend Bates) said, boys looks like you will have to go out there and give Junior James a push. He actually thought he was a car.

Joe Bates; "When Junior James came out of the house you would hear him cranking it up. Then he would start running to school. As soon as he would get right in the middle of the hill he would change gears. He was thought to be quite intelligent but we'll never know. I never will forget when Corbin Smartt sang in the Methodist church choir. When the choir would sing "In the sweet, bye and bye" . . . he would reply bring me some meat, "Bye and Bye," Bring me some pie."

James Bates; "Buster Bean . . . was a fellow that could pick up the front of a car, just to show how strong he was."

Jewel Bates; "Herbert Ramsey married Ginny and would follow her everywhere. Sometimes he would even go as far as Leesburg to find her. Mary McGregor a.k.a/Snuff Dipper' was to enter a beauty contest, and all of the mothers made sure she would win because they wouldn't let their children enter. This goes to show you that she must have looked pretty bad, because the others felt sorry for her.

James; "My parents entered me in a beauty contest once and I cried and cried because I came in second. There were only one entry." (Smile)

Paul; "There is one thing people just don't think about; I have found out after all these years, who the prettiest man in the world is. Do you know who that person is? Why . . . it's me! (Of course) (Smile)!!! The reason I say so is because I'm the only man that can see me and I can see all of you, but I don't see me, so how can I get tired of looking at me?"

Paul; "Ain't nobody gonna die tomorrow, because I have never seen tomorrow."

James; "In our younger days here at home there wasn't too much trouble to get into, because Dad took care of that."

Jewel: "Every family in this town controlled us, because if we did anything outside this house, somebody would tell Dad."

James; "One time I said darnit, and Dad said don't say that again, so I said darn it, I felt that left hand upside my head and I never said it again."

Jewel; "We had two mules to work with; Bell was blind, and Lumber had three good legs. We lived high on the hog. We milked cows and sold the milk. We sold buttermilk for ten cents a gallon. One lady was six months behind on her payments. (Smile) Mr. Hughes had some cows at the end of what used to be Edgefield Street, now across from the fire station. There was a small pasture that held five cows that Joe milked them twice a day, for a dollar a week pay. When I was a senior two years later I asked for a raise. I wanted a dollar and a quarter. He wouldn't give me a raise, so I quit."

Paul; "Joe was the only one in our family (boys) that had a job when we were coming up. I remember he was taking care of an old woman that lived about four or five doors down from us. Taking care of Ginny Irvin, bringing in firewood, building a fire, and Joe was only making fifty cents a month. Ginny was a former slave."

Jewel; "Johnny Nance, who was a former salve, jumped off the bridge and killed himself. He had a bad leg. I remember he was always complaining about being in pain.

One night he folded is clothes nice and neat and laid them on the train tracks, and jumped off the bridge. He was a very neat man, and this the way he died."

Joe recalled that the swinging bridge was located down on Beersheba Street before the present one was built. "We used to jump off there and swim too. I really don't think I should be here today because of one incident that happened. The bridge where the train goes across the river down by the dam was loaded with a group of us boys; R. C. Brown, Carl T. Rowan and the whole bunch of us were jumping off of that bridge into the water. I didn't like to dive, but I couldn't be chicken, so I jumped off. A couple of telephone poles were tied together way down under the water, but you cannot see them from the top of the water. About five of us jump in. I came so close to hitting those poles with my head that my toe hit it and knocked off my toe nail. So from then on, I don't think I dove into anything head first."

"In New Guinea, there was a boy when we get off the ship (the U.S. United States), the largest cruise ship afloat in the United States, then it was converted into a troop ship, so you didn't need destroyers and things to take you to Australia. They detected a submarine so they cut out all of the engines, and when we woke up the next morning, instead of going to New Guinea, we ended up in Australia.

They had changed our route. We had been on the water about fourteen days, and a lot of young cats jumped off due to pressure. One guy named Davis, jumped in and I dove in after him. He had pushed the panic button and tried to entangle me, so took my fist and knocked him out, and grabbed him by his chin and brought him up. This was the first time any of my brothers knew of my heroic act, per Joe Bates."

Joe Bates; "When I was in a service company, this service company that I was in loaded and unloaded ships. Blacks were mostly in service companies. We had to keep the supplies moved to the front of the ship. We landed in the middle of the day of all times. The Japanese were at Miller Bay. We went to Harslansia. Our grandmothers could have taken Harslansia. There were Japanese there. They changed that, and we had to go to the B. R. Islands in the South Statton Islands Group."

"I went up on the U. S. Invasion, you come up and you got about 50 feet of nothing but rock core cliffs, and as much beach as from here to across the street (approx. 150 yards).

That's where we had to land; we went in behind the 41st Infantry Division. At this time the service company was the only group that was not captured on the beach, they had surrounded the 41st Infantry Division and almost killed all of them; all we had were carbines."

Joe said, "I was on the beach one night where we camped and we had a cave to go in. There wasn't much room on the beach close to the cave. They had an Anti-Artillery Unit that guarded the beach 90 millimeters. The Japanese were sending a bomber out of range of the 90 millimeter. The sound was like the sound of a washing board, the plane just circled out of range just to keep us awake, but one night I was standing talking to the 90 millimeter circle men, when the Japs sent that bomber over (he made sounds of the bomber), we had supplies, gasoline stacked up all over the beach, suddenly the gun operator detected the bomber coming in across the beach. He was coming in to drop bombs ok? The gunner switched the 90-millimeter gun around and hit that thing head on. There was a big explosion. I'm standing up and I bet I went about five feet in the air."

"Another day the Japanese sent over 23 Zero's (fighter planes), Do you know our guys knocked down 22 of them. One of them got away and the Destroyer knocked it down, because they started coming over (suicide planes), can you imagine here's this LST parked on the shore, our company down there unloading 90 millimeter shells and things of this nature, and this plane comes over (this had to be a suicide plane) and just misses this ship. The tail barely grazed the ship, and crashes in the water. He was planning to hit the ship with the airplane. Just missed it, and here I was hiding between 90-millimeter shells (smile). If he had hit, you could see red and white traces. Now when it happened you know, we call all clear. We came out to look at the airplane. There's a Japanese pilot dead, with his leg blown off, what do you know what some of them cats did? They shook his leg out of the boots and kept the boot. See these things happened, and that's the way it was. When I look back, I think somebody up there (pointing upward) was watching over me through all these experiences."

"We went in, Joe says, on the invasion that morning, we were on (LCI) Landing Craft Infantry, that's the one where we go in as far as we can, open those doors you have to come out. We were going in. We were traveling all night at about 2:30 a.m. we move up into the Gulf, one side was one island and about 2 mi. separate the two islands, right in the middle of a Gulf. By the time he arrived in the middle it was about five in the morning. We heard something go boom! It was a dab URN cruiser about fifteen or 20 mi. in the ocean shooting over our heads at the beach. O.K! We heard shells going close overhead. If you heard a shell come over you, you were all right, but if it hit close by you knew it was over. They (U.S. Navy) did that about five or ten minutes, as soon as that ended, here comes the fighter planes, and as soon as that ended, here comes the destroyers shelling the beach. Soon after that was over, bombers came dropping the bombs, now we've got to get ready to go to shore. O.K! I'm coming off the dad burn boat with a carbine in one hand, and a typewriter in the other."

"225 enlisted man plus a crew on this LCI, I finagled my way because I didn't want to go down in a hole. If I'm going to go, let me see it. So I slipped out on the deck, and I stayed out on the deck. I hung around one of those poles with my leg in a chain, and another guy out there was from Alabama and his name was Lou Cell Seaman. We sat out there and talked from 2:30 a.m. until all this was over. I came to know him as the lyingest man in the world. He could tell a lie one after the other, and kept you entertained, but when we neared to beach, the Japanese started shooting 75 m. m., and I saw a shell hit one of those landing points, you know the points you down when you board the LCT? One hit the supplies and they were going every which way. Now we were still going, we can't stop now. So when we got to the beach, there was the Captain saying, "rush toward the gun, Lou Cell panicked, the Captain wouldn't let me go get him. The next morning I had to check up and do the morning report, Lou Cell's stomach was all they found of him. Now what did that do for me? It's only two of us (blacks) so I figured I was next."

Joe's brothers were surprised to learn all this about Joe. Joe's military job was the company clerk. Joe said, "Nobody really knew about all the things I experienced, (meaning family).

Edith L. Bates

(November 10, 1914-May 13, 2002)

Edith became the first child born to Ben S. and Pearl ( ) Bates.

It was at the homestead in McMinnville, Tennessee that she nurtured, supported and happily interacted with eight fun-loving brothers and sisters. She fondly thought of as the surrogate mother.

Edith accepted Christ at an early age at Clark Chapel Methodist Church of Christ. After moving to Cleveland, Ohio she found joy at Mt. Pleasant Church of Christ, where she remained active until she became a resident of Manor Care Nursing Home in Willoughby Ohio.

Edith graduated with honors from Bernard High School, and continued her education at Tennessee A & I University in Nashville, Tennessee. She earned a Bachelors Degree from Case Western Reserve University. As an exemplary educator, she dedicated herself to children and staff for fifty-five years.

Edith passed after a lingering illness. She was the beloved sister of Henrietta B. (Bates) Curtis, Mary E. (Bates) Ivy, Paul W. Bates of (Vernola) Springfield, Ohio, Joseph B. Bates (Chicago, Il.), Jewel T. and Dorothy Bates Dayton, Ohio, James L. and Mayrene Bates Fairfield, California, and sister-in-law Vera Bates of Houston, Texas.

She was buried at Gardens of Memory Cemetery.

Edith L. Bates Gets Masters Degree In Arts

Miss Edith L. Bates, a primary grade teacher in the Cleveland Public Schools, received a Masters of Arts Degree in Education Wednesday morning, June 12, 1957, during commencement ceremonies at Western Reserve University, Cleveland, Ohio.

She is the daughter of Mr. And Mrs. Ben Bates 315 Beersheba street who witnessed the occasion.

Before joining the Cleveland School system, she was a member of the Bernard School Faculty.

She received her B. S. from Tennessee A. & I. State Teacher's College, Nashville.

Jewel T. Bates (1929-)

Jewel was born in Warren County in the town of McMinnville Tennessee. He graduated from Bernard High School in 1948. While attending school he performed duties at the Brown Hotel as a short order cook.

After serving his country for two years in the United States Army during the Korean Conflict, he proceeded to further his education. He attended Central State University in Wilberforce, Ohio. Jewel earned a B.S. degree in Industrial Arts Education. He received a Master's degree in Elementary and Secondary School Administration from Xavier University in Cincinnati, Ohio. He also received a second Master's degree in Educational Leadership and Supervision from Wright State University in Dayton, Ohio. Other Post Graduate work was done at Miami University, Oxford, Ohio and Ohio University in Athens, Ohio.

Jewel was instrumental in forming a Veterans Club at Central State University.

Some of the work experiences were full-time with the Defense Electronic Air Force in Kettering. He also worked as a teacher, Associate Director of a title VIII Dropout Prevention Program, Coordinator of a school/work program for slow learning students, Assistant Elementary School Principal, Elementary School Principal, Middle School Principal, Assistant High School Principal, High School Dean of Students and coordinator of a student work programs for the Dayton City Wide Priority Boards.

He has various memberships with International Young Men's Clubs, Member of American Legion Post #208 in McMinnville, Tennessee, Central State Alumni Association, Procrastinator's Club and Alphas Phi Alpha Fraternity INC.

Mr. Bates is married to Dorothy (McClearin) Bates and is the father of Carol, Thomas, and Kevin Bates.

Jewel is presently retired and enjoying it. He loves to hunt rabbits; he comes to McMinnville several times a year to visit fish and enjoy seeing dear friends and relatives in Warren County.

The Bates family is presently restoring the home place in which they helped their father make bricks and build the home place. Some of the original studs and bricks are still in place. By the year 2001 the renovation should be complete.

Mrs. Sydna Ruth Cope Batey (Martin)

Born in McMinnville, Tennessee in 1906, Sydna went to Bernard High School were she graduated with two other students. Later she went to College the summer after High School.

She was sixteen years old when she attended (A & I), now Tennessee State University and received her teaching certificate. She taught for the first time at an East Tennessee school for one year. Then she returned home to Warren County to teach. After settling down and sinking roots she met and married Livingston 'Livy' Cope. She would later marry Sam Batey around the 1950's.

Her first few years teaching were at Smartt Station School then at Cummings Chapel. The schoolhouse for blacks was one room. The Copes lived a quarter of a mile away in a country home during the week, and on the weekends they'd return to their house in McMinnville. This went on for about six or seven years. Underprivileged black children were taught at this school also.

Mrs. Sydna later joined the Bernard teaching staff. She taught fifth and sixth grades until the school closed because of school integration.

Mrs. Sydna Batey at this time taught at West Elementary School from 1968 until 1971. She could have retired in 1968 but choose to continue on. She began teaching at home with Adult Students, after leaving West Elementary.

Mrs. Sydna sang in the church choir and played piano, fished when having the chance and enjoyed life to the fullest. This woman taught up until her untimely death in 1987. She lived to be eighty-one years old. "She was another influence on my life," says Wayne Wolford. "I was one of her students in 1960 in the sixth grade before moving back to Saint Louis." She was a warm caring individual, and when she spoke, you listened. It was pretty hard to teach a group of youngsters when just a few feet away stood a playground where football, basketball or softball were being played. There were times when someone would climb the fences in order to retrieve a ball off the roof of the school. Mrs. Sydna accomplished a feat that is hard to reckon with. She taught in Warren County for sixty-four of the sixty-five years as a teacher. There are a lot of her students living here today. She has made a wonderful impact on us all. Mrs. Sydna was definitely a teacher's teacher.

Clarence Delton Bolden Sr.

June 5, 2011

Clarence D. Sr. was born in Birmingham Alabama, to William Clarence and Della Bolden, he attended Butler University and Indiana University law school, graduating from the latter in 1953. He was an honorable discharge veteran of the United States Army and a member of the American Legion Post number 249.

He served the Marion County Municipal and Superior Courts with distinction as a Judge for over 30 years and was the first African-American so appointed, having been appointed to the bench in Marion County by Gov. Otis Bowen. He was an active member of Witherspoon Presbyterian Church for over 60 years. Bolden was active in Democratic politics, having served in many capacities and was an active member of Kappa Alpha Psi Fraternity and the Bachelor Benedict for many years.

Clarence was preceded in death by his wife, Mildred J. (Beamon) Bolden (March 25, 2011).

Dec. 27, 1969 Indianapolis Indiana

"Bolden becomes first non white magistrate"

Governor Edgar D. Whitecomb was the first state executive to name a black to a magistrate court judgeship. Prominent attorney Clarence D. Bolden, former secretary of the county democratic central committee assumed the part time position of Maywood magistrate court judge Thursday Jan.1, 1969.

He succeeded Marshall Williams in the $4,000.00 position.

The former criminal court, division two public defender, Bolden graduated from McMinnville Tn. Bernard High School in 1941, and a graduate of Indiana University School of Law. Bolden was a deputy city prosecutor in 1956 to 1960.

Born in 1924 he resides in Indianapolis, Indiana with his wife Mildred, and children; Rev. Maxie D. Bolden, Clarence D. Bolden Jr., Collesta Hosinski, Colleen Smith, and Clyde Nickerson Bolden.

Clarence joined the United States Army in April 1943 and received an honorable discharge in December 17, 1948. Served in the European theater as a Sergeant.

Friday August 28, 1999 the Marion County bar association and special friends held a retirement celebration dinner at the Ritz Charles establishment. The celebration was for 26 years behind the bench. The song "I did it my way" was sung, plus the many remarks to the honorable Judge Clarence D. Bolden Sr.

Judge Bolden served for 40 years in Indiana law practice.

Judge Clarence D. Bolden and wife (writer) Mildred Bolden have plans for returning to the Bolden Green community to live. Bolden Green community was established around the 1870's in North Warren county, near McMinnville Tn.

Clarence's great grandfather came to McMinnville from North Carolina. Judge Bolden's parents were Rev. William C. Bolden and Della Bolden who resided in the Bolden green community for many years.

Clarence inductee (NBA) hall of fame 1999 National Bar Association

"The Honorable Judge Clarence Delton Bolden"

Marjorie L. Bolden

(Aug. 4, 1907-Feb. 21, 1983)

Marjorie Lillian (Bolden) Wolford Thacker was born to the union of Reverend Walter and Mrs. Ruby Virginia (Johnson) Bolden in Saint Louis, Missouri on August 4, 1907. She was the eldest and the last surviving of three children. Some of her formative years were spent in McMinnville, Tennessee; but much of her adult life was in St. Louis, Mo. where she was first united in marriage to Robert E. Wolford. She gave birth to two sons and one daughter. In later years she and Ramey Thacker were married after the death of Robert. Several years following, they moved to the Bolden Green site in 1958 located in Warren County.

Marjorie was educated in St. Louis and took up the trade of secretary for an Insurance firm. After retiring, she and then husband Ramey decided to move to Tennessee and enjoy the four seasons of this beautiful county. In Warren County they tried to do all of the things good country people enjoy, hunting, fishing, building, raising a garden etc . . .

During Marjorie's residence in McMinnville, she became a household name throughout the town. She was active in Church work, performed volunteer services, held an office as secretary in the local NAACP Organization and was always willing to lend a helping hand when and wherever needed. She helped the sick and elderly when they were in need.

Survivors include her husband Ramey Thacker, two sons: Robert O'Neal Wolford of San Diego, Ca.: Helen and John Lee Polsen Wolford of St. Louis, Mo., one daughter: Ruby Emerald Wolford who lived with her. Marjorie's stepfather was Arthur Ransom Sr., (St. Louis, Mo.). She had three grandchildren: Monica, Valerie, and Wayne Wolford Sr. (U.S. Army Retired) and later became an author. She also had three great grandchildren and a host of other relatives and friends.

'Mom' as she was called by grandson Wayne was always keeping records and pictures. She would write in detail the dates, times, places and connection of various things. This is what inspired Wayne Wolford to do his history work.

'Mom' was a soft-spoken lady with the heart of pure gold, she was only 5' foot 4" tall and weighted approximately 100 pounds.

Marjorie was buried in the family cemetery located in the Bolden Green community.

REV. WILLIAM CLARENCE BOLDEN

Nov. 15, 1892-Sat. Feb. 8, 1972

Reverend William C. Bolden was born on November 15, 1892 in McMinnville, Tennessee. He was one of eleven (11) children born to Reverend George T. Bolden Sr. and Sarah (Webb) Bolden. He departed this life on February 8, 1972 in River Park Hospital, McMinnville, Tennessee.

He was reared in a Christian home and saw several of his brothers follow the foot steps of their father, becoming ministers, dedicating their lives to service to the Lord. Reverend Bolden was ordained as a Baptist Minister in Whitwell, Tennessee more than thirty three (33) years ago as the last member of his immediate family to follow the calling of the Lord and his ministry.

His entire life was spent in the South, that he loved, in service to his family, his God and his fellow man. He was a father, not only to his immediate family but to all needing his assistance; He was a neighbor to all; His life was devoted to service to his fellow man, unselfishly. He does not really leave any mourners, only loved ones who truly believe that he was a man that placed his hand in the hand of the man from "Galilee".

Survivors include a wife Della Bolden, three (3) sons, William Cardell Bolden, Carl B. Bolden, and Clarence D. Bolden, a sister Mollie Agnes Tucker, a brother, Livingston Bolden, several grandchildren, great-grandchildren and a host of other relatives and friends.

William Clarence Bolden, 80 years old Bolden Green community Baptist minister, succumbed to a lingering illness at River Park Hospital at 7:30 a.m. Tuesday. A native of this county and a Saint Mary's Baptist Church, he was married to the former Della (Hawkins).

Frances (Martin) Bonner

(1905-2001)

Frances was born in Warren County to Thomas and Lillie (Savage) Martin in 1905. Her husband was Harrison Bonner; he died in 1940. Sons: Harrison Jr., and Franklin and Thomas Bonner. Daughters: Betty Frances (Bonner) Favors and Dorothy (Bonner) Biles. Her brother was Ernest Martin and her sisters were Martha Martin, Ruby Spencer, Mary Etter Martin, and Laura Freeman.

She attended school in McMinnville, Tennessee. She was actively involved in community and civic organizations such as serving as PTA president of Bernard School, troop leader for the Girl Scouts American Legion Ladies Auxiliary and as an officer for the NAA CP.

She was survived by sons: Tartlon Martin (OH.) and Robert ('Bub') Bonner of Warren County and daughters and sons-in-law Mary A. Elam (G.A.), Evelyn and E. B. Malone, Lillie J. Hill, Patty Sue (Bonner) Martin, and Martha A. Robertson (Warren County).

Frances had thirty-six grandchildren, forty-six great grandchildren, and seventeen great great grandchildren. She died at River Park Hospital (Warren County) after an extended illness.

She was a retired cook with the Senior Citizens Center as well as a member of East End Church of Christ. She was not only a volunteer worker but a community leader as well, and a homemaker.

Mrs. Bonner was buried at Gardens of Memory Cemetery.

Thomas Harrison Bonner (1941-2000)

'Tom' as we remember him, was raised and born in McMinnville, Tennessee. He attended and graduated from the well known school called Bernard high school. Tom was a very gifted young man but somewhere down the road of life he didn't put these gifts together. He was Valedictorian of the graduating class, and the Quarterback of the football team.

Tom played Semi-Pro baseball for the McMinnville 'Rockets' baseball team. Thomas joined the United States Army as a Medic in the Vietnam War. Tom saw so many injuries and deaths during his time in the Vietnam War. It later took a toll because he tried to wash away most of these bad memories. When you are a medic in the war you see a lot more than the normal soldier would. Tom got along with everyone.

Tom joined the American Legion Post #208 located in the Leesburg community, and maintained his membership for over twenty years.

Thomas H. was the son of Harrison and Frances (Martin) Bonner. At the age of 59, Tom contacted cancer for an extended period of time. The illness final took its toll on June 10, 2000. He passed away at Alvin C. York Medical Center in Murfressboro, Tennessee.

Georgia 'Kate' Mae Smartt

Born in Warren County with her older sister Maude. 'Kate' is the name she is known by and because it was given to her by her grandfather. She wants to be known as just Kate Curtis.

She attended Bernard School before she moved and graduated from Attuck High School in Hopkinsville, Kentucky. After she got married to L.V. Curtis, she entered and finished business school, now known as Motlow. She received a two year certificate in Business Administration. L.V. always joked about putting her through school, but Kate says, "I paid for my training."

Kate held down a job at the McMinnville Garment Company for two years, and also worked at the Oster plant on Cadillac Lane in McMinnville, Tennessee, for twenty years. She did not retire from Oster's because her grandmother became ill. Kate stopped working in order to care for her sick grandmother. Kate has two sons one's name is Clarence Roy Curtis, and the other son is Richard Borum. Kate later moved to Murfreesboro Tennessee, where she is presently living, Kate is approximately 85 years old.

Charles A. 'Coach' Dalton

Sept. 1936-June 1998

Charles Allen Dalton, son of Ella Lyles and Melvin Dalton was born September 30, 1936 in Sumner County, TN.

'Coach' Dalton could have been a Harlem Globetrotters if he had chosen, but stayed home, preferring to spend his life helping others.

Dalton began his career in Warren County at the age of twenty-two, when fresh out of College, he took the job of teacher/coach at Bernard High School in 1957, then an all Black school. This was the start of a lustrous career.

He was a standout athlete at Mississippi Valley State, where he excelled in Basketball and Track. He was inducted into the Mississippi Valley State Sports Hall of Fame. Dalton was named to the All-State Basketball Team in Mississippi during his four years of college eligibility, and most importantly an Honor Student. Dalton was part of the school's first graduating class in 1957.

His accomplishments on the baseball diamond caught the eye of Big League scouts, who offered him a job with the Chicago Cubs. He turned the offer down.
A little known team of traveling basketball players then approached 'Coach'. The Harlem Clowns offered him a lucrative contract to play with the team, but he turned that down to continue his education. The team would later become known as the world famous Harlem Globetrotters.

Sometimes during a basketball practice at Bernard, 'Coach' Dalton would show one of his many skills, such as dunking two basketballs at the same time.

Dalton served as coach for thirty-nine years in the Warren County school system before he retired in 1994. During his career, he taught and coached at Bernard High School, Southside

Elementary, Warren County Middle School and Warren County High Schools.

His coaching spanned several sports including basketball, track, softball and football. He also taught Industrial Arts and Physical Education.

'Coach' Dalton did show McMinnville his baseball talents with the McMinnville 'Rocket' Semi-Pro Baseball team for two years in 1972 and 1973, playing the outfield and first base.

A good friend in sports was Lester Caldwell, the retired Vice President of First National Bank in McMinnville. Lester remembers when 'Coach' started playing fast pitch softball over at the fairgrounds. "He thought it would be easy to hit this kind of pitch, says Lester, compared to a regular baseball, but he found out different. I watched him in the first game we played and he was so frustrated, because he struck out all three times at bat." Charlie was a competitor, and there was no way this was going to get the best of him, so he started to bunt his way on base and found out he was almost unstoppable. Charlie was a left handed batter, and had exceptional speed, so by the time he laid down a bunt he was already at first base before a play was made on him, because of his long strides."

'Coach' was a kid person. If a kid needed help in any way 'Coach' was there. During the 1950's and 60's, kids would eagerly wait by the swimming pool for a late model 'Beetle' (Volkswagen) to turn the corner so they could enjoy the water activities for the day. They knew the moment they saw the 'Beetle,' 'Coach' was in it. This was just like someone waiting for Christmas everyday. There weren't many activities for young Blacks in Warren County during these years, but 'Coach' always opened the Bernard Pool and the Leroy Ramsey Gym so that the kids would have something to do. There was basketball, inside the gym when it wasn't too hot, and when the weather permitted the courts were used outside. Swimming was a good pass time. There was also time for boxing, and dancing the latest dance craze to the 'Juke Box.' Mr. Dalton was a very good role model, and person. We thought the world of 'Coach' Dalton.

He knew his sports, but was not listened to by his peers in the school system. He could have easily been a head coach at the High school, but was not given the opportunity. Instead he was always called upon to be an assistant at the City High. Warren County wasn't ready for a Black Head Coach.

This man could stand flat-footed under the basket and jump straight up and dunk a basketball. The most amazing thing I'd ever seen was this man could dunk two (2) basketballs at one time. He would put on a show for us sometimes. This was an attention getter. Just seeing, talking to, and having the privilege to know this great man was a dream comes true for many who felt his presence. He was our Michael Jordan.

'Coach' did some volunteer coaching after he retired from the school system. He was always helping out the junior league teams.

In addition to his school coaching and teaching duties, Dalton officiated and directed various sports leagues around the county and was involved in youth basketball camps.

In light of his devotion to athletics in Warren County, The Warren County High School Gymnasium was named in Dalton's honor. This showed that he did what he said while he was alive—earned respect. The gym is one of the few known public buildings named after a Black American in Warren County, the first being Huddleston-Jennings American Legion Post #208. (Noted as a large establishment). A photo and short story in plaque form are mounted on the wall in front of the gymnasium.

Dalton was married to Frankie Mae (Biles) Dalton, they had two sons, Allen & Charles Dalton Jr.; three daughters, Liesa, Terri, and Debra.

'Coach' died in the summer of 1998 at River Park Hospital from a bout with cancer. With his passing, he leaves behind a legacy of public service and an indelible mark on Warren County Sports. Helping others and attain respect were his main goals in life. He loved kids, and because of his influence over them, their lives were changed for the better.

He was a member of East End Drive Church of Christ. 'Coach' Charles Allen Dalton rests in peace at Gardens of Memorial Cemetery.

'Coach' Charlie A. Dalton believed that respect was most important; respect is something that had to be earned. He was well respected in Warren County.

Barron A. Garrett

On November 5, 2004, Barron attended this years last Tennessee Council on Developmental Disabilities in a conference room at the Brentwood Holiday Inn in Nashville, Tenn.

Barron was employed at the McMinnville Wal-Mart for 13 years, and a Board member of Pacesetters in which he was a Governor's Board Council member also. Some of the discussions he was involved in are reviewing the Council's purpose and responsibilities, efforts to contact State Legislation, current system of services for Tennesseans with developmental disabilities, and Federal Disability Legislation.

Barron was a member of the Planning and Priorities Committee. One of the functions of this committee is to plan a concept for the next (5) five years.

This portion of the council are involved with: transportation, education, child care, home ownership just to name a few.

'Easy Living Home Program' is one of the components that Barron was interested in, because this program is one that many Tennesseans will be effected by. Barron brought up a point about larger wheelchairs, and the difficulty of getting in and out of different rooms throughout a home. This will be a problem in the future, because more and more Americans are gaining weight, and getting larger. This will be a problem in the near future for person confined to a wheelchair. This is a new program that the Council wanted new home builders to be aware of. This was in the (5) five year plan.

Pacesetter Board member Barron Garrett and Trent Miller Director

Augustus L. Guerard Jr.

Augustus L. Geurard Jr. was a Stewards man in the United States Navy, and son of Mr. And Mrs. Guerard Sr., which reside at 212 Etter Street in McMinnville, Tenn.

Jr. returned to San Diego, California, **May 14, 1956** after completing a tour of duty in the Far East aboard amphibious task force flag ship USS Estes.

During the Far East cruise the Estes participated in Operation Beacon Hill, Luzon, P. I. It was the largest landing exercise since World War II.

Ports in Japan, Hong Kong, B. C. C. and Philippines were recreational visits for the crew. Returning to the United States the Estes also stopped at Peal Harbor.

Bessie Taylor Gwynn (1895-1980)

Bessie was born in Athens, Alabama on February 17, 1895. Born into poverty only thirty-two years after the emancipation proclamation freed her ancestors. Gwynn like most other blacks of her time, had little hope of an education or advancement beyond some form of menial labor. Her father was a tenant farmer whose yearly income barely provided the necessities to survive, but somehow her parents saw fit that she would obtain a basic education by sending her to Trinity School, a private institution for blacks run by the American Missionary Association.

While she attained a basic elementary education, the experience also whetted her appetite for more learning. She moved to Nashville in 1911 and graduated from a normal school in 1915, which was actually the High school of Fisk University. Her Warren County ties came when she was contacted by Professor Spears from McMINNVILLE in regard to a teaching job at the black high school. Gwynn accepted at once, realizing the need to repay her school debts, thus starting her on a lifelong career.

The teaching conditions facing a female teacher in Warren County in 1915 were bleak at best. The school building was a small frame structure located on the south side of Egypt Alley an area now owned by Burroughs-Ross and Colville Company. The building had no electricity and contained approximately 250students, when everyone attended, which was rare, because most kids had to help at home in order to survive. From all indications, she accepted the conditions with optimism and enthusiasm. It was a difficult task to inspire her students to obtain a good education. Some of the parents of those attending could neither read nor write, and had never had employment requiring those skills. With little urging or inspiration from parents, students were not likely to have a great desire to get an education.

Motivation required a unique person to instill the students with a desire to better their role in life. Bessie Gwynn was just that person. Former United States Ambassador to Finland and former student, Carl T. Rowan, had this to say about Mrs. Gwynn: "Among the things that I did not have was electricity in the little frame house that my father built. It was her inspiration that inspired me to spend many hours squinting beside a kerosene lamp reading Shakespeare and Thoreau".

Mrs. Gwynn seemed to have complete control of any situation she endeavored. I remember as a child admiring this thin-framed lady, (and I do mean lady). The way she talked, smiled, and walked. It was almost impossible to keep up; with the rapid pace she maintained. If I had stayed in McMINNVILLE instead of returning to St. Louis I would have had the honor of being taught by this extraordinary human being. "Such is life" (Wayne Wolford). Bessie T. Gwynn, teacher of Home Economics and English plus Music, married Roy Gwynn and was buried by his side in 1980.

Dr. Franklin Leroy Hawthorne

(1900-1979)

Dr. Hawthorne was born in Montgomery, Alabama in 1900. After he completed his high school education, he attended Howard University, located in Washington, D. C. Later Franklin enrolled at MeHarry Medical College in Nashville, Tennessee, where he received his Medical Degree. In 1933 he started practicing medicine in the **Warren County area**, and also established some business in the Manchester region.

In 1938, after practicing medicine in **McMinnville**, he moved to Columbia, TN. The good Doctor loved the community in which he lived, and served for forty (40) years with much love and compassion.

Frank Hawthorne M. D. was first married to Irene Hawthorne.

Doctor Hawthorne later married Sarah Laura (Rowan) in 1968 at Nashville, Tennessee. Sarah 'Sue' was a Warren County native. When she reached her nineteenth birthday, she decided to live in Nashville, Tennessee for a while. She owned a Catering Service in Nashville in the 1940's, and did quite well. 'Sue' as she was called, lived in Columbia, TN. At the time of her death.

Dr. Hawthorne has a daughter from his first wife. His daughter's name is 'Bettye' Irene (Hawthorne) Pillor, and she lives in Nashville with her two children: Frank and Connie Pillor.

The Doctor delivered many babies and took care of the sick in Warren County. There were times when Whites would seek the assistance of the good doctor. There was a White lady that gave Dr. Hawthorne a Quilt that she had sown, because he saw to it that she did receive help at MeHarry Medical College Center. The woman was operated on for appendicitis, and come out just fine, thanks to the Doc. Mrs. Hawthorne has the Quilt in her possession until this day. People didn't have much money; so many times they would pay their debts with whatever was available. Doctor

Hawthorne received gifts for payment of his services such as; pigs, chickens, eggs, Quilts etc . . .

When Doctor Hawthorne moved to McMinnville, he lived in the old funeral home (Fred and Gail Locke's present home) for a short time. It was just a resident at that time (1933), than later it became a Black Funeral Home.

When he was practicing in **McMinnville**, he would have to send most of his patience's to Nashville, because of better treatment then the Faulkner Springs facility. The Faulkner Springs Hospital (now Falcon Manor, a bed and breakfast building) was one of the closest hospitals around this area, but for Blacks the service was very poor, so most patients were sent to Nashville by Dr. Hawthorne.

Franklin's mother passed away when he was in attendance at Me Harry Medical College. He dropped out of school for a short period of time while getting his goals in order. He returned to Me Harry and finished. He worked his way through school, not making much money. He would sometimes go all day long with just a pack of peanuts. Franklin then found out that regular work was too hard. (Smile)

"Greatness is never something conferred; it is something achieved." Dr. Frank L. Hawthorne achieved greatness through his community involvement.

Sheila (Johnson) Hicks

(1957-2007)

Born July 25th, 1957 to Thomas William Johnson and Hilma Jean (Roberts) Johnson in Harriman, Tennessee; Sheila resided in Harriman with her parents until they divorced when she was thirteen years of age. Her mother Jean moved to McMinnville and married Jack Strode.

Sheila graduated from Warren County Senior High School in May of 1975 and headed for Tennessee State University in Nashville, Tennessee in August of 1975 on a Theatre and Drama Scholarship.

She held a 3.5 grade point average out of a 4.0 and acted in several productions. Her most memorable acting role was the part of Mrs. Phelps in the play 'The Silver Cord.' She received a standing ovation for her performance and rave reviews from her peers. Later her Professor and Drama Coach, Dr. W. Dury Cox would arrange for her to perform on stage at the famed Tivoli Theatre in Chattanooga, Tennessee. Again Ms. Hick received a standing ovation and rave reviews from the local Theatre Critics.

In April of 1978 Sheila was inducted into the T.E. Poag's Players Guild: Tennessee State's elite Drama Society She won the Children's Theatre Award in the spring of 1979 at Tennessee State University for her performance as the wicked witch in the production of Hansel and Gretel. In March 1980 she competed in the National Academe of Dramatic Speech Arts in Chicago, Illinois, where she won 2nd place in the extemporaneous speaking competition. After graduation in August of 1980, Sheila worked at Vanderbilt University Library in the T.V. News Archives department as a typist and substitute secretary.

Ms. Hicks was awarded a partial scholarship by Indiana University in Bloomington, Indiana in August of 1981 to work on her Master's in Theatre and Drama. This was quite a challenge since the white professors of that department didn't think black students had what it took academically to compete and get a Masters in their elite program. Sheila proved them wrong by graduating with a 3.2 average out of a 4.0. Ms. Hicks later resided in McMinnville where she had her own ministry called 'A Thousand Friends Outreach.' Part of her ministry work included writing a newsletter and teaching bible study classes at

NHC Health Care, Raintree Manor, Clark United Methodist Church, and mini workshops at Harmony House located in McMinnville.

She worked on her Bachelor's in Biblical Studies and Theology thru Trinity Bible College and Theological Seminary external home studies program.

> Her love for writing and the Bible has Sheila working on her Christian novel entitled "A Vessel of Dishonor." Sheila said: "I'm just waiting on the Lord to show me what is the next step to take." Clark Methodist Church awarded her with a plaque for her service to church and community at their Women's Day on May 27, 2001.

Sheila has had her share of success and failure, ups and downs, but she says she is going on in the power of Jesus Christ.

Her mother Jean Strode and son Jonathan Strode give her the inspiration to keep on keeping on.

Shelia was always a giving and caring person in her more mature years. She was always giving money and gifts to the support of the Young Men United, Warren County High School Black History Club and anyone who needed help. If it was her last $5 to her name, she would give it up gladly to know that she was helping some one.

Shelia Hicks was the proud grandmother of Jamicheal Strode, born: December 3, 2007 to Bobbi and Jonathan. He was 6 pounds and 19.5 inches.

Shelia (Johnson) Hicks was hit and killed by several vehicles on a dark road in Arlington, Texas on the night of October 11, 2008. She was having some mental problems and the fact of not taking her medicine might have come into play as to Shelia being so far away from home. She is at rest at Martin Charge Cemetery.

Sheila was one of the driving forces for me (Wayne Wolford) to continue to work on this History Book. She was always pushing me and inspiring me to finish. Sheila typed quite a bit of this book that I had hand written and interview people on tapes.

Georgia Mae (Martin) Etter Huggins

Georgia was born to George and Stella (Savage) Martin on April 1, 1929 in McMinnville, Tennessee.

On her Mothers side of the family, her grandparents were Cornelius and Charlotte (Ramsey) Savage.

Mrs. Huggins attended Bernard High School, A & I State College (now Tennessee State University) Tennessee Technology Center (McMinnville, Tenn.) for a nursing Course. She was a Registered Nurse working in the Warren County Area.

Georgia has two children, one girl: Professor Gwendolyn E. Etter, and son Dr. Terry L. Etter. Gwen was born on Jan. 5, 1950 in Earlington. Ky. and Terry was born on May 28, 1956 in Madisonville, Ky.

Georgia attends the Bahai Faith. She is married to Ray Huggins and they reside in the Leesburg community. Ray was born in McMinnville also on July 22, 1929.

In 2009 Georgia was responsible for starting the 'Senior Prom'. This event was held for people that were 35 or older. You can't just up in your Sunday best, you dance to the music, and you eat the best food. Georgia and a few other people on the committee decided this would be a good thing for the community. So it is been hailed all way up to 2011.

Georgia was also one of the founding members of the 'Black Fox's organization. She was an auxiliary member of American Legion Post 208 for many years. One of the founders of the 'Senior Prom.'

Georgia married Ray Huggins, and are life partners, both in their 80's around 2012.

Minnie Irene (Hammonds) Jackson

May 25, 1921-Oct. 17, 2002

81 years of age

Irene as many knew her, was born to the union of Joe Johnson and Nellie (Scott) Hammonds in Warren County. Irene's grandparents were Belle and Henry Scott. Joe later married second wife Maggie Johnson.

She married William Harvey Jackson, and they had one daughter; Carolyn Sue (Jackson) Meeks (married David Meeks), three sons; James (Jimmy) William, Lee Roy and Gary Floyd Jackson.

Mrs. Jackson cooked at the Kracker Barrel in Manchester, Knight's Truck Stop, the Holiday Inn and Cumberland Hotel in Manchester. Highway 70 Café in Smithville. She also did house work for Hubert Boyd. In McMinnville Irene was the head cook and **ran** the kitchens at **Denny Moore's**, Brown Hotel, Sed Berry Hotel, **Holiday Inn**, and the Hillcrest Hotel.

Mrs. Irene ran a booth at the Warren County Fair from 1981 until 1985, she and the family would keep the booth open for 24 hours to accommodate the fair workers.

Mrs. Irene and husband William started selling plate lunches out of her home. She would have William carry out lunches, and soon people would start to come to the house, so she built on to the existing house.

There was a sewage company out of Fayetteville, Tennessee named M.F. W. that contracted a sewage system in Morrison. Some of the workers boarded at the Jackson's resident until the job was completed. She also ran a little Café behind the house in the 1950's. While owning the café, she started baking cakes, doing weddings and adding on a little more and more. This portion of the house was used to accommodate parties and a restaurant for many years.

During her later years on earth she ran a State Nursing Home for unassisted patiences at the Jackson home. This facility held approximately eighteen people at a time.

Mrs. Irene Jackson seemed to find just two times in her life to take a vacation and travel to Florida, other wise she was hard at work.

She was involved in a car accident with a big truck on this side of the Warren County line in the 1960's.

Irene became an entrepreneur even though she only completed the eleventh grade, she was self taught, and encouraged her children to continue their education.

During the last ten years of her life she became sick and her legs started to bother her. She was a strong woman and held out as long as she could with a happy out look on life.

Lusk Winner of the Jaycee Award

McMinnville Central High School full-back Charlie Lusk, who led the Bulldogs in scoring during the 1965 football season with 51 points.

Lusk was the recipient of Warren Inter-scholastic "Player-of-the-Month" citation. Despite being slowed by an injured foot for a couple of games, scored eight touchdowns and three extra points, and was one of the top ground gainers in the mid-state.

Charlie carried the ball 119 times and was credited with 873 yards, a nifty average of 7.3 yards per carry. In addition to the eight touchdowns he scored, he had six long touchdown runs called back because of penalties, including runs of 39, 32, and 52 yards in the Baxter game. This was one of the games where there was a police escort, and the visiting team was not supposed to win, but they did.

Lusk, a Central Junior playing his first year of varsity football after transferring from Bernard High School, had three different games in which he scored two touchdowns.

His best offensive performance of the season was against Lafayette when, in a 47-12 Bulldog defeat, he gained 160 yards in 23 cracks at the line, scored one 60-yard touchdown, and had a 65 yard touchdown scamper called back by a penalty.

Lusk is 6' 1, weighs 165, and is the son of Mr. Frank and Mrs. Ada Lusk of Edgefield Street.

He was honored in a special assembly program on a Wednesday morning at McMinnville Central High School. Making the presentation was Ed Porter, President of the McMinnville Jaycees, and project chairman Emanuel Brewer. The Jaycees sponsor the Player-of-the-Month awards program.

Lusk was accorded honorable mention on the All-Midstate team.

Charles later joined the U. S. Army in 1968, going on to become a Sergeant. Charlie went to Vietnam in 1969. By 1972, he became one of McMinnville's finest on the Police force. He ran for Sherriff later and came in third place out of 12 candidates. Charles has owned a few nightclubs in the Warren County area.

He is married to Georgia (Strode) Lusk and they have a son named, C. J. Lusk. Charlie is a Member of the American Legion Post 208.

Charlie worked for Batesville Casket Company in Manchester for 39 years until he retired.

Barbara (Hughes) Martin

Barbara (Hughes) Martin was born June 4, 1934 in Lynchburg, Virginia to Alice and Walter Hughes. She is one of two children; sister to firstborn, Walter Hughes Jr.

Barbara met Clarence Martin in Philadelphia, Pennsylvania. They have two sons: Michael and Douglas. They are also the proud grandparents of Michael Jr., Arielle, David, and Victoria Martin.

Mrs. Martin attended the Campbell County Schools and graduated from Payne Elementary in 1948 and in 1952 from Dunbar High School. Despite the fact that the family had very few monetary resources, life was good.

School was just a pleasure. Schools were separate and unequal, but the teaching staff was exceptional. Most every faculty member either had or was working on a Master's Degree. The French teacher honed her craft in France. The staff visited the students' homes, and took a personal interest in the students.

Barbara remembers her mother having difficulty sewing an outfit needed for a school play. So she and her Mother just took the outfit to the French teacher's house, and the dear lady was happy to finish the needed costume. The teachers set high standards, and accepted no excuses for less than the best in student performances.

After High School Barbara matriculated and graduated from Hampton University in 1956 with a major in Speech Pathology. She had spent the summers working as a waitress in Ocean City, Maryland and had waited tables in the teacher's dining room during this school sessions, which was a good deal. Besides the income, teachers ate well, and of course, the waitresses ate the same kind of food as the teaching staff. With resources from Barbara's employment during the school years, and from mother, father, uncle, aunt, grandmother, whoever could chip in a few dollars, she was able to graduate from college.

Barbara remembers, "It was not a good time for finding a job in her chosen field in Lynchburg, Va. Lynchburg was a very segregated town, and most of the professional positions open to blacks were in the teaching field. There were a lawyer or two, a dentist, and there were a couple of family practitioners, so I decided to do some graduate work at Temple University." "This schools reputation was first rate in Speech Pathology, and was well established. After matriculating for a summer, money was almost nil, so I put the graduate degree on hold and secured a position at Episcopal Hospital in Philadelphia as a Speech Language Pathologist in the Rehabilitation Department, working mostly with stroke patients." Barbara admits, "it was an exciting job, one that I relished." "Philadelphia was also a life changing setting, in that en route to her job, she met a fellow en route to his job who captured her fancy; one Clarence Martin from McMinnville, Tennessee. The happy results were love and marriage shortly thereafter. Clarence secured a position in New Jersey and we relocated to New Jersey." Other happy life changing events occurred with the arrival of son, Douglas and shortly thereafter, son Michael joined the family.

When Barbara rejoined the work force some years later, she found employment in the New Jersey school system so that she could be on a schedule close to those of the children. In 1977 she decided to secure that long ago sought after Master's Degree in Speech Pathology and graduate from Rutger's University in 1979.

Barbara Martin is a nationally certified Speech Language Pathologist and authored a speech workbook for children with speech disorders.

Barbara was further honored as "Teacher of the Year" at Young School in Burlington, New Jersey in 1990.

The years flew by and retirement came, and with retirement, relocation to McMinnville, Tennessee. She was employed as a Speech Language-Pathologist in the Preschool Language Program at Warren County High School. Following that experience she became a volunteer at the National Health care Center, and at the Magness library.

Barbara is a member of Clark United Methodist Church, and she is also affiliated with Christ United Methodist Church. The time was spent enjoying the company of her husband, the travels that they took time to time, visiting her children and grandchildren, teaching an Adult Sunday school, computer card making, baking and reading.

Mrs. Martin is truly a credit to her family and Warren County.

Eulous Martin

(July 8, 1907-Dec. 24, 1991)

Eulous Martin was a World War II Veteran.

Eulous Martin was one of seven children born to the late Theodore and Martha E. Martin on July 8, 1907.

He received his elementary and secondary education in Warren County, Tennessee, attended Morrison Junior College in Morrison town, Tennessee and furthered his education at A & I Normal College (TSU) in Nashville, Tennessee.

He was married on August 29, 1942 to Juanita (Stubblefield) and to this union three children were born. One daughter, Mary Jane Martin and two sons, Jerry and Donald Martin. Eulous had a twin brother named Euford.

During the early years of his life he operated the family farm in Rock Island, Tennessee. Shortly after moving into the city of McMinnville he was inducted into the United States Army during World War II and served in the European Theatre of operations. At the conclusion of the war he returned to McMinnville and was employed by the Warren County Board of Education as custodian at Bernard High and City Elementary Schools.

Martin began cutting hair in 1919 at the age of (12) twelve. Eulous opened his first shop in 1924. He was also known for his wonderful Stone Mason and Carpentry.

All of the kids called him 'Mr. Eulous.' He was one to gain respect, and he didn't have to say a word.

It's been said you can tell a lot about a person by the way they handle children. If that's the case, then Eulous Martin was truly a great man.

A custodian at Bernard and City Grammar School for many years, children just loved Martin and were always eager to flock in his direction. The children's adoration for Martin was color blind, as he was a black janitor at the all white school (City Grammar). Martin played the piano and was quite the entertainer when children wanted to hear a catchy tune.

Martin was also said to be very generous towards under privileged school children. If he saw a particular child was in need, he made sure to pass along a coat during chilly winter days or provide an extra shirt if he noticed one filled with holes. It was that compassion which made him one of Warren County's most Honorable and respected citizens.

Eulous was a faithful life long member of the Clark United Methodist Church were he was an Adult Sunday school teacher, a choir member, and served as Chairman of the Board of Trustees. Eulous was one of the driving forces behind building a new parsonage for the church back in the early 1970's. In his spare time, Martin ran his own business on the side; a barber shop that was a popular spot. Martin didn't actually have a separate building for cutting hair. Instead it was attached to the side of his house, which was located on East Main Street. This was a smart decision because whenever a customer came in it was easy to serve the person without going anywhere. Martin eventually settled in a house on Couch Street then Beersheba Street after he lost his home on East Main Street because of an Urban Renewal project. Many blacks were affected by this project in McMinnville.

In addition to conducting business in his shop, Martin was also a traveling barber of sorts. Shut-ins or people unable to leave their homes, didn't have to visit 'Mr. Martin' to get a haircut, he came to them. He'd make house calls by going to their homes and cutting hair there. This service mainly benefited the Senior Citizens and disabled clients.

I can truly say that this individual was a role model for me; because of him I now own and operate a Barber Shop.

He was a Commander and Adjutant for American Legion Post #208, and I have been the Commander of the same Post for several years.

Eulous Martin departed this life on Tuesday, December 24, 1991. His son Reverend Jerry E. Martin officiated at McMinnville Funeral Home Chapel. He was buried in the Gardens of Memory Cemetery in Morrison, Tennessee.

JERRY ALEXANDER MARTIN 'GOOBIE'

Jerry was born to Jerry Edward Martin and Hardina (Cope) Locke on March 15, 1972 in Warren County. He is the grandson of Ella Mae Martin, and Hardy Cope.

Jerry is married to Kimberly (Rowland) Martin. She was born July 15, 1976 in Warren County. They have two children Baily Martin and stepson Dillon Rowland. Bailey was born in Cookeville May 10, 1998, and Dillion was born in McMinnville, Tennessee on March 16, 1994.

Jerry attended McMinnville City High School and graduated. He later went to Shelby State College for 2 years. Kimberly graduated from McMinnville City High and has 2 years at Motlow College.

McMinnville has been good to Jerry, he feels that he has been to various places in the world but this is home.

Jerry remembers one high school incident with a substitute teacher during his senior year. The story began with lying .50 on the table of the fast food service class and getting a soda from the fridge. "So I laid my .50 down and she said, "You didn't pay," and I said, "I did pay". "Naw I paid". "Usually I didn't carry much money with me but at the time I was carrying about $3.00, so I said, "Why would I want to steal a coke when I've got $3.00 on me? "So, I said, "I'm not paying you again, you keep the .50 and I put the coke back in the fridge." "So she took me to the principal and said that I cussed at her. I almost did but I knew better. Well, the principal gave me a lick (with the paddle) and that was the only paddling that I had in high school. That kinda rubbed me the wrong way." "I didn't speak to the principal or nobody that year. That wasn't right."

Jerry remembers this family from Memphis, Tennessee called the McCarter's. The McCarter's took special pride with the black kids of my day. They formed a baseball team that traveled and brought us together. We were treated as one of the family. The name of the traveling team was 'The McMinnville American's.' Players such as myself, Gary Cope, Keith Martin and everybody played on this team.

The McCarter's got me into college, there were no dorms for junior college, so Bob McCarter moved to Memphis and his son and I were best friends and I stayed with them for two years. He put me up to stay with them for two years rent free and food free, I appreciate and respect them to this day for helping me.

"The McCarter's also made sure Bill Rutledge had a place to stay because he was attending Memphis State where he was playing football, and they took care of us just like we were their own."

The McCarter's owned an auto parts store named (Sunnyside Auto Parts) in McMinnville not too far from the New Smithville Highway. They took good care of us. I grew up in the projects and didn't have much and they lived in West Wood in a big old house, so I felt like one of theirs. They have always been like that. They didn't care if you were Black or White. They were different from the people we were used to. They would load a few of us up and take us to Memphis to football games. During our baseball years and the traveling baseball times, they supported us with $200 per player. There were even times we made trips to Florida to play ball. The time frame I played was from 13 to 17 years of age. Eric Martin was known as a very good player.

I finally got to play with the McMinnville 'Rockets' in the final season with players Randy Nowlin, Gary Cope, Reggie Pinchoen, Thomas Martin, Teddy Martin, Terry Cope, Al Martin and Steve Harvey.

When I was in college, I went to a tryout camp in Millington, Tennessee. My coach said, why don't you go and try out, you've got nothing to lose. This was the Olympic tryout team, so I made like the first two cuts. My coach said that it was a good experience. A scout from Long Beach State University was present at the tryouts. The scout later contacted me at home and advised me to go play in the summer team in Texas and he wanted me there. It won't cost anything, we'll get you a job and you can stay with a host family. I said, I don't know, but Mama said, Yeah! Go ahead and go! So I went to Texas. I tried out for the Texas Rangers, they drafted me.

They came to me at the age of 19 years old. They wanted me to go to school another year, and then would offer me a deal, so I said that's fine. I was pitching pretty good at that time, so they came back after that year and said we want you to sign. *I* declined to sign then and decided to go back to school another year. So after my sophomore year right before the draft they had to sign me again where as I could go back into the draft. They pursued me and I signed a scholarship to play for Memphis State University, and then that's when I signed for Texas. They increased my scholarship to get more money. I was the Junior College All-American of Tennessee my freshman and sophomore years.

The first game I was real nervous, the nervous part came in from the idea of going there. Being black at the airport with the other two players was an uncomfortable feeling. We were on our way to Florida, so when I got to Florida there were tons of us (Blacks) so I felt relieved.

As you can guess, I was nervous the first game, since I was a pitcher. I had to throw a fast ball, curve ball and change up. Change up! I said, I don't even know what a change up is. So the pitching coach said, "You just hold it like this and then throw it. I didn't know how to hold it, so I just did it." The first inning I struck out 3 batters (the side). After that I was a starting pitcher. I guess that was a lasting impression. The club liked my attitude so they made me a starter.

Rookie ball is tough. The first day out we just ran. Run, Run, and Run was all you did. Later that day, I called my mother and said, "I don't know if I can do this, it's 100 degrees and we have been running all morning: since 7 a.m., and get home at 1 p.m. I can remember after the first practice, I went to the store across the street and got an alarm clock, got home, went to bed and didn't eat supper or anything, I was dead tired. It was tough, and what they tried to do was weed out the soft ones. A bunch of people quit, and they tried to test you. Just to see how tough you are and if you really want it or not.

I was scouted by several teams during my college days. Such team scouts as: Yankees, White Sox, Milwaukee Brewers, and then the Texas Rangers drafted me. All of these scouts called me. I went to one try out camp and I guess word travels fast, they used to come to the ball park to see me.

The scouts look for body types too. I was 6' 2" about 175 pounds.

I got drafted in 1991 and Gary Cope (L. A. Dodgers) did also. But Gary went earlier than I did, he went in after his sophomore year. I used to talk to him about playing when I came home. 'Cat' Walker played ball with us and we grew up together, but I was a year younger. We also worked out together. We all were pitchers.

Jerry is at home now and doing a great job as head coach.

Stella M. (Savage) Martin

Stella M. Martin, the daughter of the late Cornelius and Charlotte (Ramsey) Savage was born April 18, 1907 in Warren County, Tennessee and departed this World June 14, 2002. She was ninety-five (95) years of age. She was married to George Martin who preceded her in death in 1956.

She leaves to cherish her memory her daughter and son-in law, Georgia and Ray Huggins, and son and daughter-in-law, Clarence C. and Margie Martin both of McMinnville. Four grandchildren, Dr. Gwendolyn Etter—Lewis of West Chester, Ohio, Dr. Terry L. Etter of Nashville, Master Sergeant Clarence C. Martin, Jr. and Sharon of Goldsboro, N.C. and Tina L. Martin of McMinnville. Five great-grandchildren, Ariel S. Lewis of Ypsilanti, Michigan, Maurice Martin of Memphis, Anneka L. Martin of McMinnville, and Cynthia N. and Laniece Martin both of Goldsboro, N.C. Two nieces, Helen Brown of McMinnville and Vera Bates of Houston, Texas.

She was a member of the Clark United Methodist Church in McMinnville.

William Lawrence Martin Jr.

Born on the 27th of February in 1925, 'Lawrence Jr.' as he was known; played third base for the Rockets from 1942 until 1952.

His most memorable moment of his career was when he was chosen to play in the All-Star Game in Carthage Tennessee. Along with Billy Smith, Herman Martin, James 'Mule' Hennegar, they purchased cotton uniforms with their personal money to play in. Some of the locations Jr. remembered playing in where: in the area of the old **Garment Factory** (on Sparta Road.) The players cleared the field and mowed the area themselves in order for it to be presentable enough to play on.

Magnetek (on Red Road) was once the old fair grounds and later lights were added. All games charged a twenty-five cents admission fee. This fee was charged in order to help with the expense of purchasing balls and bats. A cold drink was only five cents at this time.

In the late 1940's All-Stars were picked from the Middle Tennessee area to participate in the All-Star Game in Carthage Tennessee.

Transportation to these games was in cars. Some of the key areas in McMinnville that were playing fields in the early 1940's are as follows: Beersheba Springs Road where the old Dairy Queen was located which is now a Pawn Shop. There was a swinging bridge near that area, now a new bridge in 2012. Permission was given to the players by the owner of the old Garment Factory property to hold their games on, provided they would clean and mow the field themselves.

Nelson O. Ramsey

Nelson Ramsey has become a household name within the community. There are too many of the youth turning to the dimmer things in life, such as drugs, alcohol, and crime. Our community needs people that are willing to spend their time, money and efforts on the betterment of today's youth.

Nelson and brother Alex established the Young Men United organization Nov. 1, 1998. Presently the membership stands at 13 strong. The ages vary from the twenties to the fifties.

He is committed to helping others in the community and any individual or family who needs help due to health, disaster or financial reasons.

Nelson knows the meaning and values that it takes to be a mentor, and wants to pass it on to the next generation.

Mr. Ramsey has taken kids on field trips such as; Coaches luncheons and to see the Harlem Globetrotters. Nelson has participated in many functions such as; Mini-fest, Basketball Classic, winter sports in the gym, Christmas dinners. He has been involved with the sponsorship of many activities and organizations.

Nelson is the son of Joe and Mary Ramsey, the husband of Gale Ramsey, and the father of two lovely children. He worked with C & M Trucking Company, and owns a local business. Nelson is always thinking of ways to better the youth, and he is relentless in his efforts.

Jon Officer

Approaching a dark car in the middle of the night is not something many people like doing.

For Tennessee Highway Patrol Trooper Jon Officer, it's something he does almost every day. As a trooper determined to keep the roadways of Warren and Cannon counties as safe as possible, Officer frequently finds himself in potentially dangerous situations. The funny thing is, he likes it.

"I prefer to work at night," said Officer. "There's more meanness out at night. If given the choice to work days or nights, I'll chose nights. There's more chances to make that DUI traffic stop."

The fact he likes to work nights-and often makes traffic stops on isolated roads-isn't much of a bother for Officer.

"This job is always something different every day", he said. "You never know what you're going to get into when you make that traffic stop. You've got to be careful.

Martin Luther King, Jr. Day, which is recognized throughout the nation tomorrow, Officer realizes it was the tireless efforts of King that have helped his right to receive an equal chance.

"The struggle that he went through, and the people went through back then, is what made it possible for me to get into law enforcement," said Officer.

He's found law enforcement to be right up his alley and takes particular pleasure in keeping drunk drivers off the road.

"We make a lot of traffic stops for speeding, but our main thing is getting DUI's and trying to get DUI's off the roadways", said Officer, who says most drinkers are fairly predictable. "When I ask them if they've had anything to drink, it's always two beers. That's the same old story whether they've had two beers or two packs."

This New Year's was an exception to the rule. Usually holiday weekends produce more disorderly conduct, which in turn leads to more arrests and citations. When he's not out monitoring the roads, Officer finds time to serve on the highway patrol's Honor Guard, which is available for special functions such as the Tennessee Titans' playoff game against the Buffalo Bills. Officer is a rifleman on the seven-man unit that shows the colors of the U.S. flag, the Tennessee state flag and the highway patrol flag.

As far as career goals, Officer said he'd like to stay with the highway patrol and get promoted to sergeant, but he said those promotions are few and far between.

"Some people can go their whole career and never get promoted," said Officer.

Jon is married to Lisa whom works in the medical field.

Albert Eugene Pleasant Sr., 59

Rock Island resident and Warren County native Albert Eugene Pleasant Sr. 59, died Feb. 24, 2005 in Nashville after a two-year illness.

A construction worker and a member of the Church of Christ, he was the son of Elmer Louise Carr Pleasant of McMinnville and the late Emerson Pleasant.

He is survived by daughter Belinda Pleasant of McMinnville; sons, Albert Eugene Pleasant Jr. and Corey Eugene Pleasant of McMinnville, brothers, William (Buster) Pleasant and Charles Edward Pleasant, both of Rock Island; sister, Betty Louise Pleasant of McMinnville; six grandchildren, several nieces, nephews and Cousins.

Graveside services will be held at 2 p.m. Monday at Martin Charge Cemetery with Frank Smith officiating. Visitation will be held from noon until time of service Monday at Love-Cantrell & Cope.

Love-Cantrell & Cope Funeral Home is in charge of arrangements.

Betty Ramsey

Mrs. Betty Jean Ramsey 26, died at her Leesburg Road residence at 8:30 a.m. Sunday.

A native of Warren County and a member of Hiawassee Church of Christ, Mrs. Ramsey was employed at Century Electric Company (now known as A. O. Smith, Inc.).

Married to Kenneth Ramsey, she was a daughter of Fred and Maggie Mae (Wood) Locke Sr.

In addition to her husband and parents, a son, Calvin Dwight Ramsey, survives her. She is also survived by three brothers; Fred Locke Jr., Larry Randolph Locke and Melvin Eugene Locke, all of McMinnville. Her maternal grandmother and parental step-grandmother, Gertrude Wood and Gertrude Locke of McMinnville.

George King officiated services at High's Funeral Chapel at 2pm Wednesday. Interment was in Gardens of Memory Cemetery.

Joe Edward Ramsey (Donahue Ancestors)

Joe lived in Arcade back in 1940, walking or riding mules were the mode of transportation.

'Rocket' Ball Field was cleared in the late 1950's. A wooden fence on one side of a house and bleachers on the other side. Jack and Clinton Strode got the lumber for the fence. The City gave the ball field to the 'Rockets'. "We worked on the field until dark every evening. Urban Renewal helped fund the field with $3,000. Brown Elcain, Marcellous Sutton and team helped to build the present building.

"Principal Woods lived across from Bernard School. Football was in existence. We had a good marching band in 1949. Farthest team played was Chattanooga, Booker T. Washington High School. The Players were: Ramsey's, James Grayson, Copes and Browns. We had poor equipment from the white high school. They furnished pads and helmets. Girls in Economics sewed numbers on uniforms." Practice field was on the side were Joe used to live.

"It was rumored that Ray Roberts helped support Edward Jr. and Clarence Martin to help get him into college. Blacks could play on Ray Roberts Croquet yard, when the yard wasn't in use. Spencer boys worked out smooth spots on Croquet yard they played on the other side. Ray Roberts was a good man. His store was owned by his wife. "I helped clean that thing up a many of times. We rode on the street in an American Legion Train and Ambulance. Charles would get mad at his mother and stay with Ray two or three days and she would bring groceries because she knew where he was."

Joe bought his land from the Wallings, Bill and Rockstone. "There was a ball field in Leesburg where the girls played with the boys without gloves. It was located across the street where Mojo's house is now. Arcade played Leesburg on Sundays. Arcade was located near Clements Bridge."

"During the period of time between 1930's and 1950's black women did house work and black men either worked in lumberyards or worked on railroad tracks.We raised our own food and owned nearly twenty acres of land." Joe's mother worked at the hospital as a mid-wife and dad worked in the lumberyard. His father was Clarence Spite Ramsey and his mother was Mary Elizabeth (Donahue) Ramsey.

Joe says, "The train bridge was a famous place to jump off and swim. A cotton gin was there on the hill, and Reverend Frank Ford raised a lot of cotton. He leased the field next to our house. He was a good hard worker. He didn't mind helping people just don't mess with his mules. He had a shuddering problem. He would have Charlie White slaughter hogs for him for about five dollars a hog in the building next to the cheese plant down by the river. We washed clothes for a living, and Joe carried many loads across town. We washed them on a washboard." Sometimes in order to raise money for the fourth of July at Clark Methodist Church, Joe would get up at daybreak and pick blackberries. Back then blackberries sold for $.25 a gallon. He was afraid of snakes and so was his dog 'Spot', which would lie down near the bushes. The money he raised at picking blackberries was spent on double ice cream cones, which sold for a nickel (5cent). The ice cream was made at the church lot.

"On 3rd of July People would stay up all night cooking and preparing food and shelter for the celebration. The church was located on what was known as Cope Lane 'Church on the Hill'. However, the Church was destroyed when Urban Renewal came through. Depot Bottom was under the hill from the church. Elcain Brown, Marcellus Sutton and Team helped to build the present church building, located on Bernard Street."

Facts:

Ivy Joe Ramsey ran 'Serve All' next to the Park Theater movie house up until 1940. Hamburgers cost a nickel so did coke cola and ice cream cones. The restaurant would sponsor a hamburger contest to see who would be the most hamburgers. The contestants paid for their own food.

Ivy Joe Ramsey opened the 'Pan Am Grill' and cooked for the Greyhound bus station on Main Street for many years.

Bernard High School; Woods (Principal) lived across from Bernard School, Mae Belle (Wood) Locust.

J. L. Reedy 1932-2001

Born August 16, 1935. July 11, 2001. Mr. J. L. Reedy passed away Wednesday in the Vanderbilt University Medical Center in Nashville, Tennessee. He was a member of the Clark United Methodist church and the husband of the late Mary Alice Quinn Reedy and the son of the late Wilburn and Notie Shockley Reedy. Two sons Barry and Jerry Quinn also preceded him in death.

He is survived by: Three Sisters: Aline Wood, Willene Martin & Georgia Officer, all of Sparta, Tennessee. One Brother: James Crisp, Cleveland, Ohio.

Four Daughters: Fernanda Reedy, Kandice Reedy & Roxanne Reedy, McMinnville, Tennessee and Treetar Reedy, Murfreesboro, Tennessee.

Four Sons: Terry Allen Reedy, McMinnville, Tn., Ronal Reedy, Morrison, Tn., J. L. Reedy Jr., Bristol, Virginia, & Jami Reedy, Nashville, Tn.

Lifelong friend: Norma Jean Coonrod & a host of loving nieces, nephews, cousins and friends.

J.L. was buried at Sparkman cemetery.

J.L. Reedy was a gentle giant, soft-spoken, with a laugh that could lighten up the room. J.L. had many friends; he worked for a bridge building contractor for many years. J.L. loved outdoor life; he didn't spend much time inside the building. He loved trucks and he loved his cars. He and his wife, Mary Alice spent their later years in the Bolden Green community.

Carl Thomas Rowan

Rowan's career spanned more than a half a century. He started as a reporter covering desegregation in the South during the 1950's then became a newspaper and television commentator. Whether in journalism or in government, Carl sounded a persistent challenge to the status quo. He wasn't just a critic; he was a champion of the people he met and saw social solutions around every corner.

In 1961, Kennedy appointed Rowan deputy assistant secretary of State to help integrate that department. He served in several other posts, including director of the U. S. Information Agency, which made him the first Black American to serve on a President's Cabinet. Rowan served on the board of Gannett Co., which owns USA TODAY, from 1990 to 1996. He was also trustee of The Freedom Forum and First Amendment Center since 1993.

Born in Ravenscroft in 1925, he was a small town kid that his family moved to McMinnville, Tennessee, who was surprised by how far he had come. Rowan grew up poor during the Great Depression. He was one of the first black commissioned officers in the U.S. Navy; he went to college and majored in journalism. He was an inspiring pioneer for black journalist. If one takes a look at Rowan's distinguishing resume, it can be said he was always first or only. For years, Rowan appeared as a guest on Inside Washington, a TV show hosted by Washington news anchor Gordon Peterson. Peterson describes Rowan as "an extraordinary guy, with an extreme sense of courage. Friends and family said Rowan would want to be remembered for the scholarship fund he started in 1987, Project Excellence. The fund has provided 3,000 students with $80 million in scholarships. The Project Excellence foundation was begun to encourage black youngsters to finish high school and go on to college.

James Rowan

(1880-1957)

James Rowan died at the age of 77 years old at his home on 265 Cora Street, in McMinnville, Tenn. He had a lingering illness for about 10 months.

James was born September 15, 1880 to Ben and Sarah (Wilson) Rowan. His wife; Leona (Reasonover) Rowan passed away before him. They had one son; Robert Rowan and one daughter; Daisy Rowan. James had three sisters: Mary (Rowan) Foster, Bertha (Rowan) Keele and Laura (Rowan) Rowe. Three brothers; Ben, McKinley and Tom.

James was a native of Warren County and was buried at Riverside Cemetery.

Béatrice (Grayson) Savage

Born in 1915, she will be eighty-six years old in 2001. Married to Fred Savage, her mother's name was Ethel (Buchannon) Grayson. Her father's name is Alexander A. Grayson. Beatrice lived in McMinnville, Tennessee all of her life. She was one of seven children: three boys and four girls.

She worked at the Brown Hotel as a maid and cook. She was the first to open up and cook at the Hillcrest Restaurant with Hazel Young. She worked at ARA, private homes, Oster's Factory for three years. While employed at Oster's she purchased her first car. She also worked as a cook at William Biles School (which is now the County Building).

Mr. Ellick Grayson sold the American Legion members the land that the ruins are on. This building was known as the 'Hall' for years. He was a tight man says Beatrice. He didn't give anything away.

Beatrice was an avid baseball fan. She attended all of the black and white games. Anytime she was asked to donate some pies and cakes she would do so willingly. She remembers the time when her father persuaded her to sell her three lots that were adjacent to his near Beersheba Street. Her dad sold his so he thought it would be a good idea for her to sell too. Little did they know that this was a plot to make good of a vulnerable situation. The Smith's owned a machine shop nearby so they bought all of this property. Beatrice sold each lot for$350.00. She explains that wasn't enough money for land. She considered this a rip off.

Mrs. Grayson helped with the cooking of fish at the 'Hall' American Legion Post 208, when they held fish fries. There was a school for the local colored kids across from Ray Huggins (Leesburg School). Beatrice walked to school before the school buses was introduced. Cars were used for transportation. She quit school at an early age (11th grade) because of the humiliation from teachers and students. She said "they layed down and laughed at us (her brothers and sisters) because of the poor condition the clothes and shoes were in." She couldn't take it anymore. Times were hard for them during the depression. Her dad made $1.50 a day and her mom washed and ironed clothes for little or nothing.

They once owned land in the Shells Ford Leesburg area, but it was lost to foreclosure because someone saw a better need for it. At the price it was sold for, she says, a paperboy could have afforded it. Mr. Grayson didn't want his kids to work because of moral reasons, so when Beatrice was old enough she ventured out and started making her own money and living. This started by going door-to-door asking for clothes to wash. As a young girl growing up in Warren County Beatrice Savage never thought about having to drink water from only certain designated fountains. The fact that her family couldn't eat in the restaurants in town or sit in seats downstairs at the Park Theater never crossed her mind.

Looking back on those times today the eighty-four year old woman with a quick wit and sharp mind said it was only natural. "When you don't know better, you don't think anything's wrong with it." Most of the time we just didn't go to those places, cause we knew we weren't welcome. But I never really thought too much about it: that's just how things were".

Mrs. Savage thought things had improved greatly for black Americans from the days when her grandfather was a slave here. "I had a lot of white friends that lived in my neighborhood and we all got along. We had to because we were all poor. If you're poor, you're poor. "Though it was literally spelled out for her on signs around town, it wasn't until she was old enough to work that she was confronted by blatant racism. "I heard the word 'N' all of my life, but was never called that to my face until a girl I worked with let it slip one day. Beatrice dropped out of school in the 11th grade to go to work for a local white family. She did that because opportunity rarely knocked on the door of local blacks in her day. "My daddy always told me, you treat people the way you want to be treated. If we did that, there'd be no more problems. Everybody puts their clothes on the same as me, and I've never met anybody I was afraid of, but I never thought Tennessee was as racist as some other states."

Her great grandfather, Henry Buchannon is buried at Bolden Green Cemetery. Great grandmother married George T. Bolden's brother, her name was Sarah (Safely) Bolden. Her grandmother's name: Sarah (Webb) Bolden married George T. Bolden Sr. Sarah (Webb) Bolden is buried at Bolden Green Cemetery.

Doctor Reverend Eugene M. Scott

In the summer of 1991, I had the distinct privilege of talking to one of the most modest citizens of Brownstown Community, here in McMinnville, Tennessee.

Reverend Scott was a pro golfer and semi-pro baseball player. He started playing baseball with (T.C.I.) Tennessee Coal and Iron. This team traveled to Georgia, Alabama, and Los Angeles to play baseball. He started playing at the age of fifteen years old. His love for the game was great. Since he is a modest person, he doesn't like the idea of bragging on his baseball accomplishments. Scott played for the Birmingham Black Barons semi-pro team in the Negro League, at the ages of sixteen and seventeen. Later, he went out West and played with the Watts Giants. Chuck Brewer, who was a scout and manager for the L.A. Dodgers at that time, had the philosophy that losing was almost a no-no. Scott could play all positions but preferred being a catcher.

He joined the army in 1943-1947 and afterwards joined the Giant Team (Watts). Josh Gibson inspired him, and taught him a lot. He was helped because he was small in stature. "They really didn't want to give me a shot, until they found out that I wouldn't take no for an answer. Once I got on the field, I took my own time getting off. I wanted to play ball, that was my life. My father preferred me to become a doctor, but being a ball player was my greatest desire so he decided to go with whatever I wanted."

Scott started golfing when he was nine years old. He use to caddy in Birmingham, and received 75 cent for eighteen holes. "The golf clubs were made with wooden shaft, so some of the rich fellows would make bad shots and would break them or throw the clubs against a tree so I would get them, replace the club with a wooden shaft and start my own club set. That's how I got started by the age of eleven or twelve. I knew what I wanted to play golf just as much as baseball. I played baseball over twenty years and played golf all along. I didn't let one interfere with the other, so I let golf go for a while."

"I had a chance to make it to the majors and busted my leg. While at the Cleveland Farm Team I tried to make extra money for camp, but the man forfeited my contract with my present team."

Blacks were in organized ball at this time. Scouts were checking him out after three weeks that they played exhibition game in Mexico. He recalls that "Jackie Robinson was playing with the Brooklyn Dodgers at second base. About five or six years before Jim Gilliam a young second baseman in the Farm League, was moved up to play second and move Jackie Robinson to first base, because he could cover so much more territory. Blacks were in organized ball at this time."

"Kinney Washington, quarterback for UCLA in 1940's holds record for the longest touchdown, one hundred yards to present." Scott was also a member of The Masonic Hall Lodge. He had some money in those days. Jim Gilliam was his best friend for thirty years. His other friends included Oscar Walker (Business man) Don Newcomb first black umpire in the majors who played with Jackie Robinson and Roy Campbenella, who caught him when he played and won thirty games in one season. "I gave Don Newcomb a rough time on some of the close calls when he umpired our games, before he went to the majors. Man you're as blind as a bat I'd say, but if you looked back he would throw you out of the game. Scott and Oscar Shaw were designed to go to the Big League. So George Roller taught the School of Umpires at this time (1949 to 1955). Scott umpired the majors for about seven years during time off from work. He got paid very little and wore the suits, with the short brim cap, thick coat, white shirt, black tie, button up and ball pockets, shin guards, chest protectors were under our shirts (plate). You had to wear a very clean pressed professional uniform. It was beautiful and I loved it all."

Scott played golf with the United States Golfing Association and played in California, Nevada, Colorado, Arizona, and Texas, where he played for money. He played by his nickname (mighty mouse) in the tournaments. He was self composed, stayed in there and mapped out shots. "You've got to remember you are playing the course not the competitors," Scott says, "Carl T. Rowan (1943) first member of Black Naval Officer, radio announcer of his own show and official to United States Embassy."

Mrs. Era Tennie (Locke) Smith

(1884-1955) 71 years old.

Era was born in Warren County April 17, 1884 to Lafayette and Sallie (Potter) Locke. She was married to W.F. Smith. He died February 15, 1954. Era was a member of the Church of Christ.

They had three sons: Arthur and Lafayette of Warren County and Dr. Lloyd Smith of Murfreesboro, Tennessee. Their daughters: Mrs. W.B. Womack and Mrs. Bernice Waldman reside in Los Angeles, California.

Era had two sisters: Mrs. W.A. (Locke) Fuston of Chicago, Illinois and Mrs. O.B. (Locke) Payne of Atlanta, Georgia. Her two brothers: V.S. Locke of the Campaign Community and Dan Locke of McMinnville.

Mrs. Tennie died suddenly at her home located on Sparta Road.

Rufe Huggins was the minister of the East End Drive Church of

Christ and joined by Joe D. Gray of Bybee Branch Church of

Christ. She was buried in the Mt. View Cemetery.

S. M. Stamps Sr.

Principal: S. M. Stamps, Born in Winchester, Tennessee: reared in Sallisaw, Oklahoma. Professor Stamps was married to a teacher by the name of Nina Dobbins. In 1948 the Superintendent of (Black) education in Tennessee contacted Professor Stamps. Stamps was appointed Principal of the segregated Bernard High School, where he remained until school integration got under way at McMinnville City High School, and Central High School. Stamps served two years as Assistant Principal at City High before he retired in 1966. Professor was the first black person to become assistant Principal in Warren County after schools were integrated.

In the early 1950's Professor Stamps and Eulous Martin were instrumental in starting the Pleasant Hill Fair. Howard Martin was the Principal of the Pleasant Hill School.

The (Leroy Ramsey Gym) was erected in 1951 and the site was used for Bernard's very first basketball team. Football had already been a part of the students few extra curricular activities. In the summer months, students in the community around Bernard swam in the Collins River, and there was a history of drownings. In the 1950's a swimming pool was put on the school property, so the gymnasium opened all summer to provide recreation for the black children.

Professor S. M. Stamps was the driving force behind the success of Bernard High School.

We don't remember anytime when he was out of uniform; a suit, white shirt, bow tie and dress shoes.

Estie 'Jack' Strode

February 6, 1924-2000

Jack was a hard working ball player. Third base was his position. He eventually turned to coaching. Frank Bonner was a pitcher for the Rockets at the time. He laid out most of the night one Saturday. Jack caught Frank and five more players out past their curfew. They cried because they got caught staying out all night and didn't get to play in the line-up Sunday. Some thought he would slip around to catch the players doing wrong. Harold Thomas remembers the saying Jack used, "I can win with you, and I can lose without you. He let us dress out for the game and after the rest of the players arrived, he sent us home."

"Well I was born to raise mules. Everybody had mules back when I was born: they were a necessity. It was a must that you had a mule." Before tractors were commonplace, Jack's father, Cliffton Strode logged and farmed with mules. They planted crops in the spring; logged in the spring, summer, and fall; then harvested the crops with mules. Jack joined his two brothers in assisting with the logging and farming, but his brothers never really liked mules and didn't take up with them like he did. Jack's dedication to working with the intelligent, long-eared creatures was recognized early in life.

When he was five or six years old, he and his family lived in a cove on an old dirt road about three miles off the main road. Jack's dad used mules in his public job hauling gravel to cover the county roads. "Back then they worked from daylight till dark. I can remember the excitement I felt every night when I heard dad coming home. I could hear those mules and wagon about a mile from the house, because the wheels would be bumping up against those rocks. It was dark, but I'd take off down the road barefooted. I'd run to meet him so I could drive the mules back to the barn." Jack's determination to smoothly control the sturdy animals escalated, as he grew older. As a small seven-year-old boy, Jack found no more pleasure than using his father's old gentle mule to work the garden. He would continually plow the dirt up and then drag it back down over and over again. At his father's urging, as soon as Jack was barely big enough to handle spunkier animals the youngster stayed busy breaking young mules. "I guess I was pretty good with mules as a boy, because my dad kept me breaking them. I was good with them anyway. I don't know if he was bragging on me to keep me at it or what—but it worked. I stuck with them; and to this day I still enjoy training them. I like to start with one that doesn't know anything, and teach him. I respect them, they are real smart animals. You won't find an animal any smarter than a mule. You can teach them to do anything you want them to do, and they'll teach you a lot too."

Throughout his life, Jack worked and broke mules. Even when he served his country in World War II, then later worked public jobs for thirty-five years; he always kept his barn full of mules. When the weathered building wasn't filled with his own mules, it was full of mules owned by people who wanted Jack to train them. Word-of-mouth referrals about the skilled Tennessean spread quickly among mule enthusiasts. While Jack has long been well known in the Volunteer State for his unusual specialization, it wasn't until the 1980's that his name became recognized throughout the nation. "I broke some mules for a friend who liked to show in halter and hitch classes," Jack said. "One day in 1975 he invited me to go with him to a show and asked if I'd be interested in showing mules. Since I'd never been to a show, I told him I didn't know about showing, but I'd go with him to watch. When he finished showing, he got a blue ribbon from the judges. Well, I didn't know the mules were supposed to be doing, but I knew whatever it was didn't look good to me. So when we got home, I asked him, what did they give you that blue ribbon for? He said, 50% went to the appearance of the harness and hitch and the grade of the mules, and the other 50% was on the driving." I sat there thinking, and then said to him, "they must have given you 75% on your mules' harnesses, because you didn't do nothing for the driving." He said, "Well do you think you can beat it?" I sat thinking a minute, and then said, "I tell you what, if I couldn't I wouldn't go out there, I said. If I had me some mules, the right kind of mules, I'd do it. See, I was handling work mules and he was handling show mules."

Jack was eager to learn more about showing mules. He was puzzled as to how people could win blue ribbons and a name for themselves based on what he saw in that show ring. A year or two later, Jack and a pair of his smaller work mules accompanied his friend and friend's show mules to the Warren County Fair. Jack became an instant success. Long time top exhibitors recognized the unusual skill he demonstrated in the show ring with his team of work mules. He quickly became the crowd favorite, leaving the show with none other than a big blue ribbon. "That's when I began showing mules." Jack says. "I showed them all over Tennessee, Kentucky, Alabama, Georgia, and as far as Michigan. Yes sir, I've had my share of blue ribbons and trophies."

At the 1990 Michigan Great Lakes International show, Jack and his mules took first place in six of the seven classes offered. The next year he won all seven classes, amazing the crowd with his unequaled showmanship in the areas of single mule hitch to a cart, tandem mule hitch to a cart, two mule hitch, unicorn hitch to a cart, four mule hitch, and six mule hitch. "On the six mule hitch, the lead mules couldn't even see him," says James Grayson, a close friend who attended the show, "but they minded his every command."

Although Jack enjoyed the limelight of show events, he really was content training work mules. When he wasn't busy training other people's teams, he and his constant companion and partner—Malcolm Jessup bought their young mules from individuals or public sales. They would train them and then sell them. Any mules not sold in the South are taken to Pennsylvania Amish Farming Communities where strong work mules are needed regularly. Malcolm and Jack were partners for several years.

Before they met, Malcolm had been breaking a few mules to sell. One time he bought a young, wild and mean team he felt had lots of potential and they ended up being the wildest team he'd ever worked with. He mentioned the pair to another enthusiast who referred him to Jack Strode. Malcolm had heard Jack's name mentioned in mule circles, but he had never met the legendary muleteer. He decided to call Jack and put him to the test. "The first time I saw Jack break a team, I saw right away he knew what he was doing. I'd been breaking mules by myself for quite some time but I wasn't doing it like he was. No one broke mules like he did. Jack didn't even harness them quite like anyone else. Everything he did was different, and it was better."

"After seeing him, I wanted to learn more about his unique technique, so I asked him to show me. He started teaching me his way of training and I've been working with him ever since. We've broken and sold some sixty to seventy mules. The time it takes to break a team varies with each pair. Jack took about thirty days to train a team from the halter up. He worked them daily. Sometimes he would get a team that required only two weeks of his attention. At other times he'd get a wild pair that had never been caught, and that might take anywhere from sixty to ninety days to break them. Jack strongly believed, "You've got to work 'em' to break 'em'. He didn't waste time when he trained a team, as soon as he caught them, harnessed them, hitched them to a working cart, he would calmly climb aboard and prepare for the ride of his life. He would drag a six hundred to seven hundred industrial tire or maybe three or four telephone poles behind the working cart." Jack said, "That weight behind the cart would slow them down. If they took a notion to run toward the field or into the woods, they couldn't run too easily. Most of the time they'll pick the easiest way to go, which is downhill, and they'll run into trees and bushes and that weight behind there will help to guide them. You have to be careful not to attach too heavy a load to the cart, because mules being trained haven't learned how to pull yet."

Jack believed a mule trained to pull logs or plow a field all day should be at least two years old. Most mules he trained were two years old and sixteen hands high. "When you start breaking a team don't get in a hurry, they are dangerous. Young mules that are gentle are no problem, but every once in a while you'll get hold of an 'outlaw'—one that has never been caught or has hardly ever seen anybody. Jack would take his lasso, pull them up to the barn, and tie them. Then start putting the harness on them. They'll throw a fit and they'll get down paw you, bite, kick or do anything else they can. So always remember to be careful and don't get in a hurry.

"When you get them worn down to where you can get the harness on them, then hook them to a working cart, get on board, pull your hat down to your eyes, say "get up!" and have someone around to tell others which way you went, because they'll sure enough take off with you. The main thing is to start driving them, teach them commands and that when you pull on the line, they need to go that way. They're smart, they'll catch on pretty quick. When hooking them up, put the one you think is the smartest, or the smallest, if you can't tell right off which is the smartest, you can usually tell when you are catching them which is which. It doesn't take but a few minutes. They're as smart as you are. They learn real fast what you're doing."

"You can take an unbroken mule and an inexperienced man fooling with mules, and the mule will catch on before the man will. The mule is smarter and will generally be a two year old mule and a forty year old man, and the mule will still catch on before the man will."

****

"Papa didn't go to college, nor did he ever win a Nobel Prize, but he served his country in the Army from 1942 to 1944," says grandson Jonathan Strode. He was a member of American Legion Post #208. Jack worked at DeZurik Southern Company from 1967 to 1991, after retirement he spent most of his time at his barn; breaking and training his mules. He was often sitting in the garage, barn, or kitchen, cutting leather whips belts, harnesses, lines and even brass rings on his mule harnesses.

Jack resided in the Bolden Green Community with his lovely wife Jean Strode and grandson Jonathan. The barn still stands today. Those who've seen him work say he could take the most stubborn or wildest mule into training, and after just a couple of months, make him perk up his head and stand at attention: ears and eyes eagerly awaiting the next command.

Jack didn't own a fancy barn or training facility. This mule man kept a few mules in his old gray, weathered barn near his home in (the Bolden Green community) McMinnville, Tennessee. It was the smart, highly trained mules that come from there that win the respect and admiration of knowledge Amish farmers and respected show judges alike. For years Jack wowed on lookers with such feats as working a twenty-mule jerk-line hitch to perfection and guiding a team just by the sound of his voice. How did he do it? Many people wondered. Some have visited Jack's farm to watch him in action.

All admit that no one could train a mule quite like Jack Strode could. Estie Jack Strode rests in peace at Gardens of Memory Cemetery in McMinnville, Tennessee.

Jean Strode, wife of Jack

Harold Thomas 'Lefty'

Born July 2, 1937, Harold pitched his way into all the hearts of the sluggers that faced him. Number eight (8) which he wore his uniform was probably the best pitcher McMinnville and Viola has ever seen. He pitched from 1957 until 1973. "When we started playing baseball in Viola Tennessee as the Viola 'Clowns' everyone called us little boys, but we beat every team we played."

Harold remembers when he played with the McMinnville 'Rockets' in later years, when Jack Strode was the manager of the 'Rockets' six players had stayed out all night long and he wouldn't let us play. Jack said, "That if I can win with you, I can lose without you. I will never forget that, says Harold. Jack put the second string in and sent us home."

"The stars that were worn on the front of the uniforms represented home runs. Jack Strode, then manager/coach would tell you to do something one time, and that was that."

Fred 'Mousy' Winton was watching his girlfriend when she called out, "Come on Fred." About that time when he turned back around and the pitcher had thrown the ball and popped him upside the head and knocked him out. He came too sometime later, but we laughed until we cried afterwards."

Roy Webb 1889-1989

Roy Webb was a Native of Warren County; he was employed in the coalmines in Alabama for a few years until he returned to Tennessee to work for over 50 years with the Warren County Highway Department.

Roy was a prominent resident of Route 5. The community was named Bolden Green. He was a member and a founder of the Bolden Green United Methodist Church, and donated plenty of time for the church. Roy took care of the up keep of the church after Rev. William C. Bolden passed away. Together they repaired the church, cut grass, cleaned the Bolden Green cemetery and served as elders and leaders in the community.

Roy's Parents were Richard and Sue (Faulkner) Webb. They were slaves to Asa Faulkner. Richard Sr. was known to be the driver for Asa Faulkner on the plantation. Richard was also used for breeding purposes. Roy played with the Faulkner children and when it was time to work, he did a lot of the yard work. He had two sisters and two brothers. They were Richard Jr., Mary, Dovie, and Robert Webb. Roy had four more stepbrothers and stepsisters. Their names were George, Sarah, Thomas and Hazel. Their mothers name was Tyree (Faulkner) Webb.

Roy married a very loving and kind woman by the name Georgia (Wood) Williams Webb; she died in 1984, four years before him.

Roy Webb was to have owned enough land in order to help 24 families build homes on. The Webb's either sold or gave some of the approximately 400 acres to different families. Richard left the land that he had owned to be divided among the children.

While working with the Transportation Department in Warren County, he also was hired by John High to dig graves for the funeral home. It would take one man all day long to dig one grave, so Roy would hire out Clifton Strode, J. L. Reedy and Rev. William C. Bolden to help out. This was more like part-time work for these gentlemen. Roy was a very busy person, always finding something to do around their farm, even when he retired, he would find time to go to the place where he used to work and sit around talking, and would help out whenever he could. This was just his nature; he was the kind of man that you would like to model after.

Georgia and Roy's house was erected in the Bolden Green community in about 1870, by a nice running brook where the water was so sweet, cold and clear. The Webb's found time to raise children, cows, pigs, chickens, dogs and ducks. The garden was also grown every year; this helped off set the food bill. The Webb's were also very giving when it came to food, and giving a helping hand.

Roy had no need for any other drinking fluids except water. No coffee, tea, milk nor sodas. No one ever remembers him drinking anything else.

The Webb's also owned land in the Martin Charge community. A house was built on the property and some years later, sold to the Wood family.

The Webb's were God's chosen people to take in a person in need. It is known that The Webb's adopted an elderly woman, which happened to be blind and let her live with them for most of thirty years, until her death. She was known as 'Aunt Callie'. Aunt Callie was buried in the Pikes hill Cemetery.

Roy and Georgia had two daughters. The daughter's names were Laura and Maude. Laura Webb Ramsey later married William "Pops" Ramsey. Maude Webb later married into the Smartt family.

Georgia (Wood) Webb was born in 1889, and departed this earth in 1984 at the age of 96. Georgia was buried beside her husband at the Pikes hill Cemetery.

Roy's great-great grandfather was a full-blooded Cherokee Indian. He was known to wear his hair in two long braids. The name differs from the family tree. He was called Larkin Leftrict.

Roy's father was a slave on a plantation, and his name was Richard. Richard's first wife name was Sue (Faulkner) Webb.

Roy had a very rich back ground in morals, religion; he was a man of his word. He married a woman with the same values, plus she loved to cook. The more people she cooked for the merrier. Some of the neighborhood children from around the community, black and white would stop over to the Webb's to see what kind of baked goodies Mrs. Webb had on hand. The Webb's had visitors from all over the County on any given day. They had just as many white visitors as black. It was nothing to see a yard full of people enjoying the company of the Webb's. People would come and share tales and receipts, especially on Sundays.

Georgia and Roy Webb

Robert Aaron Whitaker

'Bob Whitaker'

Robert Aaron Whitaker, the son of Richard E. and Jimmie Lee Reese Whitaker was born July 4, 1931 in Lincoln Co., TN. and died April 9, 2002. He was seventy years of age.

Robert leaves to cherish his memory three sisters and devoted brothers-in-law, Ola Mae King, and Ruth & George King, Jr. both of McMinnville and Annie Muhammad of California, two brothers and sisters-in-law, David E. & Mary E. Whitaker of Morrison, and Leon & Mandy Whitaker of McMinnville. A host of nieces, nephews, and cousins also survive.

Devoted friend, Annie Ruth Brown of Cannon Co., Two aunts, Ordea Whitaker and Ella B. Reese, and one uncle, Aaron L. Whitaker all of Lynchburg, TN.

He worked at the Dr. Pepper Bottling Co. of McMinnville and was a member of the Hiawassee Church of Christ. Bob had a speech defect, but you could understand him. He was a very pleasing person to be around.

Mary Virginia (Espenschied) Wolford

Mary was born to Virgil and Mildred Espenschied on September 29, 1957 in Belleville, Illinois. Mary has two brothers, Gary and David, one sister, Nina (Espenschied) Fulscher.

Mary is a very intelligent and hard workingwoman. She is married to Wayne R. Wolford Sr. since 1984; they have a daughter Named Erin Marissa Wolford. When she's not working, Mary enjoys the great outdoors, such as gardening and yard work. Mary decided to leave her resent job working with the State of Illinois Internal Revenue Service to venture with her husband as he served in the armed forces. Mary and Erin moved to McMinnville from Lawton, Oklahoma where Wayne was stationed while in the Army. A year later Wayne retired from Uncle Sam and began his final years in McMinnville.

Mary started working at River Park Hospital in the accounting department, as an Accounts Payable Clerk, two years later she got a chance to better herself and applied for a job 22 mile up the road in a town called Woodbury, Tennessee. Within a two year period she was promoted to Materials Management and housekeeping Supervisor, along with Accounting Finance Analyst at Stones River Hospital.

She has tried her hand at Massage Therapy, Cosmetologist recruiter, owned her own business. Mary enjoys working at Wal-Mart Super Center. She has helped Wayne with many organizational activities.

Mary has been an inspiration to Wayne on many of his endeavors. Sometimes she has put her life style on hold in order to please her man. Wayne is always asking his beloved wife for her thoughts, ideas and opinions, which he values so much.

Mary was a member of American Legion Post Auxiliary #208, McMinnville Chapter of the NAACP, and SOCM, and varies church groups.

Wayne Richard Graves Wolford Sr.

(Feb. 25, 1948-)

Born to Ms. Ruby Emerald Wolford on the 25th day of February 1948 in Alton, Madison County, Illinois. My grandmother was Marjorie Bolden Wolford Thacker and my grandfather was Robert Wolford of Chicago. My step-grandfather was Ramey Thacker. Great grandmother: Ruby V. Bolden, great great-great grandfather: John Bolden. Great-great grand Mother was Sarah Webb Bolden Great great-grand father: George Thomas Bolden Sr.

I am married to a beautiful Mary Virginia Espenschied Wolford, and have a lovely daughter Erin Wolford and two great sons: Wayne Jr. and Matthew Wolford by a previous marriage, and a wonderful grand-daughter Brittany Wolford.

We moved to St. Louis Missouri when I was a mere lad of six years old, from my birth place Alton, IL. My grandmother wanted to return to her roots in McMinnville, Tennessee, so in 1958 my grandparents (Ramey and Marjorie Thacker) moved to Bolden Green Community in McMinnville, Tenn. Mother (Ruby) and I lived in St. Louis but she blessed me with the gift of coming to school every other year in Tennessee. I'm a little bit country and a little bit city. I attended Bernard, Pleasant Hill and Central High Schools in Tenn., and several schools in St. Louis Missouri. Saint Louis was a rough place for an only child. There were gangs, Prostitutes, drunks, wineos, just to name a few crime related life styles to get involved in. The nickname 'Wolf' was given to me in elementary school.

In Tennessee I learned so much about the country life. Uncle Will Bolden have a 100 acre farm with just about all of the animals that you can have on a farm. I just loved being with him as a kid at ten years old. Learning how to farm was the best thing for a growing boy. I did it all, from milking cows to plowing behind mules. Getting up at the crack of day was a wonderful feeling to know that you were going to milk cows, and feed the animals. Now once I got in my teens this wasn't so glamorous. The best cooks in the world came from a kitchen with wood stoves. Meal time was always anticipated, delicious food and all kinds of deserts. The main part I don't miss is the outdoor plumbing. (Out house)

In 1965 I played with a local Semi-Pro Baseball team in McMinnville, Tenn. This team was named the 'Rockets'.

After finishing Central High school in 1966, went to Nashville, Tennessee to attend Barber College. In one year, I cleaned floors at Vanderbilt Hospital, moved furniture for Caster-Knott's Company, worked at Purity Dairies, washed pots and pans at Fisk University and had three other jobs while in Nashville attending Barber College.

After finishing there, I completed training at (Vo-Tech) McMinnville Tech-Center in Industrial Electricity.

In 1970 I moved back to St. Louis, Missouri. I worked at McDonnell Douglas Aircraft as a mail carrier, later applied for a job working as an Electrical Blueprint Analyzer.

While in St. Louis I played Semi-Pro Baseball with the 'Browns' and Semi-Pro Football with the 'Panthers.' We played in St. Louis, Missouri and Illinois. I was accepted for try outs with the then NFL Saint Louis 'Cardinals' football team in 1972.They selected 12 of us out of 250 to go down to the stadium to try out for the team. I was cut from the team after two weeks due to bad knees. In 1973 I tried out for the St. Louis, Cincinnati, and Pittsburg baseball teams and did not get the go ahead.

During my early years I moved back to Tennessee. This is where I cut hair, shined shoes, cleaned churches, worked in night clubs VFW, Country Club, carried groceries at Cooper-Martin grocery store, and picked up trash and any other kind of odd jobs to make a living for my family.

In 1975 my life had changed for the better. No more Ghetto life, bars on the school windows and policemen at the high school, or either running every time you see a gang coming your way. There was no more alley stick ball, hippie days, wandering were my next dollar was coming from. No more, 'just existing.' The break of a life time came when I joined the United States Army, in July of 1975. ('Three hots and a cot.')

While successfully completing a military career of over twenty years, I directly supervised, trained and counseled electronics instructors. There was hands-on experience performing maintenance on surveillance radars and meteorological equipment. Over eight years as a classroom instructor and fully qualified to assume the duties and responsibilities as a Basic Electronic Instructor. I earned several outstanding ribbons, badges, awards including reduced operational expenses on $2 Million worth of equipment by saving over $800,000 in repairs.

I supervised and trained numerous instructors for the Target Acquisition/Surveillance Radar Repair Course. I've instructed hundreds of soldiers, Marines, civilians and foreign students. I wrote and revised the curriculum, training plans, and exams for the course.

By 1982 I was selected as an Army Recruiter in Springfield and Mattoon, Illinois. I excelled at working with youth activities; such as assisting coaching high school football and baseball teams. Recognition for superb Public Relations, I was in demand by JROTC, High School and Eastern Illinois University ROTC Administrators to present career orientation programs, pep rallies, and individual counseling. I participated in local a Big Brothers Program in Lawton, Oklahoma before moving to Illinois to recruit.

While in the military service, I not only did coaching and playing in numerous post championships, such as, softball, football, basketball and track; I also found time to attend college.

Some of the educational institutions and training schools I attended, are as follows: Cameron University, Lawton, Oklahoma; Kansas State University, Ft. Riley, Kansas; Vo-Tech, McMinnville, Tennessee; Instructor Training Course, Oklahoma; Recruiter Supervisor Course Ft. Ben Harrison, Indiana Target Radar Repair, Ft. Sill, Oklahoma . . . (etc.).

After leaving the Army in September of 1995, I retired and have enjoyed the relaxing life of: Cosmetologist, Farmer, Historian, Author—Writer, full and part-time Substitute Teacher, Bridgestone/Firestone Security Guard, High School and Middle School Coach football, soccer, track, baseball, Community Leader, member of Kiwanis Club, member of Warren County Drug Task Force Alliance, (SOCM) Save Our Cumberland Mountains member, Warren County Health Council, Upper Cumberland Regional Health Council, Young Men United Spokesman, 4-H Club Leader, Red Cross Volunteer, Warren County High School Black History Club, Faith in Action Cares Coalition, Senior Center Volunteer, American Legion Commander of Post 208, Personal assistant for individuals at Pacesetters Inc. for mentally and physically challenged adults, Husband Father and Grandfather.

If I had it to do all over again, there would be very little that I would change. My main mentors were my grandmother Marjorie Thacker, my Uncle Rev. William C. Bolden and Uncle Roy Webb. We all need guidance in our lives, and the better our role models are, we can become also. They all have told me many times, "Wayne, you can be anything you want as long as you put your mind to it." All I ever wanted out of this life, was to be a good man and role model. The good Lord has blessed me with both.

I am very proud of my wife Mary, which keeps me in line and focused. I spend quite a bit of my time writing about the history of Warren County, and reading history in general, so she is very patient with me and my work. I truly thank her for allowing me to follow my passion, without showing any signs of jealousy or regret towards my work.

I say this every morning that I wake up. "Thank you for another day." Then when I rest at night, "Thank you heavenly Father, for another blessed day."

Lillian Young (November 17, 1923-) &
Mack Young (1910-1997)

Born in Clarksville, Tennessee, Lillian a high school graduate and former graduate of McMinnville Vo-Tech Book-keeping and Accounting class was married to Mack Leftrict Young. Their sons: Samuel McCly Young and Alfred Bernard Young were born in Muncie Indiana.

When Lillian moved to McMinnville, Samuel was only three years old and Alfred was three months. Samuel went to high school in Little Rock Arkansas, grade school here, and attended college at the University of Arkansas, then known as Pine Bluff A & M College (Grad.). Alfred went to grade school here, high school at Riverside and Howard in Chattanooga, TN. He served his country in the Air Force and Army; he got his bachelor's at Tennessee State University and his Master's Degree from Georgetown.

Sam had a construction company: 'Little Rock Arkansas Design and Construction Association, Inc.'

"Mack moved us to McMinnville with the understanding that a school job was available, says Mrs. Young. No contract was signed. We sold our home in Muncie, Indiana. Once we got to McMinnville Mr. Stamps was already hired. I guess they signed his contract. I can kind of understand why. Mr. Stamps and his wife went as a team. I'm not a college grad, so they would have had Mack and not the second person."

"We lived in a rent house with Mack's mother until we built a house were the high-rise building is now (Beersheba Towers). We were not working at this time; we lived off the money we sold from the house, in Muncie."

"A covered truck took several veterans to school in Murfreesboro, they taught Vocational Education classes at a private school. Mack taught carpentry and brick masonry there, and made more money there then in the public school system. The owner of the school was killed in a car accident, so the wife kept the school going until the year's end then closed the school. Paul Howard Officer was a driver of the transportation truck. At this particular time Blacks weren't allowed to join the union, so Mack would go to Detroit, Michigan or Cleveland, Ohio and join the union up there, until it got cold, so he could draw his unemployment, and then return home to McMinnville, Tn. Mack would draw more money than the average person made here (During the late 1940's). Mack taught for a total of thirty-one years within the school system."

Sometimes Lillian and the children would go to Cleveland, Ohio to visit Mack while he was working up there.

"After Professor Stamps was hired as principal at Bernard High School, Mack would go over and help out in his spare time with coaching and carpentry work; later, he would get a job as a teacher here, for fifteen years. Mack took his personal machine equipment over to Bernard High School when they finally hired him to teach the kids. When he went to Cleveland, Ohio to work during the summer, it was noticed that Mack's name wasn't in the paper to be re-hired to teach. Lillian called Dr. Clark and found out that Mack wasn't hired. Dr. Clark was The Chairman of the educational board. Black teachers didn't make nearly as much as they're cross-town counter parts. Professor Stamps did not re-hire Mack for whatever reason."

Mack worked until he was sixty-five years of age (retired); Lillian and Mack owned and operated a homework shop. Refinished furniture antiques until his eyesight went bad.

Mrs. Young was on the Board of Directors of McMinnville Senior Citizens. Transportation program (wrote grant for City County and federal fund for approximately $5,000 a year. She was a member of Clark United Methodist Church choir since 1947, member of Warren County Cares Program and Community leader until her passing.

Lillian Young; was a High school graduate, housewife, one of the first students at Vo-Tech in McMinnville, Bookkeeping / Accounting class.

Lillian's mother and father were Glenn and Mattie (Johnson) Young. Her grandmother was Hattie Johnson Suggs. Half brothers and sisters were; Henry L. Johnson, Al Wendell Johnson, Dewayne Johnson, Robert Young and Betty Young. Mack's father was named Alpha Omega Young and his mother was Hattie (Leftrict) Young. Mack Young was buried at Riverside Cemetery (December 28, 1910-May 20, 1997) also buried there are: Sam Leftrict, Irene Young, his little sister named Loretta (who died at a young age). Blacks as well as Whites were buried at Riverside Cemetery. Most Blacks were buried on the low side of the hill. (About 1947).

"I used to work at the Magness Memorial Library checking books, shelving them, and doing stock. This was my first job! Hazel and Irene said "Humph!" Girl you need a job, I said "Why?" Hazel and Irene took Lillian to the unemployment office for a job interview; they thought I wasn't working a real job in their eyes."

Irene was a very smart woman. Buddy Young was known for his masonry work. L.V. Curtis and Harry Cope worked for him.

Mack's first wife wasn't as friendly as I was, so McMinnville just took to me! I would go to town with Juanita Martin and she knew everybody.

Facts: Found in 1945-46 Bernard High School Annual in the 1920's Young, Alpha helped build and fund Bernard High School. Tom Howell, Ellen Teacher of 7th and 8th grade—Rhodes, Edna (Etter) Teacher of 3rd and 4th grades—Bates, Edith Teacher (BHS) 1st & 2nd grade.

Interesting Bits of Info on the Young Family

(1) Hazel Young worked as a cook at City Grammar School.
(2) Lillian's first job was at Magness Library.
(3) Lillian has no full brothers or sisters.
(4) Lillian won 'Miss Senior' Warren County Pageant.
(5) Mack's sister Irene went to Tennessee Normal College in Nashville, Tennessee, which was later, called Tennessee A & I.
(6) Mack's sister Clara Young attended Fisk University; taught in Little Rock and she taught Trichonometry.

Diagnosed with Alzheimer's, was dying from a heart attack but managed to drive self to the hospital. She is buried here in Warren County.

Chapter 6

Churches

Part 1
Many Churches

Bolden Green Methodist: (Bolden Green)

Browns' Chapel: Brown Town (Nashville highway)

Clark Chapel United Methodist: 'Church on the Hill' (city)

Clark Chapel United Methodist (city)

Church of Prophesy (city)

Cummings' Chapel: Brown Town

Foot Washing Baptist: (Leesburg)

Hiawassee Church of Christ: (Morrison)

Leesburg Methodist

Martin Charge Methodist: Pleasant Hill 'Shady Rest'

Mount Zion Baptist: (City)

Philadelphia: (Morrison)

South High Baptist: (city)

Saint Mary's Baptist: (city)

South High Street Methodist: (city)

Bro. George King

Bro. Eugene Wilkerson

Rev. Arnold and Rev. Bolden at Saint Mary's Baptist Church

Inside of Church on the Hill 1975—Clark United Methodist

The First Clark United Methodist Church—Leesburg

CLARK UNITED METHODIST CHURCH

104 Bernard Drive
McMinnville, TN 37110

South High Baptist Church

Old Philadelphia Church

East End Drive Church of Christ est. Built in1941

Dr. Eugene M. Scott

Brown Chapel Baptist Church—on N. Johnson Road

Martin Chapel Methodist Church est. 1960

Bro. Michael and Eunice Harris
North Hills Church of God of Prophecy (city)

Bro. Phillips Smith Jr.

East End Drive Church of Christ: Built in 1941 (city)

Part 2
History of Clark United Methodist Church

McMINNVILLE, TENNESSEE

On December 2, 1869, a lot from H. Stevens to J.W. Johnston, which was known as the property of the Methodist Episcopal Church, became the home of Clark United Methodist Church as we now know it. This location was on College Street. For over eight years services were held there, although there were tests of the Congregation's faith. On August 30, 1886, a conveyance was made between a Board of Church Extension of The Methodist Episcopal Incorporated by the Legislature of Pennsylvania and The Corporation of the town of McMinnville, Warren County and the State of Tennessee, Witnessed: Whereas the Corporation of McMinnville, TN. have at the request of the Methodist Episcopal Church Extension conveyed to Mack Young, Alfred White, T.N. Mabry, S.M. Leftwich and Joseph Gross: Trustees of the Church, A certain property known as 'The Waters and Walling College Lot.

The first Pastor of this church was sent from the Conference and served the charge with sincerity. He was Rev. S.P. Bell. The Membership was growing rapidly, when a fire destroyed the building, leaving the congregation literally out of doors. Pooling their money and labor, the members began the erection of a new church. Just as the walls were completed, a storm leveled one side and end. But with religious fervor, more funds and labor were contributed. Under the efficient leadership of Rev. T. J. Johnson the church was completed, which served the community until was remodeled in 1950, with Rev. J.C. Johnson as pastor.

Worship was held at this location until 1974, the old building was raised for renovation. The church congregation re-located to Leesburg. Services were held at Leesburg until the building was constructed on Colville Street. The old building was made of handmade bricks that some of the Black Stone Masons made. Many bricks were taken as mementos.

The memorial stained glass windows, the pews and the old bell, which rang many years ago, are being preserved in the new church. It was sad to see the old church go, but they hoped prayed and thrived to grow in the new church and in the hearts of all the people. Urban renewal came through and removed many buildings in this area.

Under the leadership of Rev. Luther Allen, they had their first worship service at the present location on October 4, 1977. This church location is on Bernard Street. At that time the trustees were: Lillian Young, Eulous Martin, Mack L. Young, Lottie Crisp, Jonah Patterson, Bessie T. Gwynn, Juanita Martin, Edna Etter and Roy Spencer.

With the Bishop and District Superintendent participating in the ceremony, ground was broken Sunday 3, April 1977 for the new $75,500 sanctuary of Clark Methodist Church.

The modern, new worship center will be located on a 2 acre tract of land near Bernard School, now Bernard Street.

According to Mack L. Young, chairman of the Building Committee, the building will be measure 36 x 60 and will contain an auditorium seating 175 persons, three classrooms a kitchen, nursery, ladies and men's lounge, and Baptistery.

Wayman E. Hillis, a member of First United Methodist Church drew the plans for the church, and the contract to construct the building has been awarded to Jewell Hale, a local contractor.

Young said plans call for the building to be completed by the last of July.

Serving on the building committee with Mack Young are Roy Spencer, Eulous Martin, Jonah Patterson and Mrs. Lottie Crisp. Mrs. Crisp is Secretary of Finance.

The congregation's original building was in the area cleared for redevelopment as a part of the Beersheba Heights Urban Renewal Project. Members at some time in changing conference and mergers, they became known as Clark United Methodist Church.

The ministerial leadership has been provided by: Reverends S.P. Bell, T.J. Johnson, Miles Williams, H.M. Prim, Alfred Martin, D.T. Burch, T.W. Johnson S.M. Tetley, J.W. Richmond, W.A. Rodgers, W.T. Travis, John H. Houston,

J.T. Paitllo, John R. Gray, I.R. Irving, Daniel L. Garrett, J. R. Booth, Jared 0. Dixon, Jury E. Turner, James M. Hayden, Major M.

League, William R. Smith, D.S. Harkness Julius C. Johnson, Rev. Blackwell, Edwin Sanders, J.R. Royal, Lynwood

Parker, Dean W. Simmons, Robert V. Green, Henry Walter, Willis, John P. Willis, Marcellus Caldwell, Joe K. Shelton, Luther Allen, Glen Lyles, Frederick Yebuak, Daniel Hayes, Nathanial Williams, Ezell Garner. At one time there were two local associate preachers: Rev. Jake Anderson and Albert Huddleston, Rev. Ernest Howse and Rev Hilton of the congregation have been holding worship services at Leesburg for the past several months.

Participants in the ceremony Sunday afternoon of the ground breaking were: Senator Ernest Crouch, Jonah Patterson, Rev. Luther Allen, Rev. Charles G. Poole, Rev. John B. Sessoms Jr. Eulous Martin, Rev. Luther Allen, Mack L. Young,

Jewell M. Hale, Bishop Earl G. Hunt Jr., Roy Spencer, Clinton Shockley, George and Carl Allen.

Chapter 7

List of Warren County Blacks Residents

Master List of Warren County History Names

(A-Ar)

Adams, Henry; Blacksmith during 1870 in the Smartt, Verville, Morrison area.

Adcock, Horace; WWI Vet., O/S (Pvt), 1918-19.

Alexander, Joseph; Stone Mason early 1900's.

Alexander, Mary (Biles)

Alexander, Paul; Rocket baseball player, Husband of Virginia (Womack).

Alexander, Virginia (Womack); wife of Paul Alexander, Daughter of Ernest

Sr. & Lucile (Smith).

Allen, Lena Mrs. R.; lived in Yankeetown in 1942.

Allen, Robert

Allen, Vivian

Allison, Jane; widow to W. Henry, 334 South High in 1942.

Ajamu, Waleed Bakari; Pastor of Church of Prophesy (1990's).

Anderson, Emma; Died 1934 76 yrs.

Anderson, Jake; caretaker for W. Vance Whitson, lived on 108 East Colville in 1942.

Anderson, Joseph; Stonemason in 1900's.

Armluett, Lena; 19? 4, 70 yrs. old.

Armstrong, Ben; Stonemason, early 1900's.

Arnold, Cora (); Wife of Rev. Horace Sr.

Arnold, Doris: died March 2002, Daughter of H. D. Sr.

Arnold, Henry: son of Horace Sr.

Arnold, Horace D. Sr.; Rev. Minister, Carpenter.

Arnold, Horace D. Jr.

Arnold, Nora (); Wife of Henry Arnold.

Arnold, Rufus; Son of Rev. Horace D. Arnold Sr.

Arnold, Shannon R.: daughter of Henry & Nora.

Arnold, Thomas Jr.

Arnold, Virginia Mai

(B-Bo)

Bain, Samuel; WW1, DD214. Original member of Post 208, lived in city in 1945. [story]

Baker, Amiel (Alice); Janitor at City Bank & Trust Co. in 1942, lived on 111 East End Drive Ave.

Baker, Chad; Soph. WCHS 2001.

Baker, Chassidy

Baker, Michael; Son of Nancy Baker. Vet. Panama 1980.

Baker, Phyllis

Barnes, Henry (Addie); laborer, lived on Carney in 1942.

Barnes, John; WW1 Vet, 1918-19 (Pvt), O/S Born in Viola

Barnhill, Carolyn; wife of Dwight, Social worker.

Barnhill, Dareus; Freshman, WCHS 2001.

Barnhill, William Dwight 'Sug'; Rocket Baseball player, Vietnam-Navy [Story]

Barnhill, William 'Poochie' 1940's.

Bartley, Robert D.; WW1 Vet. 1918-19 (Pvt), Born in Rock Island 6/30/1893, Farmer, not married, Parent: (Mother) Lige Bartley.

Bass, Marie Lorene

Bass, Willie

Bates, Benjamin M. Sr.; Elder in church in the 1950's, built church in Sparta, & Smithville, TN. (Rev.), husband to Pearl () Bates. They owned a restaurant on Egypt Alley and East Colville in 1942.

Bates, Benjamin Jr.; Pearl Harbor Vet. U. S. Navy. [story]

Bates, David

Bates, Dorothy; Daughter of Ben Sr. and Pearl ().

Bates, Edith L.; (1914-2002) Educator, 1st & 2nd grades, wife of Morton

Lived on Egypt Alley in 1942. [story] Daughter of Ben Bates

Sr. and Pearl ().

Bates, Earnest Wade; WW1, (Pfc), 1918-19, born: 12/17/1891 in

McMinnville, Laborer, not married, Ed: 5th grade, Parent: Law Bates.

Bates, Harrison; WW1, 1918-19

Bates, Henrietta B.; Daughter of Rev. Bates and Pearl ().

Bates, James Lloyd; 1950 BHS Valedictorian, Korean Vet. [story]

Bates, Jennie (Womack); Died 1949, 68 yrs. old

Bates, Jewel 'Johnny' Thomas; Korean Vet. B. H. S. Class President 1948,

Captain of the football team, Fullback. [story]

Bates, 'Joe' Joseph Brown; DD214, WW2 Vet. Lived on Egypt in 1942. [story] Born; Oct. 25, 1924.

Bates, Law; Son of Earnest W.

Bates, Lizzie (Flanigan)

Bates, Mark

Bates, Mary (Calvin)

Bates, Mary Evelyn: married name is Ivy. Daughter of Pearl () and Ben Sr.

Bates, Myrene

Bates, Paul W.; DD214, WW2 in the Army in 1942. Address on Egypt Alley in 1942. [story] Born; Nov. 7, 1919.

Bates, Pearl; wife of Benjamin Sr.

Bates, Samuel

Bates, William 'Will': (1875-1944)

Bates, Willie Randolph.; (Dec. 25, 1925-) DD214, WW2, Vet. BHS football 1947, [story] Born; Dec. 25, 1925.

Batey, Sam; Sydna's 2nd husband.

Batey, Sydna (Martin); Educator. [story]

Battles, Fred

Battles, Gail; wife of Nelson Ramsey, Business owner Thrift store.

Battles, Larry

Battles, Louis; 'Turkey' (1944-) Civil Service worker for over 35 years. [story]

Battles, Martisha: 1998 WCHS Sr.

Battles, Mary

Beard, Irene; member of East End Church of Christ (2002)

Beasley, Alda J. (); wife to Ellis in 1942.

Beasley, Cleveland; U. S. Navy in 1942, WWII, (Vet) lived on S. African St.

Beasley, Ellis; lived on S. African St in 1942 with his wife; Alda J.)

Beatrice, Willena

Bedford, Frankie C.; lived on Lane St. in 1942.

Bedford, Katie P.; lived on Lane St. in 1942.

Bell, Maggie; lived on 501 Beersheba in 1942.

Biles, Andrew R.

Biles, Anthony; member of East End Church of Christ (2002)

Biles Aries Dwayne; son of 'Butch' Biles, WCHS Jr. 2002

Biles, Barbara 'Beth'

Biles, Bertha (); widow of Harrison, lived on 122 Edgefield Street in 1942.

Biles, Betty Louise; 1st grade BHS 1945.

Biles, Billy

Biles, Bobby; Korean Vet. 1947 BHS 8th grade student, Semi-Pro baseball player.

Biles, Brown A.; husband to Helen L. He was an electrician and lived on 120 Murphy Street in 1942.

Biles, Catherine ()

Biles, Chris

Biles, David

Biles, Dorothy (Bonner) ; 1929-Nov. 9, 1974. Daughter of Harrison & Frances (___) Bonner, wife of Fred Biles. [story]

Biles, Eugene; husband to Cathrine () in 1942, they also lived on 107 East End Drive in 1942. A porter at Puckett Motors. Bellhop at Brown Hotel 1960's.

Biles, Eural (Leola); Caretaker, lived in Yankeetown in 1942

Biles, Florence; wife of Nick Biles, mother of Harrison E.

Biles, Frankie Mae Dalton; BHS 1955 Grad, wife of Charles Dalton. 2nd grade BHS 1945.

Biles, Fred; Korean Vet., 1946 BHS 6th grade student.

Biles, Fred; 1932-Jun. 26, 1980. WW II Vet. Son of Eural & Leola

(Ramsey) Biles, husband of Dorothy Bonner.

Biles, Harrison E.; WW1, (Pvt), 1918-19, Army, Born in Warren County 2/1889, Farmer, Parents: Nick & Florence Biles.

Biles, Harrison 'Son'; [story]

Biles, Harrison E. Jr. 'Butch'; Vet.

Bales, Harrison, E. Sr.; Korean Vet. Dad of 'Butch'.

Biles, Beth; daughter of Katherine ().

Biles, George; son of Katherine ().

Biles, Helen L. (); wife of Brown Biles in 1942.

Biles, Jason

Biles, Joe

Biles, Josephine; wife of Charles 'Scooky' Crabtree. 4th grade BHS 1945.

Biles, Josh

Biles, Katherine

Biles, Lera

Biles, Marjorie Ruth; 1st grade BHS 1945.

Biles, Mary (); (1788-1828)

Biles, Paul

Biles, Robert : Vet.

Biles, Sara Francis; BHS 1955 Grad.

Biles, Tonya; Daughter of 'Butch', WCHS 1999 Sr.

Bishop, Darius

Bishop, Thelma (Grayson);daughter of Dorothy Womack.

Bishop, Reese: son of Thelma

Black Foxes; [story]

Blevins, Casandra: daughter of Ronnie Blevins.

Blevins, Johnnie (Woodard); lives in Detriot.

Blevins, LaMont; Son of Ronnie Blevins.

Blevins, Robert

Blevins, Ronnie; Rockets Baseball player, [story]

Blue, Clarence; WW2 Vet.

Blue, Genevia Lucile

Blue, Jas A.; lived at 110 East End Drive in 1942.

Blue, Jim; 1958, 68 yrs. old. [story]

Blue, John Burr (Eldora); WW2 Vet. Class of 1939 BHS. Lived at
    110 East End Drive in 1942.

Blue, Virginia L.; student, lived at 110 East End Drive in 1942.

Bohannon, Gaskell; employed at Southern Standard in 1942.

Bolden, Betty; wife of John.

Bolden, Cardell

Bolden, Clarence Delton; Korean Vet. Judge, [story]

Bolden, C. B. Carl; Sr.

Bolden, Carl Jr.; Son of Carl Sr. Bolden.

Bolden, Clara May; Daughter of George & Sarah.

Bolden, Della; Housewife, Clarence Delton's mother. Wife of Rev.
William C. Bolden. [story]

Bolden, Edward; Son of George & Sarah.

Bolden, George Thomas; Feb. 3, 1862-Jan. 18, 1946. Husband of
    Sarah (Webb), Preacher at Bolden Green.

Bolden, George Thomas Jr.; Dec. 2, 1893-Feb. 12, 1916.

Bolden, Helen (); wife of John Bolden, 1870 census. 1910-
Bolden, Isaac

Bolden, John; Bolden community named after. Husband of Betty ()

Bolden, Livingston 'Liv' Son of George & Sarah.

Bolden, Lillie Pearl; Daughter of George & Sarah.

Bolden, Mattie Lee; Daughter of George & Sarah.

Bolden, Roscoe; Son of George & Sarah.

Bolden, Ruby (Johnson): Wayne Wolford's Great-grandmother.

Bolden, Sarah (Webb); Wife of George T. Bolden, Wayne Wolford's Great-great-grandmother. [story]

Bolden, Tyree (Faulkner) Webb

Bolden, Walter (Rev.): 1887-Jun. 13, 1915. Marjorie Bolden's father, husband of Ruby (Johnson). Son of George & Sarah.

Bolden, William Clarence 'Will'; (Rev.) Son of George & Sarah Bolden.

Bonner, Alford

Bonner, Alex

Bonner, Berry Lynn

Bonner, Brenda

Bonner, Brewster; Vet. Military Police.

Bonner, Buford Franklin; Korean Vet. [DD214].

Bonner, Callie

Bonner, Dean

Bonner, Delli

Bonner, Dorothy Lee; BHS 1949 Grad.

Bonner, Edward; WW1, (Pvt) 1918-19.

Bonner, Emery

Bonner, Eric

Bonner, Ernestine (Womack); Daughter of Ernest Sr. & Lucille () Womack.

Bonner, Evelyn; Wife of E.B. Malone.

Bonner, Frances (Martin); wife of Harrison Bonner. [story]

Bonner, Frank Harrison; Korean Vet., BHS 1959 Salutatorian.

Bonner, Frank T.; Vet. [story]

Bonner, Gene Louis; [story]

Bonner, George; Waiter at Sedberry Hotel on 319 South High Street in 1942.

Bonner, Harrison; husband of Frances (Martin)

Bonner, Harrison 'Bub'

Bonner, Ida (Webb)

Bonner, Inez Willie M.; 4th grade BHS 1945.

Bonner, Irene L.; Maid at Brown Hotel in 1942.

Bonner, Isaac

Bonner, Jerry

Bonner, Jess

Bonner, Jordan; East End Drive Church of Christ in 2012.

Bonner, Lillie Hill

Bonner, Lilly; 4th grade BHS 1945.

Bonner; Louise (Hunter); Wife of 'Bub' Bonner.

Bonner, Louis (Woods): Mother of Gene Louis

Bonner, Martha Agnes; 1st grade BHS 1945.

Bonner, Mary Arden; Born: Sept. 27, 1936-Jan. 30, 2011. BHS 1955 Valedictorian, basketball player. Married name (Elam).

Bonner, Mary Louise (Leftrict)

Bonner, Patty Sue; married Roosevelt Martin, Social worker.

Bonner, Polly

Bonner, Reginald 'Reggie,' Rocket ball player

Bonner, Robert 'Bud'; BHS 1947 8th grade student, Korean Vet. [story]

Bonner, Robert E. 'Bob'

Bonner, Robert; Father of Gene Louis

Bonner, Sydney

Bonner, Thomas Harrison 'Tom'; Vietnam (1941-2000), 59 yrs. 1959 Salutatorian BHS [story]

Bonner, Thomas Ray

Bonner, Tommy; East End Drive Church of Christ in 2012.

Bonner, William; husband of Irene, porter in 1942.

Bonner, William Paul 'Pee Wee'; lives in Hawaii.

Bonner, Willie M. Inez; 4th grade at BHS in 1945

Bonner, Xavier

Boren, Landon: WCHS Freshman 2002

Borum, Carolyn (Crabtree); Employee of Technology Center. [story]

Borum, Richard Allen Jr.; Vietnam Vet. [DD214]

Bowman, Hollie; (1889-1911)

Bowman, Jackson; (1850-1906)

Boyd, Brandon

Boyd, Charles Emery Jr.; YMU Vice president

Boyd, Charles Emery Sr.; husband of Mary (League) Boyd, Vietnam Vet. 1st grade BHS 1945. [DD214]

Boyd, Christopher Todd; son of Charles Sr. and Mary F. League. [story]

Boyd, Deanna (Thomas)

Boyd, Homer; husband of Lula M., Waiter at Smith Hotel, lived on 109 Etter St. in 1942

Boyd, James: Korean Vet.

Boyd, Laveda Danielle: WCHS 2000 Sr.

Boyd, Lula Mae: Church of Christ member 2002, daughter of Will & Lizzie

Ramsey (Hopkins), wife of Homer Boyd. [story]

Boyd, Mary (League): wife of Charles Sr.

(Br-Bz)

Bradford, Harrison; WW1, 1918-19. (Pvt), O/S

Bragg, Bob

Braston, Maxine (Terry)

Brewington, Bettie (Brown); May 16, 1870-Oct. 8, 1915. Bettie E. Brown, wife of William Brewington.

Brewington, Joe; Husband of Pearl (Foster)

Brewington, Pearl (Foster); (1894-1978), wife of Joe Brewington

Brewington, William; Apr. 16, 1862-Sep. 14, 1938. Husband of Bettie E. Brown.

Brooks, Mary L. (Rucker); (1898-1989), 90 yrs, old.

Brown, Albert; (1865-1956), 111 Edgefield in 1942, husband of Annie.

Brown, Ammie E. (French); (1881-1973), wife of Herbert Brown, maid, lived in Leesburg in 1942.

Brown, Amos; Cook at Brown Hotel in 1942.

Brown, Andy; 1934, 74yrs old

Brown, Annie (Winton); (1871-1945), wife of Walter.

Brown, Annie Mae (Thomas); (1917-1970

Brown, Annie S. T. (Smartt); (1874-1959)

Brown, Arthur; Died 1929-37 yrs old

Brown, Ary; (1882-1943)

Brown, Bell; (1855-1955), wife of Charles, lived at 115 Murphy in 1942. [story]

Brown, Bertha; lived at 115 Murphy in 1942.

Brown, Betty Jane; 4th grade BHS 1945.

Brown, Bobby Sue; 1946 BHS 6th grade student.

Brown, Catherine (): wife of Horace F. Brown

Brown, Charles

Brown, Christie: WCHS Soph. 2001

Brown, Clarence; 1970-56 yrs. old

Brown, Cora (Brown): mother of Earnest & William Brown.

Brown, Daisy; lived on Colville St. in 1942.

Brown, Doak A.; WW1, (Pvt), 1918-19, Born in Morrison 2/28/1891.

Brown, Don A.; Raintree Manor (2002)

Brown, Don William; (1938-2002) [story]

Brown, Dorothy

Brown, Earline G.; 'Mandy'

Brown, Earnest; (1917-1943)

Brown, Edd

Brown, Elcain; Korean Vet., BHS 1947 Grad. [DD214].

Brown, Ellen (Ramsey); 1926 61 yrs. Old

Brown, Evie; wife of Foster Lee Mercer.

Brown, Florence (Gardner); (1870-1903), wife of George W. Brown—married in 1893.

Brown, Frank; 1989-90yrs old

Brown, Frankie; Attendant at Horton Service Station in 1942.

Brown, Frank C.; (1942-1977) 1st grade BHS 1946.

Brown, Frankie C. Jr.

Brown, George; died April 17, 1918.

Brown, George Jr.; BHS 1939 Football.

Brown, George W.; born Nov. 29, 1866-Jun. 5, 1930, son of Wesley R. & Sarah (Gardner), husband of Florence (Gardner) Brown.

Brown, Gillie; WW1, (Pvt.), (1918-19), Born in Viola Apr./1/1897.

Brown, Gladys; lived on Congo Street in 1942.

Brown, Gloria; 1955 BHS student.

Brown, Harding; WW2, [DD214].

Brown, Hattie (Winton); wife of Walter.

Brown, Heather; WCHS Jr. in 2001.

Brown, Herbert; (1889-1961), husband of Ammie E. (French) Brown, Janitor at Bernard H. S. in 1942, lived in Leesburg.

Brown, Herbert; Husband of Suzie (Roberts).

Brown, Hobert; husband of Joan (Looper). 1st grade BHS 1946.

Brown, Horace Franklin; (1926-1961), husband of Catherine

Brown, J. L.; 1948-present, Viola, BHS student 1970's

Brown, James; WW2 Vet. 1951 28 yrs. old

Brown, James E.; WW2 Vet, BHS 1947 Grad. [DD214]

Brown, James O.; WW1, 1918-19, O/S, (Pvt), Born in Warren County 9/22/1912, Age; 22.

Brown, Jefferson

Brown, Jennifer Louise; 1998 WCHS senior

Brown, Jessie (Fisk); (1916-1961)

Brown, Jim; 1950-78yrs old, father of Earnest & William.

Brown, Jim; Father of (James Brown)

Brown, Joann (Looper); wife of Hobert Brown.

Brown, Joe; (1941-1956)

Brown, Larry 'Dobbie'; Rocket baseball player.

Brown, Laura; 1915-50yrs old

Brown, Lawrence; husband of Margaret, Mechanic, lived at 413 Beersheba Street in 1942.

Brown, Leatha (Smith)

Brown, Lillie (Jones)

Brown, Lucy (); mother of Ary Brown

Brown, Mandy; died in 1914, 62 yrs. old

Brown, Marshall

Brown, Martha Ann

Brown, Marvin L.; WW2, [DD 214].

Brown, Mary

Brown, Oliver

Brown, Oney; husband on Sadie, Mill worker, 513 Beersheba St. in 1942.

Brown, Pauline (McKinley)

Brown, Richmond; WW2 Vet., brother of Gladys (Brown) Terry.

Brown, Robert

Brown, Robert Charles; WW2 Vet., BHS 1947 Grad.

Brown, Rose; WW1, (Pvt) 1918-19, O/S, Born in Warren County, Age; 22

Brown, Sadie; wife of Oney Brown.

Brown, Sarah (Gardner)

Brown, Sarah (Lee); 1883-1944

Brown, Sue; Nurse in 1942.

Brown, Sue Carol (Thomas); 3rd grade BHS 1945.

Brown, Tommie (Ford); daughter of Mabel (Patterson) & Frank Ford.

Brown Tony

Brown, Tony; Vet. Charles Womack & Eva's Son

Brown, Travis

Brown, Velma C.; Housekeeping Aid, lived on 113 Edgefield St. in 1942.

Brown, Walter M.; 1976 80 yrs old, Husband of Annie.

Brown, Westley R.

Brown, William M.; (1896-1976)

Buchanan, Henry; husband of Sara (Safely). Buried in Bolden Green Cemetery.

Buchanan, Michael

Buchanan, Patricia A.

Buchanan, Alice; Clark United Methodist Church member 1969.

Buck, Clarence W.; husband of Edna, lived on Cotter Row in 1942.

Burgess, Beulah Lee; (1920-1993)

Burgess, Elmer E.; 1921-

Burk, Will; Pastor at Leesburg

Burks, John Henry

Burks, John Loanza Jr.

Burks, John Loanza Sr.

Burks, John; Soph. WCHS 2001

Burks, Emma; wife of Howard, lived on 534 Beersheba St. in 1942.

Burks, Paulette

Burnett, Summer

Burnett, Terri

Burt, Robert Tecumseh; Doctor, (1873-1955) [story]

Burton, Earnest: Land, houses, & Café owner in the 1960's. Owned a
    Barber Shop on Burton's Lane

Burton, Robert T.; (Doctor), (1890-1900's).

Bybee, Sam; Stonemason in 1880.

(Ca-Co)

Cabell, Danielle Nicole; 2000 WCHS Sr. [Story]

Cabell, Jacqueline (Martin); mother to Danielle Cabell.

Caldwell, Amanda; daughter of Debbie () Caldwell.

Caldwell, Debbie ()

Cambell, Willie Paul

Cameron, Brandon; son of Willie and Brenda.

Cameron, Brenda; Wife of Willie

Cameron, Willie; Husband of Brenda

Cammon, Perry; husband of Ada, laborer, lived on 334 S. High St. in 1942.

Campbell, Otis Jr, (Dr.); MeHarry Med. Grad.

Campbell, Willie Paul; 1946 BHS 6th grade student.

Canada, Gwin

Carr, Allie I.; 1896-1957, Wife of Gus Carr. [story]

Carr, Audie Marie; Daughter of William and Beulah.

Carr, Barbara Neil (Scott); wife of Freddie Carr. [story]

Carr, Beulah Etta (Lusk); Died Feb. 1, 2012, 88yrs. old. Wife of William.

Carr, Bob

Carr, Carl; Member of East End Church of Christ (2002)

Carr, Cassie (Southern)

Carr, Charles Edward; Died 1953

Carr, Dewayne

Carr, Dora (Bell)

Carr, Dorothy Mae; wife of Morris C. Carr. Member of East End Church of Christ (2002)

Carr, Eugene; brother of Emma Irene Beard.

Carr, Freddie; husband of Barbara N. (Scott).

Carr, Georgia Lee; 1943-1959 (single)

Carr, Gus; Husband of Allie I. () Carr

Carr, Jess; Son of William and Beulah.

Carr, Jesse Ray; Vietnam Vet.

Carr, Jesse Reed

Carr, Jessie Lee; Died 1986, 82 yrs.old, WW2 Vet.

Carr; Johnnie Sue

Carr, Lillian (Smartt) V.; Died 1987, 75 yrs.

Carr, Lottie Mae

Carr, Lula; Daughter of William and Beulah.
Carr, Markee: WCHS Soph. 2003
Carr, Mary (___)
Carr, Mary Emma; Died 1985-69 yrs. old
Carr, Mary Magdolein (Pleasant); 1900-1929
Carr, Morris C.; husband of Dorothy Mae ().
Carr, Pearlie (Mount)
Carr, Rosie (_____)
Carr, Sarah (Woods)
Carr, Will; Died in 1971, 93 yrs.
Carr, William Eugene; Husband of Beulah (Lusk).
Carr, Willie Etta (Lusk): 1914-1952
Carr, Wilma Winfree; 1927-1966-39yrs old
Carson, Amanda; 402 Spring St. in 1942.
Carter, Daniel; Porter at Dixie Theatre in 1942.
Childs, Jonathan; WCHS JR, 2001
Clark, Anita
Clark, Arie L.; 1935 BHS Grad.
Clark, Pauline L.; lived on African St. in 1942.
Clendenen, Mary M.; wife of Byron, lived on African St. in 1942.
Colley, Hassie; 103 Copes Lane in 1942.
Comer, Martha (____)
Comer, Reuben P
Conner, James
Coonrod, Andrea
Coonrod, Annie
Coonrod, Arthur
Coonrod, Billy; Vietnam Vet.
Coonrod, Chiquita; 1998 WCHS senior
Coonrod, Darlene
Coonrod, Dennis
Coonrod, Donna
Coonrod, Earley; WW1 Vet.
Coonrod, Ethel (French)
Coonrod, Freda (); wife of Arthur.
Coonrod, George; WW1 Vet 1918-19, (Pvt), Born in Morrison 4/18/1895.
Coonrod, Isaiah
Coonrod, James Steve Sr.

Coonrod, J. C.

Coonrod, Kenneth

Coonrod, Mattie (); wife of George Coonrod

Coonrod, Norma Jean ()

Coonrod, Pearl

Coonrod, Richard 'Dick'

Coonrod, Sharon; daughter of Arthur and Freda (Price) Coonrod. [story]

Coonrod, Simon; Philadelphia Church

Cope, Andrew J.; 1838-1859

Cope, Ann; daughter of Jay and Katherine

Cope, Arch; Brother to King & Kang.

Cope, Archie (Paige or Page); attended Philadelphia Church

Cope, Bell; wife of 'Buck' 420 Beersheba St. In 1942.

Cope, Bessie

Cope, Betty Harriet

Cope, Betty Harris

Cope, Bobby Jr.

Cope Bridget; Daughter of Betty, Author of several books.

Cope, Buchanan 'Buck', Barber owner in downtown McMinnville 1880's.

Cope, Cheryl; daughter of Jay and Katherine.

Cope, Elizabeth

Cope, Gary; Played Pro Baseball with the L. A. Dodgers.

Cope, Hardy Jr.; Born: Mar.7, 1921-1980, WW2, Vet. DD214

Cope, Hardy Sr.; husband of Bessie, Laborer, lived in Yankeetown in 1942.

Cope, Harris Bradford; 1810-1886

Cope, Hattie J.

Cope, Henrietta (Bates)

Cope, Herbert Lewis 'Hub'; 1940's Semi-Pro baseball player.

Cope, James; 1776-1874

Cope, Janet

Cope, Jerry Joe Louis; Korean Vet.

Cope, Jessie Mazy (____)

Cope, Jimmy; 3rd grade BHS 1945.

Cope, Joe L.; Son of Sydna (Batey) Cope, 1946 BHS student.

Cope, Kang, Brother to Arch & King.

Cope, King; Brother to Arch & Kang.

Cope, Larry

Cope, Lavina M.; (single) 1842-1851

Cope, Livingstone; husband of Sydna R., lived on 414 Beersheba St. in 1942.

Cope, Lawrence; Junk Yard owner on Cope St., lived at 420 Beersheba St. in 1942.

Cope, Lawrence 'Jay'; Husband to Mary Katherine (Ramsey) Cope

Cope, Livingston 'Livy'

Cope, Lydia (Crouch)

Cope, Margaret V.; 1849-1851

Cope, Mary Katherine (Ramsey); Wife of Jay Cope, daughter of Clara Ramsey.

Cope, Mary Polly; 1782-1850

Cope, Pricilla; lived in Yankeetown in 1942.

Cope, Rena; 503 Beersheba St. in 1942.

Cope, Rhonda L.; (single) 1843-1859

Cope, Ricky; Mayor of Woodbury, Tenn., 2 terms as the first Black Mayor.

Cope, Robert Louis 'Rob' Jr.

Cope, Robert Louis 'Bobby' Sr.

Cope, Ruth (Grayson); 1927-1962, daughter Barbara Ann.

Cope, Sarah Murray; 1809-1882

Cope, Sydna Ruth; (Batey); Educator, 5th & 6th grades, Taught for 65 yrs. [story]

Cope, Terry 'T.C.'; National known Comedian.

Cope, Vonda (Looper); Daughter of Myrene and Herman Looper

Cope, Willie King (W. K.); Husband to Vonda Cope. 1st grade BHS 1946.

Cope, Lawrence Jr. 'Jay'

Cope, Waymon; lived on 101 East Colville St. in 1942.

Coppinger, Canzada Patterson, Jones; Jonah Patterson's Mother.

Coppinger, Jones

Coppinger, Thomas B.; 1856—Died in 1939, husband of Tiller (Marbury) 1878

Coppinger, Tiller; 1857-1942, wife of Thomas 'Tom'.

Corley, Rebecca

Cowan, Catherine; wife of Robert, lived on Egypt Alley in 1942.

Cowan, Elizabeth; lived on Egypt Alley in 1942.
Cowan, Minnie
Cowan, Robert; husband of Catherine, lived on Egypt Alley in 1942.
Cowan, Sally
Cowan, T.L.

(Cp-Cz)

Crabtree, Charles 'Scooky' Jr.; Husband of Joshphine (Biles),Son of Sr. & Jessie, retired Bus driver.

Crabtree, Charles Dillard Sr.; WW2, Vet. Husband to Jessie Crabtree. [DD214]. [story]

Crabtree, Dillard Cardon 'D.C.'; WW2 Vet

Crabtree, Jessie (League); Educator, wife of Charles Sr. [story]

Crabtree, Josephine (Biles)

Crabtree, Landis Ladale; Grandson of 'Scooky'

Crabtree, Lizzie; 415 Beersheba St. in 1942.

Crabtree, Mildred; wife of Sidney in 1942, lived on Egypt Alley.

Crabtree, Robert; died in 1999, lived on 415 Beersheba in 1942.

Crabtree, Sidney; husband of Mildred, lived on Egypt Alley in 1942, Porter at Park Theatre.

Crisp, Catherine: 2000 WCHS Sr.

Crisp, Christine: 2000 WCHS Sr.

Crisp, Cora;

Crisp, Donald; Vietnam Vet. Youth Leader, Coach, YMU.

Crisp, Earline Lee (Gwynn); 1900-1954, Wife of Thurman.

Crisp, Heath

Crisp, Jennifer; Wife of Donald Crisp.

Crisp, Lottie; 1969 Clark Church member.

Crisp, Thurman William; Husband of Earline (Lee), Vet. DD214

Cummings, April

Cummings, Beulah (Grayson); 1899-1942

Cummings, Chris

Cummings, Derrick; WCHS 1999, SR.

Cummings, Donna (Coonrod)

Cummings, Gladys

Cummings, Leland

Cummings, Mary Elizabeth (McReynolds); Jul. 29, 1866-May 30, 1945. Daughter of Anderson & Percilla (Lamb). Wife of Jarrett Cummings.

Cummings, Mickie

Cummings, Rickie Vaughn

Cummings, Sedrick Darnell: 1998 WCHS Sr.

Cummings, Shawn Rickie

Cummings, Sonya; WCHS, 2001, JR

Cummings, Will

Cunningham, Jimmy

Curry, Drew; Freshman at WCHS 2012.

Curtis, Birdie (Strode); daughter of Mary and Clarence Roy Curtis.

Curtis, Bessie; lived on 510 Beersheba St. in 1942.

Curtis, Charlie; son of Mary and Clarence Roy.

Curtis, Clarence Roy 'Pee Wee'; Vietnam Vet. Husband of Mary, [DD214]

Curtis, Clarice; lived on 510 Beersheba St. in 1942.

Curtis, Henrietta (Bates); wife of William W. In 1942.

Curtis, Kate (Smartt); wife of L. V. [story]

Curtis, L.V.; Korean Vet. [story] 1922-1995

Curtis, Mary (Cunningham); wife of Clarence Roy. Business owner.

Curtis, Mary (Watson)

Curtis, Michael; son of Mary and Clarence Roy.

Curtis, Nick; son of Mary and Clarence Roy.

Curtis, Virginia Sally; 4th grade BHS 1945.

Curtis, William W.; husband of Henrietta, Bottler, lived on the Lane in 1942.

(Da-Du)

Dalton, Allen; son of Allen Sr. and Frankie.

Dalton, Charles Allen Sr. 'Coach'; [story]

Dalton, Frankie (Biles); wife of 'Coach'

Dalton, Liesa Aikens; daughter of Charles and Frankie.

Dalton, Tammie; daughter of Charles and Frankie.

Darrell, Chinae; WCHS, 2001, Freshman

Dartis, Marilyn Marie; (single)

Dartis, Sarah Frances; (single)

Davis, Diana; 1820-NA

Davis, Matt; 1818-1914.

Dean, Lee B.; Indian decent, metal finisher, lived in Yankeetown in 1942.

Dick, Robert; Driver at Pan Am service station, lived on 409 Beersheba St. in 1942.

Dick, Willie; lived on 409 Beersheba St. in 1942.

Dickey, Robert

Dillard, Betty (Looper); Wife of John Dillard, Mother of Tina & Jonathan.

Dillard, Deborah

Dillard, Herman; Vietnam Vet.

Dillard, John; husband of Betty (Looper).

Dillard, Johnnie (Lusk); wife of Walter Dillard, they lived in Bolden Green Community.

Dillard, Johnathan; son of Betty (Looper) Dillard

Dillard, Krista, 2003 WCHS Soph.

Dillard, Lacresha Donette

Dillard, Patricia

Dillard, Sarah; wife of William Kenneth Sr.

Dillard, Shirley (Carr)

Dillard, Tina; daughter of Betty (Looper), and John Dillard.

Dillard, Trista; 2003 WCHS Soph.

Dillard, Walter; husband of Johnnie C.

Dillard, William Kenneth; Vet. [DD214], Born: Oct. 15, 1938.

Dillard, William Jr.

Dodson, Remus; WW1, (Pvt), 1918-19, Born in Warren Co. Born: Mar. 26, 1890. O/S, [DD214].

Donabee, H.C.

Donabury, H.C.

Donahue, Bessie (Cope); divorced

Donahue, Bob; Died in 1940

Donahue, Dock

Donahue, Jake; husband of Sofia (Ganaway)

Donahue, Joe; 1897-1937

Donahue, Mary Bell (Gwynn); 1875-1950

Donahue, Sofia (Ganaway); 1845-1920, wife of Jake.

Donaldson, David A.; WW2, [DD214].

Donaldson, Tom; Nursery Worker, Manchester Rd. in 1942.

Doublefield, Janie; widow of Charles, lived on 110 Edgefield St. in 1942.

Dotsen, Maxey H.; WW1, (Pvt), 1918-19, Born in Morrison Feb./6/1895, [DD214].

Dowell, Calvin

Drake, David Jr.; 1924-1985

Drake, David Lynn; 1955-1980

Drake, Mabel E.; Cook, lived on Egypt Alley in 1942.

Drake, Roberta C.; 1926-

Drake, Trevin; WCHS 1999 Sr.

Draper, Julius M.

Draper, Margaret E.

Duncan, Alfred; Died 1944 65 yrs old, Barber.

Duncan, Cora B.

Duncan, Frank; Husband of Ada (Storkey)

Duncan, Lawson; Blacksmith in 1870.

Duncan, Martha (Alexander)

Duncan, Sam

Durham, James William; 1942 63 yrs old

Durham, Jim; husband of Eva, Caretaker, lived on 408 West Main in 1942.

Durham, Mattie (Stewart)

Durham, Moses

Durley, Genreanure; 1895-1908

Durley, Herman; N/A

Durley, Ida D. (Mazy); 1866-1905

Durley, James A.; WW1, 1918-19 (Pvt), O/S, Age: 31 years old.

Durley, Rufus W.

(Ed-Ev)

Ealey, James A. C.; husband of Dora, Farmer, lived on Cedar near E. Main in 1942.

Ealey, Dora; wife of James A. C. 1942.

Edge, George; Father of Jim Edge.

Edge, Jim; WW1, (Pvt), 1918-19, O/S, Born in Warren Co. on Jul./10/1895.Parents: George & Mary Edge, Married, Laborer.

Edge, Mary (); Mother of Jim Edge.

Elam, Ella; lived on 113 Edgefield St. in 1942.

Elam, Georgia; wife of Robert, lived on Egypt Alley in 1942.

Elam, James; Husband of Mattie 1st.

Elam, Mary A. (Martin)

Elam, Willie M.; Laborer, lived on 418 Beersheba St. in 1942.

Etta, Ted Louis;. 1946 BHS 6th grade student.

Etter, (Carlee or Caralee) (Gwynn); 1896-1963

Etter, Edna

Etter, George; husband of Nobie, lived on E. Main near Cedar St. in 1942.

Etter, Gwendolyn; Gwynn-Lewis, College Professor, Author of two books.

Etter, Hal; lived on Church St. in 1942.

Etter, Harold Buford; WW2.

Etter, John L.; lived on Church St. in 1942.

Etter, Johnell (Martin)

Etter, Leroy Ted Louis; 1955 Bernard H.S. Grad. Korean Vet. DD214.

Etter, Nobie; lived on E. Main near Cedar St. in 1942.

Etter, Merrel H.; husband of Mary L., Caretaker of Riverside Cemetery,

lived on 531 Beersheba St. in 1942, 1935 BHS Grad.

Etter, Olívia D. (Ramsey)

Etter, Richard; 1877-1951

Etter, Terry; Dentist, MeHarry Grad.

Etter, William; husband of Anna M., Mechanic, 503 Beersheba St. in 1942.

Evans, Ashley

Evans, Avo; Maid George M. Smith, 121 Murphy St. in 1942.

Evans, Bárbara Jean; Wife of Arbury Green, Mother of Wayne Evans. 1st grade BHS 1945.

Evans, Edward; lived on Murphy St. in 1942.

Evans, Gary; Desert Storm Vet. Son of James & Loretta (Strode). [story]

Evans, Howard 'Butch'; Son of 'Moody' & Loretta (Strode), Retired Army Vet.

Evans, James 'Moody'; Vietnam Vet. Husband of Loretta (Strode).

Evans, James Edward; 4th grade BHS 1945.

Evans, Loretta (Strode); Wife of James 'Moody' Evans.

Evans, Paige; daughter of Wayne Evans.

Evans, Robert Harold; WW2 Vet. 1946 BHS student, Football Left guard.

Evans, Shirley Ann

Evans, Shula; lived on Murphy St. in 1942.

Evans, Wayne; Son of Barbara Jean () Green.

(Fa-Fu)

Faulkner, Ann Cardwell; 1889 60 yrs old. Wife of David

Faulkner, Beulah (Martin)

Faulkner, David; Husband of Ann (Cardwell) in 1866.

Faulkner, Everette Edward; Son of Mollie Agnes

Faulkner, Harvey Lee; WW1, (Pfc), 1918-19, O/S, Born in McMinnville on 4/11/1890, Parent: Nannie Faulkner. Mill Worker, lived on 115 Etter St. In 1942.

Faulkner, Hattie Belle; daughter of Edward Jr. Faulkner & Mollie Agnes (Bolden) Faulkner Tucker. [story]

Faulkner, Hershel C.; son of Mollie Agnes.

Faulkner, James Oliver; WW1, (Pvt), 1918-19, O/S, Born in Warren Co. Sept./5/1892, 50% disable from service.

Faulkner, Leatha; Cook at Brown Hotel Café, lived on 115 Faulkner St. in 1942.

Faulkner, Luke

Faulkner, Nannie; Mother of Harvey Faulkner.

Faulkner, Robert L.; son of Mollie Agnes

Favors, Frances (Bonner); (1927-1983). [story]

Finger, Charley

Finger, Columbus; WW1, (Pvt), 1918-18, Born in Morrison 12/15/1891, Farmer, Parents: Sam & Della Finger DD214.

Finger, Della (); Mother of Columbus.

Finger, Ella; wife of Bob, Café owner down on Sloppy Rock in the 1940's, lived on524 Beersheba St. in 1942.

Finger, John

Finger, John; 1790-1860

Finger, John L.; 1820-1853

Finger, John R.; 1843-1951

Finger, Law; Father of Seba.

Finger, Malinda W. (Comer); 1821-1889

Finger, Mary

Finger, Mattie

Finger, Sam; Father of Columbus, husband of Della, Father of Winfred.

Finger, Seba; WW1, (Pvt), 1918-19, Born on 7/31/1889, Married, Chauffer, Parents: Law & Della Finger.

Finger, Stephen; Minister 1900's.

Finger, Willie

Finger, Winfred (Winford); WW1, (Pvt), 1918-19, Born in Warren Co. 8/21/1896, Auto Mechanic, Parents Sam & Della Finger, DD214.

Flint, Harold; Principal at BHS. Husband of Jessie Mae ().

Flint, Jessie Mae; Teacher at Morrison and Leesburg school, wife of Harold.

Fisk, Alex Gemond

Fisk, Anthony

Fisk, Bill

Fisk, Emma C. (___)

Fisk, Estella (Looper); 1880-1951.

Fisk, James; 1906-1964

Fisk, James L.; 1929-1979

Fisk, Mary (Carr)

Fisk, Mary (Grayson); Wife of James Fisk.

Fisk, Matt

Fisk, Mattie Pice; Died 1970

Fisk, Nellis; Died 1978-63 yrs old

Fisk, Shaneka; Freshman, WCHS, 2001

Fisk, Spencer Calvin

Fisk, Stella (Looper)

Fisk, Willie; Died in 1950

Ford, Frank; 1900-1971, WWI Vet. DD214, 106 Etter St. in 1942. [story]

Ford, Jeanette (Ford)

Ford, Mabel Louis (Patterson); 1905-1965, Wife of Frank Ford.

Ford, Paul; son of Frank and Mabel.

Ford, Tom; lived on 106 Etter in 1942.

Ford, Tommie; 1st grade BHS 1945. Lives in Leesburg Community 2007.

Foster, Herman; husband of Mary, Laborer, Lived on 114 Etter St. in 1942.

Foster, Lucy (Marbury); 1855-Dec. 22, 1929. Daughter of Jack & Lucinda (Black) Marbury, wife of Foster.

Foster, Mary; wife of Herman.

Foster, Sam; Aug. 1846-Feb. 11, 1930. Son of ___ & Mary () Foster, husband of Lucy Marbury, married Oct. 5, 1872.

Foster, Walter; WW1, (Pvt), 1918-19, Born in McMinnville May/11/1895.

France, Homer; WW1, (Pvt), 1918-19, O/S, Born in McMinnville, Age: 23 by Jan/12/1919.

France, Oliver; WW1, (Pvt), 1918-19, Born in McMinnville, Age: 26.

Frazier, Christopher

French, Clopie; wife of Frank, lived on the Lane St. in 1942.

French, Frank; Husband of Clopie.

Fults, Celeste; WCHS 1998 SR.

Fults, Even: 2000 WCHS Jr.

Fuston, Cora (Mazy)

Fuston, John

Fuston, Odie Kay; lived on 107 Edgefield in 1942.

(Ga-Gw)

Gardner, Lizzie; wife of Minor, lived on Murphy St. in 1942.

Gardner, Lucy (Patterson)

Gardner, Madison

Gardner, Mary ()

Gardner, Matt B.; Dec. 1816-Dec. 28, 1917. (101 yrs. old). Husband of Sarah A. Gardner.

Gardner, Minor; husband of Lizzie.

Gardner, Sallie Ann (Crowder); Feb. 5, 1846-May 1, 1914. Sarah Ann, daughter of Sid & Lucy (Moore) Crowder, wife of Matt Gardner, married Sep. 7, 1885.

Gardenhire, Bridgett; Warren Co. H.S. 2000 student.

Gibble, Alton; WW1, (Pvt.), 1918-19, Born in Viola 4/22/1887.

Gibson, Anna L.; wife of William, lived on Congo St. in 1942.

Gibson, Dee

Gibson, Delacy; wife of Ernest Sr.

Gibson, Ernest Jr.

Gibson, Ernest Sr.; Retired Army, Desert Storm Vet.

Gibson, Russell N.

Gibson, William; husband of Anna L.

Gilbert, Andrew M.; Prof. of Bernard H.S. 1947.

Gillespie, Ernestine; wife of Robert.

Gillespie, Robert; husband of Ernestine, Lived on 122 Edgefield St. in 1942.

Gipson, Waymon N.; WW1, (Pvt), 1918-19, Born in McMinnville Jun./9/1896.

Gooden, Katie M.; lived on 103 E. Colville St. in 1942.

Goodwin, Bryce: Member of East End Church of Christ 2002.

Gordon, Annis P.; Maid, lived on 511 E. Main St. in 1942.

Granison, William; husband of Gertrude, lived on 110 Etter St. in 1942.

Grayson, Alexander A.; 1892-1964

Grayson, Alexander; 1859-1932 Husband of Sylva Patterson.

Grayson, Beatrice; lived on Church St. in 1942.

Grayson, Beulah Bell

Grayson, Charles Aaron; Vet. [story]

Grayson, Christine (Strode); wife of Eddie G. Sr. [story]

Grayson, Crystal

Grayson, David; 1946 BHS football player.

Grayson, Dean; Father of Deanna

Grayson, Deanna Renea; High School Senior died in a fatal car wreck 2001. [story]

Grayson, DeMarrio

Grayson, Dorothy Mai; wife of Thomas H. Sr. [story]

Grayson, Dorothy (Womack); Last married to Harold Young

Grayson, Eddie G. Jr.; Desert storm

Grayson, Eddie G. Sr.; Vietnam Vet., Instructor at Vo-Tech.

Grayson, Elnora (Marbury); 1905-1936.

Grayson, Emma; wife of Isaac, lived on Cotter Row In 1942.

Grayson, Ethel (Buchanan)

Grayson, Eugene

Grayson, Evelyn (Foster); Nov. 1928-Jan. 1929, Daughter of W.L. & Susie

Grayson, George L.; 1919-1991 WW2 Vet

Grayson, Gilbert; 1857-1953.

Grayson, Goldie May (Carr); Aug. 1917-Aug. 1941. Daughter of Will & Bee.

Grayson, Hugh; (1894-1953) WW I Vet. DD214. Original member of Post 208, lived on RR6 in 1945.

Grayson, Ike Henry; 1883-1949, husband of Emma (Lindsey).

Grayson, Isaac; husband of Emma, lived on Cotter Row in 1942.

Grayson, James E.; Korean Vet.

Grayson, James William; 1905-1955, husband of Virginia (Marbury)

Grayson, Janell (Brown);

Grayson, Jessica L.; Daughter of Nathana, 1999 WCHS Sr. [story]

Grayson, Karen Ann; daughter of Ronnie Blevins and Armestine Drake. [story]

Grayson, Katherine (Marbury)

Grayson, Keith

Grayson, Krystal

Grayson, Lillian (Patterson); 1865-1944

Grayson, Mack

Grayson, Magnolia; wife of Harold Solomon.

Grayson, Margaret Ann (Strode) (Coonrod); second wife of Eddie Sr.

Grayson, Margaret; wife of Raymond.

Grayson, Marlena D.; Daughter of Nathana, 1999 WCHS Sr.

Grayson, Nathana Denise; former wife of Dean Grayson.

Grayson, Osise

Grayson, Queen E.

Grayson, Raymond; husband of Margaret, lived on 505 Beersheba St. In 1942.

Grayson, Rebecca Sue (Foster)

Grayson, Ruby; 1896-1929

Grayson, Sherlia

Grayson, Shirley (Ramsey); wife of James.

Grayson, Son

Grayson Steve; YMU, son of Shirley and James.

Grayson, Sue Emily (Ramsey)

Grayson, Sussie (Rebecca Susie) (Foster); 1895-1977

Grayson, Sylva (Patterson); 1864-1935

Grayson, Thelma; Mother of Resse Bishop.

Grayson, Thomas; WW2 Vet. DD214.

Grayson, Thomas Hilton; Vet. DD214.

Grayson, Thomas Jr.

Grayson, Tina (Woods)

Grayson, Travis

Grayson, Valerie; Daughter of Tommy.

Grayson, Viola; Died in 1935.

Grayson, Vivian (Strode); Wife of Tommy.

Grayson, Willie Lee

Green, (Rev.) Willis; 1903-1982

Green, Arbury; Korean Vet. A/Legion member Post 208.

Gribble, Alton; WW1, (Pvt) 1918-19, Born in Viola 4/22/1887.

Gribble, Ann (Gribble)

Gribble, Charles R.; WW1, (Pvt). O/S, 1918-19, Born in McMinnville 11/28/1896.

Gribble, Dovie (Hunter); 2nd wife of Murphy.

Gribble, Holly

Gribble, J.C.

Gribble, Jeff; Father of Joe.

Gribble, Jess; 1902-19

Gribble, Joe; WW1, (Pvt), 1918-19, O/S Born in McMinnville 6/15/1889, Farmer, Parents: Jeff & Jodie Gribble.

Gribble, Jodie; Wife of Jeff.

Gribble, Joseph; lived in Yankeetown in 1942

Gribble, Josie (Northcutt)

Gribble, Lena Bell (Lusk); 1st wife of Murphy, 1876-1942.

Gribble, Lucius; Died 1944, 60 yrs. Old.

Gribble, Mary (Lusk); Died 1930-70 yrs. old.

Gribble, Dovie (Hunter); 2nd Wife of Murphy

Gribble, Mary (Mitchell); Died 1932 72 yrs. old

Gribble, Murphy; WW1, 1918-19 (Pvt), O/S, Died 1950-62 yrs. old.

Gribble, Retha (Hunter)

Gribble, Rosanna; 1962 61 yrs. old.

Gribble, Will

Griswold, Nero 'Neo'

Gross, Debbie (Caldwell)

Gross, Jerry

Guerard, Augustus Lewis Sr.; Poet, Writer, Pastor [story]

Guerard, Augustus Lewis Jr.; Vet. 1st grade Bernard H.S. 1946. [story]

Guerard, Christy; WCHS 2000 Jr.

Guerard, Helen A.; Daughter of A. L. Brown is her married name, 1946 BHS 5th grade student.

Guerard, Louise (Stokes); Wife of A.L. Sr. [story]

Guerard, Marvaetta; Daughter of A. L. Sr.; 3rd grade BHS 1945.

Guerard, Robert Edwin; Son of A. L. Sr.

Guerard, Vera E.; Daughter of A. L. Sr. (single). [story]

Guerard, Victor R.; Vet. Son of A. L. Sr.

Guest, Mary Ann

Guy, Larry

Guy, Mary Lee (Wood)

Gwynn, Bertha (Rice); wife of Lawson Gwynn. [story]

Gwynn, Bessie Taylor; Educator, Home Economics, Science & English, lived on 507 Beersheba St. in 1942. (story)

Gwynn, Bobby

Gwynn, Charles Edmond; Vet. DD214.

Gwynn, Dolly Brown

Gwynn, Ellen

Gwynn, Enice; Daughter of Bessie.

Gwynn, Fannie (Brown); Mother of James Stanley, 1864-1951.

Gwynn, Herbert; 1903-1983

Gwynn, Huston; 1852-1940, 90 yrs. old. Husband of Fannie (Brown). Gwynn, James

Gwynn, James Stanley; WW1, (Pvt), 1918-19, Born in Viola 8/15/1890-1970, Teamster, Parents: Fannie & Huston Gwynn.

Gwyn, Kathy; Social Security employee.

Gwynn, Larry H.

Gwyn, Lawson 'Frog; WW1, 1918-19, Born in Viola Jun./10/1895-1908, Milling, Parents: Huston & Fannie Gwynn. DD214.

Gwynn, Leonard; WW1, 1918-19, (Pvt), O/S, Born in Viola 11/24/1892, Teamster, Parents: Huston & Fannie Gwynn. Played with the Viola Clowns Baseball team.

Gwynn, Mary Ann

Gwyn, Mark R.; Tenn. Fed. Of Investigation Director. 2007 [story]

Gwynn, Onnie B. (Northcutt); 1893-1930, Wife of Will Gwynn.

Gwynn, Robert 'Bobby'

Gwynn, Roy Richard; Son of Bessie, 1942 Semi-pro baseball player.

Gwynn, Roy; husband on Bessie, Driver, lived on 507 Beersheba St. in 1942, WW1, 1918-19 (Pvt), Born in Warren Co. 4/27/1894, O/S.

Gwynn, Sarah ()

Gwynn, Stanley; 1890-1970.

Gwynn, Tommy; 1883-1903

Gwynn, Virginia (Fuston); 1986-72 yrs. old.

Gwynn, Will 'Willie'; WW1, 1918-19, (Pvt), Born in Viola 9/23/1887, Farmer, 97 years old, husband of Onnie B. (Parents: Huston & Fannie), Died in 1984 97 yrs. old.

Gwynn, William Logan

Gwynn, William; WW1, (Pvt), 1918-19, Born in McMinnville Apr./5/1897, Laundry, Parents: William Logan & Dolly Brown Gwynn.

(Gr-Gz)

Grayson, Ashley; Daugther of Keith and Karen Grayson. Senior at WCHS in 2012.

Grayson, Alexander A.; 1892-1964

Grayson, Alexander; Dec. 1859-Apr. 28, 1932. Son of Simon Poke & Simpie () Grayson. Husband of Sylva Patterson.

Grayson, Annie Mae (Ramsey); Wife of George Grayson, Mother of George L.

Grayson, Beulah Bell

Grayson, Charles Aaron; Vet. [story]

Grayson, Christine (Strode); wife of Eddie G. Sr. [story]

Grayson, Crystal

Grayson, Dahynelia; daughter of Keith and Karen.

Grayson, David; 1946 Bernard H.S. football player.

Grayson, Dean; Father of Deanna

Grayson, Deanna Renea; High School Senior died in a fatal car wreck 2001. [story]

Grayson, DeMarrio

Grayson, Dorothy Mai; wife of Thomas H. Sr. [story]

Grayson, Dorothy (Womack); Last married to Harold Young

Grayson, Eddie G. Jr.; Desert storm

Grayson, Eddie G. Sr.; Vietnam Vet., Instructor at Vo-Tech.

Grayson, Elnora (Marbury); 1905-1936.

Grayson, Ethel (Buchanan)

Grayson, Eugene

Grayson, Evelyn (Foster); Nov. 1928-Jan. 1929, Daughter of W.L. & Susie

Grayson, George L.; 23 Aug. 1919-Jul. 1991, WW II Vet, son of Annie Mae Ramsey, and George Grayson.

Grayson, Gilbert; 1857-1953.

Grayson, Goldie May (Carr); Aug. 1917-Aug. 1941. Daughter of Will & Bee.

Grayson, Hugh; (1894-1953) WW I Vet. DD214. Original member of Post 208, lived on RR6 in 1945.

Grayson, Ike Henry; 1883-1949, husband of Emma (Lindsey)

Grayson, Jalane (Perkins); wife of Keith.

Grayson, James E.; Korean Vet. Member of American Legion Post 208.

Grayson, James William; 1905-1955, husband of Virginia (Marbury)

Grayson, Janell (Brown);

Grayson, Jessica L.; Daughter of Nathana, 1999 WCHS Sr. [story]

Grayson, Karen Ann; daughter of Ronnie Blevins and Armestine Drake. [story]

Grayson, Katherine (Marbury)

Grayson, Keith

Grayson, Krystal

Grayson, Lillian (Patterson); 1865-1944

Grayson, Mack

Grayson, Magnolia; wife of Harold Solomon.

Grayson, Margaret Ann (Strode) (Coonrod); second wife of Eddie Sr.

Grayson, Marlena D.; Daughter of Nathana, 1999 WCHS Sr.

Grayson, Nathana Denise; former wife of Dean Grayson.

Grayson, Osise

Grayson, Patricia; wife of Dean.

Grayson, Queen E.

Grayson, Rebecca Sue (Foster)

Grayson, Ruby; 1896-1929

Grayson, Sherlia

Grayson, Shirley (Ramsey); wife of James.

Grayson, Son

Grayson Steve; YMU, son of Shirley and James.

Grayson, Sue Emily (Ramsey)

Grayson, Sussie (Rebecca Susie) (Foster); 1895-Nov. 1977, Daughter of Sam & Lucy (Marbury) Foster, wife of Willie Lee Grayson.

Grayson, Sylva (Patterson); July 1864-Dec. 16, 1935. Daughter of Isaac & Sarah (Marbury) Patterson, wife of Alexander Grayson, married Mar 11, 1888.

Grayson, Thelma; Mother of Reese Bishop.

Grayson, Thomas; WWII Vet. DD214.

Grayson, Thomas Hilton; Vet. DD214, born; Oct. 14,1922.

Grayson, Thomas Jr.

Grayson, Tina (Woods)

Grayson, Travis

Grayson, Valerie; Daughter of Tommy.

Grayson, Viola; Died in 1935.

Grayson, Vivian (Strode); Wife of Tommy.

Grayson, Willie Lee

Green, (Rev.) Willis; 1903-1982

Green, Arbury; Korean Vet. A/L member Post 208.

Gribble, Alton; WW1, (Pvt) 1918-19, Born in Viola 4/22/1887.

Gribble, Ann (Gribble)

Gribble, Charles R.; WW1, (Pvt). O/S, 1918-19, Born in McMinnville 11/28/1896.

Gribble, Dovie (Hunter); 2nd wife of Murphy.

Gribble, Holly

Gribble, J.C.

Gribble, Jeff; Father of Joe.

Gribble, Jess; 1902-19

Gribble, Joe; WW1, (Pvt), 1918-19, O/S Born in McMinnville 6/15/1889, Farmer, Parents: Jeff & Jodie Gribble.

Gribble, Jodie; Wife of Jeff.

Gribble, Joe

Gribble, Josie (Northcutt)

Gribble, Lena Bell (Lusk); 1st wife of Murphy, 1876-1942.

Gribble, Lucius; Died 1944, 60 yrs. Old.

Gribble, Mary (Lusk); Died 1930-70 yrs. old.

Gribble, Dovie (Hunter); 2nd Wife of Murphy

Gribble, Mary (Mitchell); Died 1932 72 yrs. old

Gribble, Murphy; WW1, 1918-19 (Pvt), O/S, Died 1950-62 yrs. old.

Gribble, Retha (Hunter)

Gribble, Rosanna; 1962 61 yrs. old.

Gribble, Will

Griswold, Nero 'Neo'

Gross, Debbie (Caldwell)

Gross, Jerry; Blacksmith in 1870.

Guerard, Angellette

Guerard, Augustus Lewis Sr.; Poet, Writer, Rev. (story)

Guerard, Augustus Lewis Jr.; Vet. 1st grade BHS 1946. [story]

Guerard, Christy; WCHS 2000 Jr.

Guerard, Helen A.; Daughter of A. L. Brown is her married name, 1946 BHS 5th grade student.

Guerard, Louise (Stokes); Wife of A.L. Sr. [story]

Guerard, Marvaetta; Daughter of A. L. Sr.; 3rd grade BHS 1945.

Guerard, Robert Edwin; Son of A. L. Sr.

Guerard, Vera E.; Daughter of A. L. Sr. (single). [story]

Guerard, Victor R.; Vet. Son of A. L. Sr.

Guest, Mary Ann

Guest, Saint

Guy, Larry

Guy, Mary Lee (Wood)

Gwynn, Bertha (Rice); wife of Lawson Gwynn. [story]

Gwynn, Bessie Taylor; Educator, Home Economics, Science & English (story)

Gwynn, Bobby

Gwynn, Charles Edmond; Vet. DD214, born; Sept. 14, 1938.

Gwynn, Dolly Brown

Gwyn, Ellen

Gwyn, Enice; Daughter of Bessie.

Gwyn, Fannie (Brown); Mother of James Stanley, 1864-1951.

Gwyn, Herbert; 1903-1983

Gwyn, Huston; 1852-1940, 90 yrs. old. Husband of Fannie (Brown). Gwyn, James; Vet. Lives in Murfreesboro, owns food business.

Gwyn, James Stanley; WW1, (Pvt), 1918-19, Born in Viola 8/15/1890-1970, Teamster, Parents: Fannie & Huston Gwyn.

Gwyn, Kathy; married name is Officer. She works for the SSN office.

Gwyn, Larry H.; lives in Florida

Gwyn, Lawson 'Frog'; WW1, 1918-19, Born in Viola Jun. 10, 1895-1908, Milling, Parents: Huston & Fannie Gwyn. DD214.

Gwyn, Leonard; WW1, 1918-19, (Pvt), O/S, Born in Viola 11/24/1892, Teamster, Parents: Huston & Fannie Gwyn. Played with the Viola Clowns Baseball team.

Gwyn, Mary Ann

Gwyn, Mark R.; Tenn. Fed. Of Investigation Director. 2007 [story]

Gwyn, Mickey; son of Thelma and Leonard. Lives in Murfreesboro, Tn.

Gwyn, Onnie B. (Northcutt); 1893-1930, Wife of Will Gwyn.

Gwyn, Robert 'Bobby'

Gwyn, Roy Richard; Son of Bessie, 1942 Semi-pro baseball player.

Gwyn, Roy; WW1, 1918-19 (Pvt), Born in Warren Co. 4/27/1894, O/S.

Gwyn, Sarah ()

Gwyn, Stanley; 1890-1970.

Gwyn, Thelma Jean(); wife of Leonard. Mother of Mark and Kathy, Larry, Mickey.

Gwyn, Tommy; 1883-1903

Gwyn, Virginia (Fuston); wife of Lawson, 1986-72 yrs. old.

Gwyn, Will 'Willie'; WW1, 1918-19, (Pvt), Born in Viola 9/23/1887, Farmer, 97 years old, husband of Onnie B. (Parents: Huston & Fannie), Died in 1984 97 yrs. old.

Gwyn, William Logan

Gwyn, William; WW1, (Pvt), 1918-19, Born in McMinnville 4/5/1897, Laundry, Parents: William Logan & Dolly Brown Gwynn.

(Hi-Hz)

Hall, Jessica; Freshman, WCHS 2001

Hammons, John; WW1, 1918-19, (Pvt), O/S, Age: 25 by Oct. 1812.

Handcock, Clark

Handcock, Marie; Robertson is her married name.

Hanley, Dan; Barber on Main Street, lived on 508 Beersheba St. in 1942.

Hanley, David J.; Barber.

Harper, Indy; Soph. Warren Co. H.S. 2001.

Harris, Anna Jo (Thomas); Wife of Robert 'Mojo'

Harris, Annie Ruth

Harris, Betty (Thomas)

Harris, Charles

Harris, Jimmie; WW2, DD214.

Harris, Josephine

Harris, Linda Sue

Harris, Melissa Leann; 1999 WCHS SR.

Harris, Mary J.

Harris, Robert; Black History student, football player, WCHS 2006

Harris, Robert Lee 'Mojo'; Husband of Anna Jo (Thomas) [story]

Harris, Tiny; 1940's Semi-pro baseball player.

Harris, William 'Zeke'; played and owned a band in the 1960's.

Harris, Yvette; Sr. WCHS 2001.

Hart, Annie; wife of Frank, 334 S. High St. in 1942.

Hart, Frank; wife of Annie.

Hawthorne, Franklin Leroy; Doctor, (1900-1979). Husband of Sarah Laura Keel (Rowan). [story]

Hawthorne, Sarah Laura Keel (Rowan); wife of Dr. Franklin Leroy. [story]

Haynes, Barbara (Martin)

Haynes, George 'Shakey'; Semi-Pro baseball player, Husband of Margaret.

Haynes, Margaret (Thomas); wife of George. [story]

Haynes, Sarah L. (Malone); (Single), (1936-2002) [story]

Hayworth, Walter

Head, Fred; husband of Lottie, Laborer, lived on 530A Beersheba St. in 1942.

Head, Mary Virginia 'Little Bit'; daughter of Mrs. Oscar Crisp. [story]

Head, Lottie; wife of Fred in 1942.

Henderson, Notie (Woods)

Henderson, Robert Lee; (1917-1948)

Henderson, Walter

Henderson, Willie (Miller).

Henegar, Alton; husband of Lydia.

Henegar, Benjamin; Army, WW2 Vet., lived in Yankeetown in 1942.

Henegar, James; Porter at Hutchins-Davies Drug Co. in 1942.

Henegar, Lydia; wife of Alton, lived on Yankeetown St. in 1942.

Hennegar, 'Bunny; Navy WW2, Retired.

Hennegar, Benny; Brother of 'Bunny'

Hennegar, Lillie Mae; 1946 BHS student.

Hennegar, Walter 'Wall C.' (Mule); WW2 Vet. DD214.

Hennessee, Josie V.; wife of Willie E., 119 E End Drive in 1942.

Hennessee, Minnie L.; 1946 BHS 6th grade student.

Hennessee, Willie Mae;1st grade BHS 1945.

Hennessee, Willie E.; husband of Josie V., Janitor at Dr. Douglas Gunn, lived on 119 E. End Drive St. in 1942.

Hennessy, Willie

Henny, Alice (Rowan); wife of Howard Sr.

Henny, Alvin; son of Howard Sr. and Alice (Rowan)

Henny, Howard Jr.; Son of Alice (Rowan)

Henny, Howard Sr. husband of Alice (Rowan)

Henny, Kathy (Price); wife of Robert. Educator at Smithville School 2007.

Henny, Lillian; daughter of Howard Sr. and Alice (Rowan)

Henny, Mary (Price)

Henny, Micheal

Henny, Michelle; daughter of Howard Jr. & Peggy.

Henny, Mikeesha Denae; daughter of Robert and Kathy.

Henny, Paul

Henny, Peggy (Smith): Wife of Howard Jr.

Henny, Robert; husband of Kathy (Price), son of Howard Sr. and Alice (Rowan). [story]

Henny, Whitney; daughter of Howard Jr. & Peggy (Smith), 2003 WCHS Soph.

Henry, Charles 'Goat Henry'

Henson, Ada; lived on Egypt Alley in 1942.

Hicks, Sheila (Johnson); married twice, Daughter of Jean (Roberts) Strode. [story]

Higginbotham, John

Higginbotham, Lillian

Higginbotham, Maggie (Hill)

Higginbotham, Marcus Rubin; WW1, (Pv1), 1918-19, Born in McMinnville, Age: 30 by May 1912, DD214. Lived on 17 East End Drive in 1945.

Higginbottom, Juanita; lived on Egypt Alley in 1942.

Higginbottom, Maggie; wife of Marcus, 117 E. End Drive in 1942.

Higginbottom, Marcus; husband of Maggie, Driver, lived on 117 E. End Drive in 1942. DD214, WW1, Vet.

Higginbottom, Martin; husband of Willie B., lived on Egypt Alley in 1942.

Higginbottom, Willie B.; wife of Martin, Egypt Alley in 1942.

Higginbottom, Yvonnie

Higgins, George; Worked at Puckett motors for years.

Higgins, Mary; lived on African St. in 1942.

Higgins, Joe

Hill, Benjamin; husband of Martha, Chauffer, lived on Yankeetown St. in 1942.

Hill, Charles; WW1, (Pv1), 1918-19, Over Sea, husband of Margaret, Carpenter, Born in McMinnville 4/15/1895. Lived on 64 Lane Street in 1945.

Hill, Ella; wife of Ellihew, lived on Yankeetown St. in 1942.

Hill, Eugene; husband of Olivia, Helper for Ed Warren, lived on 107 E. End Drive St. in 1942.

Hill, Gwynn

Hill, Ida (); Married to Jessie in 1860.

Hill, Isabelle 'Issie' M. (Finger); 1839-1861.

Hill, Irvin

Hill, Jessie; Husband of Ida in 1860.

Hill, Leon; 1st grade BHS 1946.

Hill, Lillie

Hill, Margaret Ann; wife of Charles, lived on Lane St. in 1942.

Hill, Obie; Laborer, lived on Yankeetown St. in 1942.

Hill, Olivia; wife of Eugene, 107 E. End Drive St. in 1942.

Hill, Rohonda

Hill, Shakka; WCHS Freshman, 2001.

Hill, Theadoshia; 1855-1934 wife of Gwynn Hill.

Hill, Tracy

Hobbs, Clyde; Porter at Sedberry Hotel in 1942.

Hobbs, Loretta; 4th grade BHS 1945.

Hobson, Maggie; Cook at Melton's Café in 1942.

Hogan, Ida; lived on Lane St. in 1942.

Holland, Lucy (Marbury); 1878-1906 wife of Walter Holland married: 1898.

Holland, Walter

Holland, Will; WW1, 1918-19 (Pvt), Over Sea, Born in McMinnville.

Hopkins, Bert; lived on Yankeetown St. in 1942.

Hopkins, Maggie; lived on Yankeetown St. in 1942.

Hopkins, Docie B.; wife of Virgil, in 1942.

Hopkins, Virgil; husband of Docie, WW1, 1918-19, (Pv1), Born in McMinnville Apr./1/1890, lived on Yankeetown St. in 1942.

Houckin, William; (1843-1895) Warren Co. wealthiest man in 1895. [story]

Houseworth, Connie (Cope); Daughter of Jay Cope.

Howard, William

Howell, Ellen 'Ella); 7th & 8th grade teacher at Bernard H.S. in the 1940's.

Huddleston, Albert J.; Pastor at Leesburg, lived on 108 E. Colville St. in 1942, died in 1955 at 72 years of age.

Huddleston, Asbury or Asberry; WW1, (Pvt), 1893-1918, 1918-18, Died in service. Wife Susie Huddleston was notified by Western Union that her husband died of Pneumonia on July 22, 1918. Born in Leesburg. Age; 22 years old on 4/12/1918. He was in the Co A 521 Serv Bn. Engrs 4/15/1918, Co D 521 Serv Engrs 4/27/1918, and 31st Co 154 Dep Brig. until death.

Huddleston, Emma (Bates)

Huddleston, Isham

Huddleston, Odell; Maid, lived on 119 E. End Drive St. in 1942.

Huddleston, John; 1854-1920

Huddleston, Permelia (Smith)

Huddleston, Sue (Foster)

Hudgens, Dock

Hudgens, Lou (Bradley)

Hudgens, Robert; 1900-1937

Hudgins, Clayton; Son of Willie Mae

Hudgins, Edward Lee.; DD214, Air Force Vet. Born; Mar. 23, 1927.

Hudgins, Helen Loretta; Daughter of Willie Mae.

Hudgins, Johnnie; Son of Willie Mae.

Hudgins, Robert

Hudgins, Willie Mae; mother of Johnnie, Helen & Clayton.

Hudson, Dollie; Bolden Green resident, Fortune Teller.

Huggins, Arabella (); Mother of Ray and Kenneth.

Huggins, George E.; husband of Hattie, WW2, Army, worked for Al Puckett's Ford Dealer, pumped gas, lived on African St. in 1942. Born; Aug. 14, 1907. DD214.

Huggins, Georgia Mae (Martin) Etter; Wife of Ray Huggins. [story]

Huggins, Hattie; wife of George.

Huggins, Arabella; wife of Joseph, lived on Congo St. in 1942.

Huggins, Joseph; husband of Arabella, Deliveryman for Green's Grocery, lived on Congo St. in 1942.

Huggins, Joseph F.; Father of Ray.

Huggins, John

Huggins, Kenneth; 1946 BHS football player. [story]

Huggins, Ray Roberts 'Butch'

Huggins, Rufe; Minister 1955.

Huggins, William A.; DD214, WW2, Vet. Army, lived on African St. in 1942. Born; Aug. 19, 1910.

Huling, Charlie

Huling, Curtis

Huling, Rosanna Yvette E.

Hunt, Cleo; 1867-1962

Hunt, Isham

Hunter, Buford; 'Razz' WW2 Vet. DD214. Born; June 25, 1940.

Hunter, Carthew; husband of Mary E.

Hunter, Clarence; husband of Nora, lived on Egypt Alley in 1942.

Hunter, Ermon; lived on 103 E. Colville St. in 1942.

Hunter, Florence Jane (Martin); wife of Thomas, lived on 530A Beersheba St. in 1942.

Hunter, James; Brother of Louise (Hunter).

Hunter, Jessie L.; Teacher, lived on 410 Beersheba St. in 1942.

Hunter, Lula: Abe Thomas's school teacher at Cornith school in Viola in the 1930's.

Hunter, Nora; wife of Clarence, lived on Egypt Ally in 1942.

Hunter, Mary; wife of Carthew, lived on 410 Beersheba St. in 1942, died 1967, 93 yrs old.

Hunter, May

Hunter, Ollis; Mill Worker, lived on 410 Beersheba in 1942.

Hunter, Sarah

Hunter, Thomas; husband of Florence, WW1, DD214, Mill Worker, lived on 530A Beersheba St. in 1942.

Hunter, Tom; Vet. Original Post 208 member in 1945.

Hurd, E. F.

Hurd, John; died in March 1955.

Hurd, Lottie (Ramsey); wife of Wesley Hurd.

Hurd, Mattie

Hurd, Wesley; Husband of Lottie (Ramsey) Hurd.

(Ik-Is)

Ikeard, A. Paul Jr.
Ikeard, A. Paul Sr.
Ikeard, Betty
Ikeard, Capp
Ikeard, Charlie
Ikeard, Easter May (Mckinley)
Ikeard, Mandy Mae
Ikeard, Mary Frances (Thomas); 1927-1962
Ikeard, Maude (Hill)
Ikeard, Oscar; 1915-1979
Ikeard, Paul
Ikeard, Pearline (); Divorced
Ikeard, Raymond
Ikeard, Willie Rice; 1914-1967
Irvin, Louise Cynthia; 1907-1990
Irvin, Thomas William; DD214, WW2 Vet. Born; May 14, 1918. Lived on 107 Congo St. in 1942.
Irving, Grant; husband of Iola, lived on Egypt Alley in 1942.
Irving, Iola; wife of Grant, Egypt Alley in 1942.
Isabel, Robert; husband of Mary, Cement Worker, lived on Egypt Alley in 1942.
Isabel, Mary; wife of Robert, Egypt Alley in 1942.
Isabel, Nora; lived on Lane St. in 1942.
Isabel, Shelia; Janitor, lived at Lane St. in 1942.
Isibell, Eddridge

(Ja-Jo)

Jackson, Francine

Jackson, Gary Lewis; (Rabbitt), son of Eunice and Audie Marie (Carr). [story]

Jackson, Jimmy; [story]

Jackson, Latoya; WCHS Freshman, 2001.

Jackson, LeRoy; Nat. Guard Vet. Principal in Tullahoma, Tn.

Jackson, Minnie Irene; (story)

Jackson, William

Jaco, Mourning Dove

Jennings, Otis Falls; WW1, (Pvt), 10/3/1918-10/17/1918 time in service, Born in McMinnville 1/17/1898, military organization: Army Tng. Corps, Fisk University, Nashville Tn., until death. Died of Influenza and Pneumonia on Oct. 17, 1918. Notified: Bettie Roberson (Mother), McMinnville, Tn. 504 East Main Street.

Jennings, Thomas; 1850's, 1st Baker known in Warren Co. as a black freed man (1850's-1860's.

Johnnigan, Carrie; 1st grade Bernard H.S. in 1945.

Johnson, Andrew 'Andy'; 1880's Barber with B. Cope, downtown McMinnville.

Johnson, Clara Bell

Johnson, Bill; husband of Minnie G., Carpenter, lived on 109 E. Colville St. in 1942.

Johnson, Ella; Bank teller.

Johnson, Eldora; 1945 BHS student.

Johnson, Emma Ruth

Johnson, Eunice Jefferson.; DD214, Korean Vet. May 28, 1928. Commander of American Legion Post # 208. Employee of First Nat. Bank.

Johnson, Eunice L.; Vet.

Johnson, Helen; B.H.S. 1949 class.

Johnson, Lois

Johnson, Minnie (Murphy); wife of Bill, 109 E. Colville St. in 1942.

Johnson, Nelson; DD214, WW1, Vet. 1918-19, (Pvt) O/S, Born in McMinnville, Age 22, May/1912.

Johnson; Paul W.; DD214, WW2 Vet. Born; Sept. 3, 1921.

Johnson, Thelma

Johnson, Willie; (1873-1956). [story]

Jones, A. Elizabeth; lived on 323 S. High St. in 1942.

Jones, Birdie L.; lived on Barnes St. in 1942.

Jones, Buster; lived on 323 S. High St. in 1942.

Jones, Courtney

Jones, Ermon; Died in 1991 at 79 yrs old

Jones, George 'Buck'; Rocket baseball player, husband of Yvonne. 4th grade BHS 1945.

Jones, George, Edward

Jones, George Everet

Jones, James A.; WW1, 1918-19, (Corpal), Born in McMinnville 10/30/1891

Jones, Tennie L.

Jones, Virgil; McMinnville Police Dept.

Jones, Yvonne (); Wife of George Jones.

(K)

Keel, Bertha M.; wife of Robert, Church St. in 1942.

Keel, Dock

Keel, Harold; Korean Vet., 1946 BHS 6th grade student.

Keel, Joe; 1945, 82 yrs. old.

Keel, Martha Ann (Durley)

Keel, Robert Harold, DD214, Vet. Air Force, Born; Jun. 16, 1932.

Keel, Robert J.; husband of Bertha, Laborer, lived on Church St. in 1942.

Keel, Shirley Temple; 4th grade BHS 1945.

King, Anderson; lived on 108 E. Colville St. in 1942.

King, Brenda (Terry)

King, Freeda

King, George Jr.; Minister Church of Christ.

King, Gerdine

King, Jerry William; Vet. Marines, American Legion #208 member.

King, Martha (Northcutt); 1838-1915

King, Michael Ray; 1950's, Jerry's Son (1969-)

King, Ned III

King, Ned Jr.

King, Ned Samuel; Jerry King's father.

King, Ola Mae (Whitaker); Wife of George Jr.

King, Queen Esther; [story]

King, Tom

King, Willie Bob

King, Woodson

Knight, Annis: 1950's

Knight, Fred A. Jr.; DD214, Retired Army Vet., McMinnville Policeman. Born; Sept. 1, 1920. Lived on 511 E. Main St.in 1941.

Knighton, Chaton; 2003 WCHS Grad.

Knox Lee; WW1 Vet.

(La-Lo)

Landford, Levy; 1st Blacksmith in McMinnville.

Lane, David; Blacksmith in 1870 in the Morrison area.

Laundress, Anna; Housewife—(Rubin Higginbotham)

Laundress, Susan; Housewife (Richard Webb)

League, Alice

League, Ann

League, Bruce Edwin; (1963-2005) [story]

League, Cecelia M.; wife of Major M., Church St. in 1942.

League, D'Andre; Junior at WCHS in 2012, Basketball/Football Player.

League, Gerlene or Gereline

League, Harvey; 'Rocket' baseball player.

League, Jesse

League, Josie (____)

League, Major M.; husband of Cecelia M., Pastor of Clark's Chapel Methodist Church, lived on Church St. in 1942.

League, Mary Francies; BHS 1956 Grad.

League, Matthew

League, Minnie Virginia (Martin); Cook at Bailey's Place, in 1942.

League, Oldham; member of Pleasant Hill P. T. A. 1956.

League, Olen Matthew: husband of Willie Beatrice (Martin)

League, Olen Edward

League, Paul

League, Willie Beatrice (Martin): wife of Olen Matthew

League, William Eugene; 1941-1964

League, William H.; 1915-1989

Lee, Amanda; 1904-1944

Lee, Arthur or (Authur)

Lee, Ary; Husband of Emmaline

Lee, Carlee (); Mother of Earline

Lee, Earline

Lee, Edd David; WW1, 1918-19, (Pvt), Born in Viola in 4/11/1897. Original member of Post 208 in 1945, Waiter at Brown Hotel Café, lived on 311 High St. in 1942.

Lee, Elsie Mai

Lee, Emmaline (); Wife of Ary.

Lee, George

Lee, Jennie (Donohue); wife of John, lived on 319 S. High St. in 1942.

Lee, Joe B.; Janitor, lived on 518 Beersheba St. in 1942, 1902-1990

Lee, John; husband of Jennie.

Lee, Johnnie (Martin)

Lee, Lena

Lee, Luther; 1900-1959

Lee, Marietta (Marbury); Cook, lived on E. Main St. in 1942. (1916-)

Lee, Porter; 1905-1935

Lee, Thomas; 1880-1954

Leftrict, Charlie Franklin; DD214 WW2 Vet. Born; Apr. 9, 1911. Born in McMinnville.

Leftrict, Charles Franklin Jr.; DD214 Vet. Born; Feb. 26, 1941. Son of Charles Sr. Born in Louisville, Ky.

Leftrict, Danny

Leftrict, Donald Ray; DD214 Vietnam Vet. Born; Sept. 30, 1948.

Leftrict, Edd; DD214 WW2 Vet. Born; Aug. 29, 1909.

Leftrict, Helen Joyce

Leftrict, Larkin; Roy Webb's G-G-Grandfather.

Leftrict, Levoy

Leftrict, Margaret Lin ()

Leftrict, Robert Louis; (1927-2001) husband of Margaret Lin (). [story]

Leftrict, Thomas; Porter at Brown Hotel, lived on 528 Beersheba St. in 1942.

Leftwich, Sam; Warren County's Stonemason industry in 1880. He laid railroad piers for Rock Island which still stands today.

Leftwich, Pauline (McKinley)

Lewis, J. C.; Pastor of Primitive Baptist Church in 1942.

Lillard, Minnie W.; Maid at Brown Hotel, lived on 422 Beersheba St. in 1942.

Lisk, Wiley; lived on Carney St. in 1942.

Locke, Arthur

Locke, Bernice

Locke, Betty Jean

Locke, Brandon; 8th Grade 2001 WCMS

Locke, Cecil; husband of Nora (Burch), Laborer, lived on Yankeetown St. in 1942.

Locke, Clarence; Brother of Hugh.

Locke, Clarence Jr.; Vet, Army, Killed in a car wreck on Leave. (McMinnville).

Locke, Cora; Maid, lived on 321 S. High St. in 1942.

Locke, Dan; son of Lafayette & Sally (Potter) Locke

Locke, Earline; BHS 1956 Valedictorian.

Locke, Frank

Locke, Fred Jr.; Vietnam—Desert storm, Army, National Guard retired after 22 years of service. [story] DD214.

Locke, Fred Sr.; WW2, 1918-19, (Pvt), Army. [story] DD214.

Locke, Gail (Cope); wife of Fred Jr.

Locke, Gertrude (Rucker)

Locke, Gwen J.; wife of Hugh Locke. [story]

Locke, Hardina (Cope); wife of Larry.

Locke, Hubert Sr.; father of Hubert Jr.

Locke, Hubert Jr.; son on Hubert.

Locke, Hugh; Korean, Army. Husband of Susie (McReynolds) [story] DD214. Born; Apr. 6, 1930. Son of Harry and Hattie (King) Locke.

Locke, James; Brother of Hugh.

Locke, Jammal; son of Larry and Hardina.

Locke, John L.; son of Cecil and Nora (Burch) Locke. [story]

Locke. John R.; DD214 WW2 Vet. Born; Aug. 26, 1909.

Locke, Johnny; Army Vet.

Locke, Joyce Ann

Locke, Lafayette Jr.

Locke, LaFayette Sr.; husband of Sallie (Potter).

Locke, Larry Randolph; Vietnam—Desert Storm, Army 1yr. and 8months, Retired National Guard with 21 years.

Locke, Lawrence W.; husband of Zelma, Porter, lived on Yankeetown St. in 1942.

Locke, Lloyd

Locke, Lorena

Locke, William 'Bill'; [story] (1916-2001)

Locke, Maggie Mai (Wood); Wife of Fred Sr. [story]

Locke, Margaret

Locke, Melvin

Locke, Nora (Burch); wife of Cecil Locke, lived on Yankeetown St. in 1942.

Locke, Rodney; Son of Hugh.

Locke, Sallie (Potter); wife of Lafayette Locke.

Locke, Shauna; Daughter of Hugh. Wife of Dr. Wiley. Mother of Javier and Che'

Locke, Susie (McReynolds); wife of Hugh Locke.

Locke, Terrence Jamaal

Locke, Cora; wife of Timothy, 321 S. High St. in 1942.

Locke, Timothy; husband of Cora, Concrete Worker, lived on 321 S. High St. in 1942.

Locke, William Sr.

Locke, William Jr. (Sonny)

Locke, V. S.; son of Lafayette & Sallie (Potter).

Locke, Zelma; wife of Lawrence W., Yankeetown in 1942.

Locust, Mae Bell; Educator, History, English at Bernard High School.

Locust, Richard; DD214, WW2 Vet. Born; Aug. 22, 1907.

(Lop-Lz)

Looper, Andrew J.

Looper, Betty; mother of Tina and Johnathan

Looper, Daisy (Woo)

Looper, Foster

Looper, George

Looper, Herman Sr.; husband of Myrena (Womack)

Looper, Hilary

Looper, James Herman; son of Myrena and Herman Sr.

Looper, James Yardley; 1909-1944

Looper, Joann; daughter of Herman Sr. and Myrena.

Looper, Josie (Womack); (1877-1955), wife of Andrew J. Looper. [story]

Looper, Mamie Shirley (Martin)

Looper, Maranda (Rander) (Webb)

Looper, Myrena (Womack); wife of Herman Sr.

Looper, Norma Dale; mother of Wayne Jr. and Matthew Wolford.

Looper, Oliver C.; Died 1959 (single)

Looper, Ray Dean; son of Herman and Myrena.

Looper, Renda (Webb)

Looper, Shelby; daughter of Herman Sr. and Myrena.

Looper, Susan; 1861-1894

Looper, Vonda; daughter of Herman Sr. and Myrena.

Loper, Maude; wife of Dock, lived on Burton's Lane in 1942.

Lopez, Samuel; Army Vet., Grandson of Tommie Ford, WCHS Jr. 2001

Lopez, Shandra; Soph. WCHS 2001.

Lowe, Richard 'Rock Eyed Slim'; husband of Viola, 1930's Semi-Pro Baseball great, Porter at Puckett Motors, lived on 323 S. High St in 1942.

Lowe, Viola; wife of Richard, Cook at Sedberry Hotel, 323 S. High St. in 1942.

Lusk, Ada Rosen (Storkey); wife of Frank Duncan Lusk.

Lusk, Annie E. (Fuston); 1901-1969

Lusk, Bernard; 3rd grade BHS 1945.

Lusk, Beverly; Daughter of Marvin Sr. & Mollie Lusk.

Lusk, Burley; 3rd grade BHS 1945.

Lusk, Chantlor

Lusk, Charles Jr. 'C. J.'; Son of Sr. & Georgia (Strode). 2003 WCHS Junior, Medical Assistant 2007.

Lusk, Charles Sr.; Vietnam Vet., Night Club Owner, McMinnville Police. [story]

Lusk, Cora A.; BHS 1956 Grad.

Lusk, Curtis Eugene; Son of Ada & Frank Duncan.

Lusk, Donald Lennis; Born Feb. 22, 1922, Went to Pleasant Hill School & Central High School.

Lusk, Floyd; lived on Egypt Alley in 1942.

Lusk, Frances; daughter of Velma, Sister of Robert K.

Lusk, Frank; Son of John Lusk.

Lusk, Georgia (Gribble)

Lusk, Georgia (Strode); Wife of Charles Sr.

Lusk, Glady F.

Lusk, Harold Buford; WW2 Vet. Son of Rosena (Starkey) & Frank Duncan

Lusk, Henrietta; wife of Marvin T. Jr. Educator.

Lusk, Howard Franklin 'Sampson'; died in 2003, Son of Ada & Frank Duncan.

Lusk, James Leonard 'Flint'; Son of Rosena (Starkey) & Frank Duncan. [story] Lives in Bolden Green.

Lusk, James Eldgridge; DD214, Vietnam Vet. Born; July 22, 1944. Son of John Lusk.

Lusk, Jeff; Son of Harold & Louis (Smith)

Lusk, Jerry; Son of Rosena (Starkey) & Frank Duncan.

Lusk, Jewel; Daughter of Annie Ester Lusk. Sister to Marschel. Wife of Thomas Wood.

Lusk, Junita; Married a Taylor, Daughter of Rosena (Starkey) & Frank Duncan.

Lusk, John; Father of James, Velma, Robert, & Frank Lusk.

Lusk, John Lewis; (1933-1977), Jewel & Marschel's Brother.

Lusk, Joyce; Daughter of Mollie and Marvin Sr. Lusk.

Lusk, Kurt; Son of Harold & Louis (Smith). 2000 WCHS Sr.

Lusk, Lena Evelyn (Martin); Wife of John Lusk. Died in 1973, 63 yrs. old.

Lusk, Lewis

Lusk, Linda (Martin); Wife of Kuin Lusk, sister of Erie Jô, Ralph. Lives in Bolden Green.

Lusk, Lula; Student, lived on 128 Murphy St. in 1942.

Lusk, Margaret Elizabeth (Patterson); Wife of Donald Lusk. Works for school system for 28 years, Head start.

Lusk, Mary; Student, lived on 128 Murphy St. in 1942.

Lusk, Marschel Brady; DD214, Vietnam Vet. Son of Annie Ester () Lusk. Born; Sept. 20, 1937.

Lusk, Marshall

Lusk, Marvin T. Jr.; DD214, Vet. Son of Mollie and Marvin Sr. Lusk. [story]

Lusk, Marvin T. Sr.; WW2 Vet.

Lusk, Mary (Douglas)

Lusk, Mary (Higginbotham)

Lusk, Mary E.

Lusk, Mary Malissa (Woods)

Lusk, Missie (Bartley)

Lusk, Mollie Monroe (Paige); Wife of Marvin Sr. Educator, [story]

Lusk, Paige; daughter of Marvin T. Lusk Jr.

Lusk, Peggy Ann (Dartis); Died 2000, wife of James. [story]

Lusk, Rerha Mae; 1946 Bernard H.S. student.

Lusk, Robert Kewen.; husband of Linda (Martin) DD214, Vietnam Vet. Lives in Bolden Green. Born; Apr. 11, 1941.

Lusk, Rufus; 1933, 74 yrs old.

Lusk, Sylvia Myra Gale; 1998 Warren Co. H.S. Senior.

Lusk, Taylor; Son of Marvin T. Lusk Jr.

Lusk, Tristan; son of Linda and Robert Kewen.

Lusk, Vera; Married a Thomas, Daughter of Ada & Frank Duncan.

Lusk, Waymon; Semi-pro baseball player 1930's w/Abe Thomas.

Lusk, William T. 'Rusty'; DD214, WW1, Vet. 1879-1946

Lusk, Yvonne; Daughter of Mollie and Marvin Sr. Lusk.

(Mab)

Mabry, John or Marbury; 1887-1974

Macon, Celia

Macon, Carrie Elizabeth (Wade); wife of Walter Jr. [story]

Macon, Ethel

Macon, Jim

Macon, Roy

Macon, Walter; husband of Carrie E.

Main, Morris Monroe; WW1 Vet.

Malone, Clifton; WW1, 1918-19, (Pvt), Born in McMinnville Apr./9/1897.

Malone, E. B.; Community leader, N.A.A.C.P. Leader.

Malone, Evelyn (Bonner); Wife of E. B.

Malone, George

Malone, Harvey; husband of Janie.

Malone, James

Malone, Janie; wife of Harvey, lived on 120 Edgefield St. in 1942.

Malone, Kirk

Malone, Margarette Elizabeth (Winton) [story]

Malone, Orvil K.; WW1 Vet.

Malone, Pam

Malone, Reggie

Malone, Sarah

Manier, Channell Nicole: 1998 WCHS Sr.

Marbury, Aaron; Feb. 14, 1886-Apr. 10, 1952. Son of Cy & Jane (Side)

Marbury, husband of Ethel Gardner.

Marbury, Cora; Died Jan. 6, 1913, wife of Cyrus (Cy) Marbury.

Marbury, Cyrus 'Cy'

Marbury, Della; wife of Jack E., lived on Carney in 1942.

Marbury, Eddie M. Stuart

Marbury, Elizabeth (Grayson); 1883-1979

Marbury, Ethel (Garner); 1887-1920, Aaron Marbury's wife.

Marbury, Isabell (Walker)

Marbury, Ivy Willis; 1922-1965, DD214, WW 2 Vet. Born; Oct. 18 1922.

Marbury, Jack E.; husband of Della, Driver, lived on Carney St. in 1942.

Marbury, James E.; Vietnam Vet.

Marbury, John; 1881-1981 100yrs. old.

Marbury, Mary Ann (Rion)

Marbury, Simon Pope; 1900-1937.

Marbury, Toosie (Smith)

Marchbanks, Porcia Ashanti: daughter of Joyce, WCHS 1998 Sr.

Marks, Lula; Died in Jun. 6, 1910, (46 yrs. old).

Marshall, Booker T. Jr.; 411 Beersheba St. in 1942, 1st grade BHS 1945.

Marshall, Booker T. Sr.; husband of Claudia, Director of funeral Parlor,

Marshall & Howard, 411 Beersheba St. in 1942.

Marshall, Claudia; wife of Booker T. Sr.

Marshall, Odessa; 1st grade BHS 1945.

Maxey, George; Barber in 1880.

(Mar-Maz)

Martin, Aaron; Warren County H. S. Freshman, in 2001.

Martin, Alford

Martin, Alfred; (1825-1899), Blacksmith in 1870.

Martin, Alice R.; 1926-25 yrs old

Martin, Alice Rebecca (Bates)

Martin, Allen

Martin, Allan

Martin, Alta

Martin, Alvin

Martin, Ann; daughter of Elmer & Caroline (York).

Martin, Annie

Martin, Arthur; father of Elmer Sr. 1st wife Caroline (York), 2nd wife Belle.

Martin, Arthur Lee; husband of Myrtle, Laborer, lived on Egypt Alley St. in 1942.

Martin, Arthur Ray; 1884-1980

Martin, Asa; lived on Burton's Lane St. in 1942.

Martin, Barbara; Educator, Author of a published school book, wife of Clarence E. Martin. [story]

Martin, Barbara

Martin, Barbara; daughter of Lawrence.

Martin, Barbara Cynthia

Martin, Beatrice (Stubblefield)

Martin, Betty Jo; daughter of Elmer Sr. & Caroline (York), 4th grade BHS 1945.

Martin, Betty

Martin, Beulah (Carr)

Martin, Bradford

Martin, Bright L.

Martin, Brittany; 2000 Warren Co. H.S. Soph.

Martin, Brown

Martin, Brownloe

Martin, Bub Edward; 1921-1979, WW2 Veteran.

Martin, Calvin

Martin, Carol Thomas; wife of Harold Thomas.

Martin, Caroline (York); (1888-1921), 1st wife of Arthur Martin.

Martin, Charles Lester 'Muggin'; DD214, Vet. Son of Elmer Sr. Born; Dec. 25, 1932.

Martin, Chiquita; Daughter of Sadie & Howard.

Martin, Chiquita; Freddy Martin's sister.

Martin, Clarence C. 'Bill' Sr.; Retired Air Force, Korean & Vietnam Vet., 1946 BHS football player Right Tackle. [story]

Martin, Clarence C. Jr.; Air Force, Desert Storm Veteran.

Martin, Clarence 'Edward'; DD214, Korean Vet. Marine, Educator. Born; July 21, 1930. [story]

Martin, Clayton

Martin, Clifton; 3rd grade BHS 1945.

Martin, Clinton; DD214, WW2 Vet. 19 years old at time of enlistment. Mar. 19, 1943.

Martin, Courtney; Daughter of Jeff & Treva (Martin) Martin. College Graduate.

Martin, Danny Lewis; Played corner back during his playing days at City High School. He played all sports, and had a brilliant career at Warren County High School. Danny later went to UT to become a standout in football. Vice President at Union Planters Bank / Vice Pres. of Security Bank.

Martin, Diane; (Thomas), Married to 1st husband, Danny Martin, 2nd husband Wood.

Martin, Dilia (Wood)

Martin, Donald 'Don'; son of Eulous and Juanita, Retired Army, Desert Storm Veteran.

Martin, Donna; Worked for Ben Lomand Telephone Company over 25 years. Has worked with kids most of her life.

Martin, Dorothy Beatrice; 'Baby Sis' 1946 BHS student.

Martin, Dustin; son of Danny & Diane, College graduate.

Martin, Edward; DD214, WW2 Vet. Born; Jan. 17, 1918. Husband of Letha, Cook, lived on Egypt Alley in 1942.

Martin, Elizabeth (Flannagan) Bates

Martin, Ella Mae (____)

Martin, Ellen; wife of Joe, lived on 416 Beersheba in 1942.

Martin, Elmer Clarence Jr.; Semi-Pro Baseball player, 'Rockets' and Coach.

Martin, Elmer Clarence Sr.; DD214, WW2, Veteran, Born in May 4, 1908.

Martin, Emma (Fisk)

Martin, Erie Jo

Martin, Eulous; DD214, WW2 Vet. Barber, Stonemason. [story]

Martin, Everett; WW1, 1918-19, (Pvt), O/S, Born in McMinnville, Age: 22 in 11/1912.

Martin, Fannie; wife of Lawrence, lived on 528 Beersheba St. in 1942.

Martin, Forrest Monroe Jr.; 1932-1994. [story]

Martin, Forrest Monroe Sr.; husband of Polly, lived on 327 S. High St. in 1942.

Martin, Foster Sr.

Martin, Franklin 'Frankie' Roosevelt

Martin, Franklin Jr.

Martin, Freddie

Martin, French; WW1, 1918-19, (Mech.), Over/Seas, Born in McMinnville on Sept./16/1894.

Martin, Garland

Martin, George; (1925-2002) [story]

Martin, George W.; Father of Bill, husband of Stella, lived on Church St. in 1942.

Martin, Georgia Mae; Etter, Huggins, wife of Ray.

Martin, Glenda

Martin, Gloria (); Raintree Manor in 2012.

Martin, Grady Frank Scott

Martin, Gregory 'Greg'; Son of Elmer Sr.

Martin, Harold

Martin, Harrison

Martin, Hattie Jane (); daughter of Forrest and Pearl (Fisk). [story]

Martin, Helen (Woods);

Martin, Helen G. (Smith); Wife of Michael, Mother of Michaela and Zachery. Works at First National Bank.

Martin, Herman A. 'Buster'; DD214, WW2 Vet. (Jan. 1, 1922-1995) [story]

Martin, Hobert T.; DD214, WW2 Vet. Married, Barber.

Martin, Howard T. Sr.; husband of Sadie, Principal of Pleasant Hill School, lived on 532 Beersheba St. in 1942.

Martin, Howard; Blacksmith in 1870.

Martin, Howard Thomas. Jr.; DD214, Vietnam Vet. Born; Feb. 21, 1931.

Martin, Ida Lee (Grayson); (Single)

Martin, India; Cook, lived on Yankeetown St. in 1942.

Martin, J. B.

Martin, Jay; husband of Martha, Trucker, 207 Etter St. in 1942.

Martin, James 'Jim'

Martin, James Melton; 3rd grade BHS 1945.

Martin, James D.; WW1, 1918-19, (Corp).

Martin, James Edward; DD214, Korean War Vet. Born; Dec. 23, 1930. Lived on 405 E. Main St. in 1954. Class of 1949 BHS, football player.

Martin, Jane (Alexander)

Martin, Jane (Gribble)

Martin, Jefferson Brown; 1880-1947

Martin, Jeffery 'Chick'; Assist. Principal at WCHS, Coach, Community Leader. Founder of WCHS Black History Club. [story]

Martin, Jerome

Martin, Jerry 'Head Monster'; Father of 'Goobie' DD214, Vietnam War Vet. Born; Nov. 20, 1952.

Martin, Jerry; Son of 'Head Monster'

Martin, Jerry Alexander (Goobie); Hardina Locke's son. A lefty for the Texas Rangers. [story]

Martin, Jerry Edward; Vietnam Vet, (1952-1982)

Martin, Jerry Eulous; son of Eulous and Juanita. Pastor/Musician in New Jersey.

Martin, Jim; WW2, (1907-1980)

Martin, Jim; husband of Pearl, lived on Congo St. in 1942.

Martin, Jim Theron; WW2, Vet.

Martin, Jimmie Theron.; Korean Vet., 1946 BHS 6th grade student.

Martin, Joe; husband of Ellen.

Martin, John

Martin, John; Died 1929, 75 yrs. old.

Martin, John M.

Martin, Johnnie Lee

Martin, Josephine

Martin, Juanita (Stubblefield); 1st Wife of Elmer Martin Sr., 2nd Wife of Eulous Martin, lived on 110 Edgefield St. in 1942.

Martin, June

Martin, Katie (Jones)

Martin, Katie Lee (Smartt)

Martin, Kevin Lewis; son of Peggy Ann and Lawrence Martin. [story]

Martin, Keith 'Midnite'; Jaycee Man of the Year 2003.

Martin, Lawrence Jr.; husband of Fannie, lived on 528 Beersheba St. in 1942.WW2 Vet. Semi-pro baseball player with the Rockets.

Martin, Lelia (Hunter); 1894-1942

Martin, Letha; wife of Edward, Egypt Alley in 1942.

Martin, Lillie; wife of Thomas, lived on 207 Etter St. in 1942, 1894-1957.

Martin, Lois

Martin, Lou; Died 1909-28 yrs. old.

Martin, Lou Ada; (1870-1955) daughter of Garland and Lucinda (Christian) Martin, 103 East End Drive in 1942. [story]

Martin, Louise; wife of Thomas I., Congo St. In 1942.

Martin, Lucinda (Hunter)

Martin, Lulu (Huddleston)

Martin, Lulu Jane (Huddleston)

Martin, Luther; 1905-1941

Martin, Maggie; wife of George

Martin, Maggie; wife of Robert, lived on Congo St. in 1942.

Martin, Malissa (Walling)

Martin, Manila W.; 1898-1985, teacher, lived in Bolden Green.

Martin, Margaret; 1st grade BHS 1945.

Martin, Marjorie (Martin); Bill's Wife.

Martin, Marjorie Alaska (Savage); 2nd wife of Elmer Sr.

Martin, Markus T. (1983-1999) [story]

Martin, Martha (_____); wife of Jay, 'Toot' lived on 207 Etter St. in 1942.

Martin, Martha E. (Martin); wid. Of Theo, lived on 201 Etter St. in 1942.

Martin, Mary Jane; daughter of Eulous and Junita.

Martin, Mattie L.

Martin, Maude; lived on Egypt Alley in 1942.

Martin, Melissa (Walling)

Martin, Michael; County Commissioner, DD214, Vet. Born; Jan. 4, 1955. [story]

Martin, Michaela, Daughter of Helen & Michael John.

Martin, Monica; WCHS Jr. 2001.

Martin, Morris M.; WW1, 1918-19, (Pvt), O/S, Born in McMinnville, Age: 23 by May 1912.

Martin, Nancy Ann (Gribble)

Martin, Nancy Ann (Lusk)

Martin, Nancy Ann (Martin)

Martin, Nannie Frank

Martin, Nodie; 1913-1937 (single)

Martin, Olivia Emma Ruth (Johnson); (1932-2001) [story]

Martin, Oscar Bill; 2nd grade BHS 1945.

Martin, Parthenia

Martin, Paten

Martin, Patrice

Martin, Patty Sue (Bonner); Wife of Roosevelt, Social Worker, Community Leader.

Martin, Pearl (Fisk); wife of Jim, 1903-1979, Maid for Hillis Hunter, lived on Congo St. in 1942.

Martin, Polly; wife of Forrest Sr., 327 S. High St. in 1942.

Martin, Ralph; Lawyer.

Martin, Raymond; DD214, WW2 Vet. Born; June 1922.

Martin, Robert; husband of Maggie, Congo St. in 1942.

Martin, Rolan; 1877-1952

Martin, Roosevelt; Husband of Patty Sue. 1st grade BHS 1945.

Martin, Ruth

Martin, Sadie; Educator, Wife of Howard Martin Sr. [story]

Martin, Sam

Martin, Sanford; DD214, WW2 Vet. Born; May 13, 1922.

Martin, Sarah (Looper); 1873-1932

Martin, Sarah; 2012

Martin, Shatorra Nashay

Martin, Shawnda

Martin, Sherre Ann

Martin, Stella (Martin); Maid, 104 Church St. in 1942, Daughter of George Martin.

Martin, Spurgeon; Bernard H.S. 1955 Graduate.

Martin, Susan

Martin, Susan (Martin) 'Tootie'

Martin, T. Guss; lived on 416 Beersheba St. in 1942.

Martin, Tarlton H.; lived on Barnes St. in 1942, DD214, WW2 Vet. Born; Feb. 22, 1924.

Martin, Teddy; son of Betty Jo Martin.

Martin, Theodore; husband of Martha E.

Martin, Theron; DD214, WW2 Vet. Born; Nov. 7, 1907.

Martin, Terri (Dalton); Daughter of Charles & Frankie Dalton.

Martin, Terrin, Son of Calvin Smith.

Martin, Thelma

Martin, Theodore

Martin, Thomas; husband of Lillie, lived on 207 Etter St. in 1942.

Martin, Thomas Edward; 1937-1959.

Martin, Thomas I.; husband of Louise, Army Vet., lived on Congo St. in 1942.

Martin, Thomas Ollie; 1930-1965

Martin, Thula (Looper)

Martin, Thurman

Martin, Tiara

Martin, Tina

Martin, Tonya

Martin, Treva (Strode); Daughter of Betty Jo Martin.

Martin, Trevor Adolphus; Son of Treva & Jeff Martin.

Martin, Tyler

Martin, V. K.

Martin, Van or Vann

Martin, Vancie Ray; WW2 Vet.

Martin, Vancie; member of East End Drive Church of Christ 2012

Martin, Vanulous

Martin, Vassie Ray

Martin, Valeria (Sutton); Wife of Elmer Jr.

Martin, Veral

Martin, Victor

Martin, Victor Eugene; 1873-1955

Martin, Violet Jennie (Worthington)

Martin, Wiley; (1929-1991)-62 yrs. old. [story]

Martin, William III

Martin, William: Member of East End Church of Christ 2002

Martin, William Lawrence Jr.; Korean Vet. [story]

Martin, Willie Beatrice; Wife of Olen M. League.

Martin, Willie Etter

Martin, Willie Mai; 1910-1939, (single)

Martin, Wilson Sr.; (1934-1997) 2nd grade BHS 1945. [story]

Martin, Yonita (Stubblefield)

Martin, Zackery; Son of Helen & Michael.

Maxey, George

Maynard, Fred; Husband of Lula (), NAACP President, Community Leader, McMinnville Police force, Chef, Rocket Baseball Player.

Maynard, Lula (); Wife of Fred Maynard.

Mazy, Joe; 1910, 65 yrs. old.

Mazy, Mollie ()

Mazy, Rhoda (); 1887-1945

Mazy, William H.; lived on Congo St. in 1942.

(Mc-Mu)

McCampbell, A. L.; Saddle & Harness maker in Viola.

McClarty, Comer

McClarty, Reathy (Gardner); (1882-1981) 99 yrs. old.

McCleary, Allen: 1998 Warren Co. H.S. Sr.

McGee, Annie; 1903-1956 (single)

McGee, Bethany: 2000 WCHS Jr.

McGee, Charles Lee; Bernard H.S. Class of 1949.

McGee, Don Depriest; (1932-1988) Vet. [story]

McGee, Donald D. 'Moon'

McGee, Elsie () or McGhee; BHS Class of 1949.

McGee, Eula (Winton)

McGee, Fannie (Donahue); Wife of George.

McGee, Fred; WW1 Vet.

McGee, George; Husband to Fannie D.

McGee, Jake; 1917-1955

McGee, Justin; WCHS Freshman, 2003

McGee, Marshall; NA-1961, Husband of Lizzie (Thomas).

McGee, Nathan Lane; 1905-1979

McGee, Ryan; WCHS Freshman 2003.

McGhee, Fred

McGinnis, James H.; 1935 BHS Grad.

McGregor, Joseph; husband of Sallie, Egypt Alley in 1942.

McGregor, Sallie; wife of Joseph, Egypt Alley in 1942.

McKinley Albert; 1935 BHS Grad.

McKinley, Betsy

Mckinley, Bill

McKinley, Cindy; Business owner.

McKinley, Clara Elora; 1906-1965, wife of Raymond.

McKinley, Clara Frances (Grayson), wife of Louis McKinley.

McKinley, Deana

McKinley, Ed

McKinley, Gina

McKinley, Henry

McKinley, Jack Sr.; Jun. 10, 1882-Dec. 27, 1981. Husband of Sallie
    Gwynn.

McKinley, Laura; WCHS Freshman, 2001.

McKinley, Louis; 1916-1988, son of Jack & Sally (Patterson), husband of Clara Frances Grayson.

McKinley, Pauline ()

McKinley, Raymond K.

McKinley, Rachel Nicole; WCHS Soph. 2000.

McKinley, Sallie (Gwynn) 'Sally'; Sep. 11, 1888-Feb. 3, 1959. Daughter of George & _____ (__) Gwynn, wife of Jack McKinley.

McKinley, Shireia (Shyna) Reen

McMasey, Will; In 1954 was 62 yrs. old.

McReynolds, Anderson; Mar. 15, 1835-Mar. 4, 1912. Husband of Percilla (Lamb)

McReynolds, Elizabeth; Died Jun. 27, 1911.

McReynolds, Ernest W.; son of Wallace and Rhodie.

McReynolds, Gary; Son of Calvin Sr. & Maggie (Womack).

McReynolds, George Augusta; Died in 1935, WW1 Vet.

McReynolds, Isaac; Blacksmith in 1870. Lived in Irving College.

McReynolds, Jerry Wayne; DD214, Vet. Born; Oct. 1, 1956. Lived at 202 Yankee St. in Apr. 12, 1979.

McReynolds, Johnnie Bell (Vaughn); 1930-1990.

McReynolds, Maggie (Womack); wife of Calvin Sr.

McReynolds, Martin; 1845-Sep. 9, 1914.

McReynolds, Mary; Died Feb. 15, 1919. (26 yrs. old).

McReynolds, Michael; son of Roy Sr. and Maggie (Womack).

McReynolds, Nathaniel; Jan. 11, 1895-May 31, 1956, DD214, WW1, Vet. Original member of American Post 208, lived on 120 Murphy Street in 1945. Son of John & Saphronia (Gardner) McReynolds, husband of Odell Huddleston.

McReynolds, Neisha Patrice: 1998 WCHS Sr.

McReynolds, Odell; (): Raintree Manor Home 2002 (Mrs.) [story]

McReynolds, Patricia; daughter of Roy Sr. and Maggie (Womack).

McReynolds, Percilla (Lamb); Oct. 25, 1844-Aug. 21, 1907. Wife of Anderson McReynolds.

McReynolds, Rhodie (Grayson); Mar. 31, 1910-Mar. 27, 1945. Daughter of Mack & Susie (Ramsey) Grayson, married Wallace McReynolds on 13 Nov. 1927.

McReynolds, Robert Lynn Jr. 'Mac'; Rocket baseball player.

McReynolds, Robert Lynn Sr. 'Bozo'; Son of Jr., 1946 BHS football player Left Half back.

McReynolds, Roy Calvin Jr.; Son of Roy Calvin Sr. & Maggie (Womack).

McReynolds, Roy Calvin Sr.; husband of Maggie (Womack), DD214, Korean Vet. Born; Mar. 6, 1931.

McReynolds, Susie; daughter of Wallace and Rhodie, wife of Hugh Locke.

McReynolds, Tommy; DD214, Vietnam Vet. Son of Wallace and Rhodie. Born; Apr. 28, 1936.

McReynolds, Wallace; Aug. 11, 1897-Feb. 3, 1977. DD214, WW2, Vet. Son of John & Saphronia (Gardner) McReynolds, husband of Rhodie (Grayson).

McReynolds, William 'Will'; 1872-1931.

McReynolds, Willie; WW1, 1918-19, (Pvt), Born in McMinnville on July 7, 1896-Sept. 1974. Son of John & Saphronia (Gardner) McReynolds, husband of Alvilda Brown.

McReynolds, Willie ; DD214, WW2, Veteran, born; May 31, 1925. Lived on 120 Mulbury Street in Jul. 17, 1942.

Mendoza, Paula Aleca (Bonner) 'Squeaky'; (1958-1998) [story]

Mercer, Alex

Mercer, Foster Lee; 1877-1934, husband of Evie (Brown).

Mercer, John; Blacksmith in 1870.

Mercer, Margaret (Cell)

Miller, Bud

Miller, Charles

Miller, Cody; Son of Susan (Martin), WCHS 2001.

Miller, Dydema; Died 1939.

Miller, Finnis; husband of Mary, Laborer, lived on 508 Beersheba St. in 1942.

Miller, Jane (Jack)

Miller, Jim; Farm in Viola.

Miller, Joshua C.

Miller, Larkin

Miller, Laura; lived on Church St. in 1942.

Miller, Lillian; wife of Will T., Carney St. in 1942.

Miller, Mary; wife of Finnis, 508 Beersheba St. in 1942.

Miller, Mattie (Taylor); wife of William Hayes Miller.

Miller, Ollie M.; 1905-1939.

Miller, Pearlee; 1884-1952.

Miller, Sidney

Miller, Velma (Martin)

Miller, William Hayes; Husband of Mattie (Taylor), Korean Vet., Commander of American Legion Post #208.

Miller, Will T.; husband of Lillian, Carney St. in 1942.

Miller, Pearlee (York)

Mills, Mary Francis; 3rd grade BHS 1945.

Mitchell, Della

Mitchell, Marinda (Cummingham)

Mitchell, Jim

Mitchell, Susie

Mitchell, Zaro

Moore, Charles; husband of Ellen, lived on 108 E. Colville St. in 1942.

Moore, Ellen; Widow of Charles, lived on 108 E. Colville St. in 1942.

Moore, John; Helper, lived on 108 E. Colville St. in 1942.

Morford, Flora

Morford, Hoyt; WW1, 1918-19.

Morgan, George; Stone Mason 1900's.

Mount, Ollie; WW2

Mount, Ollie Randolph; Vet. Born; May 6, 1964

Murphy, Mattie Lee (Savage); (1909-1976) daughter of Burks and Belle () Savage [story]

(Na-Nz)

Nance, Johnny; Pastor at Leeburg.

Northcutt, Bettie (Brown); 1885-1905

Northcutt, Buddy; 1946 Bernard H.S. student.

Northcutt, Clara

Northcutt, Charles Augusta Sr.; 1905-1983, husband of Nora (Bates) Laborer, lived on 121 Edgefield St. in 1942.

Northcutt, Charles Augusta Jr. 'Buddy'; Son of Nora (Bates) & Sr.

Northcutt, Charlie

Northcutt, Clara Elizabeth; Wife of Savage.

Northcutt, David H.; DD214, WW2 Vet. Born in Viola on Jan. 26, 1920.

Nortcutt, Ellen (Smartt)

Northcutt, Enoch Hollis; 1899-1954.

Northcutt, Esther (Coonrod) 1900-1954.

Northcutt, Ester (Smartt); Wife of Horace.

Northcutt, Frank; WW1 Vet.

Northcutt, Gene

Northcutt, George

Northcutt, Hollis

Northcutt, Horace; Husband of Ester (Smartt)

Northcutt, Lester; WW1 Vet.

Northcutt, Lillie Maude (Winton); 1902-1959.

Northcutt, Lou Ann (Cope); wid. of Tom in 1942, Congo St.

Northcutt, Nathan

Northcutt, Nora Frances (Bates); (1911-2001) Wife of Charles A. Sr. She died at 89 yrs. of age. [story]

Northcutt, R. D. 'Bud'

Northcutt, Rossie

Northcutt, Roy; Son of Nora & Charles Sr.

Northcutt, Samuel Paul; Viola Clown baseball player. [story]

Northcutt, Sanford

Northcutt, Sarah Ellen; 1927-1943

Northcutt, Thomas 'Little Tom'; DD214, WW2 Vet. Born in Viola on Sept. 12, 1922.

Northcutt, Tom; 1912-1977.

Northcutt, Tom; husband of Lou Ann, 1886-1939.

Northcutt, Tom 'Booker'

Northcutt, Wayman E.; WW1 Vet.

Northcutt, Willie

Nowlin, Charles, Husband of Peggy.

Nowlin, Fred L.; WW2, Vet. DD214, Husband of Lera (Curtis). American Legion member and held the Post #208 together for many years.

Nowlin, Freddy; (single) Daughter of Fred & Lera.

Nowlin, James; Son of Fred & Lera.

Nowlin, Joyce; (single) Daughter of Fred & Lera.

Nowlin, Kelsey; daughter of Randy Nowlin.

Nowlin, Lera (Curtis); Wife of Fred. [story]

Nowlin, Peggy; Wife of Charles.

Nowlin, Phyllis K.; (single) Daughter of Fred & Lera.

Nowlin, Randy; Son of Freddy Nowlin (single).

Nowlin, Robin; Ex-wife of Steve.

Nowlin, Steve Allen.; Retired Army Desert Storm DD214, Vet. Son of Lera and Fred. Husband of Robin.

Nowlin, William Mance 'Bill'; Vietnam Vet. Marines. [story]

(O)

Oakley, Addie (Gardner); wife of Will, 1864-1945.

Oakley, Will; Husband of Addie (Gardner).

Odom, Jonah Jr.

Odom, Linnie Mae; 1st grade BHS 1945.

Odom, Susie French (); died June 1958, W. C. Bolden officiated, buried at Riverside Cemetery.

Officer, Bobby

Officer, Charles E.; Vietnam Vet., Owner of C & M Trucking Firm.

Officer, Evelyn (Womack)

Officer, Georgia F.; wife of Thomas E., lived on 311 S. High St. in 1942.

Officer, Helen (Smith); wife of Phillip Smith, daughter of John Officer.

Officer, Horace; WW1 Vet.

Officer, Jermaine

Officer, Jessie; lived on Maple Street in 1958.

Officer, John; Barber.

Officer, John; husband of Oceania Florence, Salesman, lived on 309 S. High St. in 1942.

Officer, Jon; First Black State Trooper in Warren County. [story]

Officer, Louise; Maid, lived on 309 S. High St. in 1942.

Officer, Oceania Florence; wife of John, 309 S. High St. in 1942.

Officer, Paul H.; DD214, WW2, Vet. Born; Sept. 30, 1922. Lived on 309 S. High Street in 1942.

Officer, Pauline (Patterson); Maid, lived on 407 Beersheba St. in 1942, 1898-1976. Maxwell Patterson's mother.

Officer, Peggy Eugenia 'Tick'

Officer, Robert

Officer, Thomas E.; husband of Georgia F., Waiter at Brown Hotel, lived on 311 S. High St. in 1942.

Officer, Tori

Officer, William J.; 1935 BHS Grad.

Oldom, Sissro; lived on Burton's Lane in 1942.

O'Neal, Nelson

(P)

Page, Ann (Gribble)

Page, Berry

Paige, Lena (Martin); Mother of Mollie (Lusk)

Paige, General; Father of Mollie (Paige) Lusk.

Paige, Hattie : Abe Thomas' Teacher at Cornith School in Viola.

Paige, Minnie M.; Daughter of General and Lena (Martin) Paige.

Paige, or Page, Percilla (Bowman) 1840-1895.

Paige, Thomas D. Jr.; DD214, WW2, Vet.

Parker, Emily

Parker, Jannie; June 1887-Jan. 1916. Daughter of Preston & Emily (Steve

Parker, Nelson Masy; Oct. 1893-Jun. 1914. Son of William Preston & Emily.

Parker, Preston

Patterson, Amos; died Jul. 7, 1920. (16 yrs. old).

Patterson, Annie Ruth (Tubbs); Wife of Maxwell.

Patterson, Arthelia

Patterson, Canzada (Coppinger); Wife of Jones.

Patterson, Ezaw: Brother of Jonah.

Patterson, G. A.; 1858-1900.

Patterson, Hattie (Parker); 1875-1906.

Patterson, Henry; 1869-1939.

Patterson, Isaac

Patterson, Joe; Brother of Jonah.

Patterson, Jonah: (story) DD214, WW2, Vet. Born in McMinnville TN. While on tour in the Navy, his duties were Machine gun operator and cook. [story] Born; Jun. 23, 1923.

Patterson, Jonas; 1800's.

Patterson, Jones; Nov. 15, 1872-Jul. 29, 1952. Son of Isaac & Sarah (Marbury) Patterson, (1) husband of Hattie Parker and (2) Canzada Coppinger.

Patterson, Margaret; Jonah's daughter. Wife of Donald Lusk.

Patterson, Maxwell; Husband of Annie Ruth (Tubbs), Semi-pro baseball player, Rockets. Son of Pauline Officer.

Patterson, Preston

Patterson, Ritter (Mason)

Patterson, Roberta (Carr); Jonah's 1st wife.

Patterson, Sarah (Marbury)

Patterson, Thelma (); Jonah's 3rd wife.

Patterson, Wilma (Higginbotham); Jonah's 2nd wife.

Patton, Brandy Kennetta

Patton, Wade

Peppers, Carl: Vet. 1940's

Peppers, Charles Eugene Sr.; DD214, Korean Vet. Husband of Janie Lois (Martin) [story]. Born; Apr. 26, 1928.

Peppers, Dick

Peppers, George; husband of Rachel.

Peppers, Janie Lois; wife of Charles Eugene Sr. [story]

Peppers, John Robert; 1946 Bernard H.S. student.

Peppers, Lizzie (Gardner)

Peppers, Nannie; wife of Raleigh, 217 East End Drive, in 1942.

Peppers, Rachel; widow of George, 518 Beersheba St. in 1942.

Peppers, Raleigh; 'Rollie' husband of Nannie, WW1 Vet., DD214, 1946 BHS football player. Original Post 208 member, lived on 217 East End Drive in 1945.

Peppers, Robert E.; Artist of oil paintings.

Perkins, Alan; Son of Lane & Brenda.

Perkins, Angie; Daughter of Lane & Brenda.

Perkins, Brenda Jean (Lamoine); wife to Lane.

Perkins, Daim; Son of Lane & Brenda.

Perkins, Damon; Son of Lane & Brenda.

Perkins, Ella Mae (Crisp)

Perkins, Henry Lane; Husband of Brenda Jean (Lamoine).

Perkins, Jalane; Daughter of Lane & Brenda.

Perkins, James; Son of Lane & Brenda.

Perkins, Mandi

Perkins, Michael; Son of Lane & Brenda.

Perkins, Michelle Renee; Daughter of Lane & Brenda.

Perkins, Nathan; WCHS Freshman 2001.

Perkins, Shana; Daughter of Lane & Brenda.

Perkins, Troy

Perry, Laura; widow of Bost, lived on 109 East End Drive, in 1942.

Phillips, Etta; wife of Vernon, Egypt Alley in 1942.

Phillips, Vernon; husband of Etta, Laborer, lived on Egypt Alley in 1942.

Pincheon, Jeffery

Pincheon, Reggie

Pleasant, Albert Eugene; Husband of Suzie (). [story]

Pleasant, Alex; died in 1937.

Pleasant, Betty Louise; daughter of Emerson & Elmer Louise (Carr) Pleasant. [story]

Pleasant, Bonnie

Pleasant, Charles

Pleasant, Dick; died 1908, 70 yrs. old.

Pleasant, L. Elmer; Member of Pleasant Hill PTA in 1956.

Pleasant, Jonah; 1939 32 yrs. old.

Pleasant, Kayla; WCHS Soph. 2001.

Pleasant, Kelly Denise; daughter of William Buster & Ruby Nell (Wade) Pleasant. [story]

Pleasant, Kinette; WCHS Jr. 2001.

Pleasant, Malvina (___); 1872-1932.

Pleasant, Mary Whitsker (Maxwell)

Pleasant, Melvina; 1872-1932.

Pleasant, Prince Albert; 1906-1988.

Pleasant, Sadie; 1908-1928 (single).

Pleasant, Shantay; WCHS Jr. 2001.

Pleasant, Suzie; (1901-2003), she wore a cowboy outfit and carried a guitar at all times.

Pleasant, Ruby Nell (Wade); (1939-1994) [story]

Pleasant, Vina (Gribble)

Pleasant, William Emerson; 1915-1987.

Prater, Benjamin; husband of Sinda, WW1 Vet., died in 1936.

Prater, Sinda, widow of Benjamin, lived on 115 Edgefield St. in 1942.

Price, Herman Lee Jr.

Price, Lillian

Purden, Ernest; husband of Elizabeth, Restaurant, lived on 130 Murphy St. in 1942.

Purden, Elizabeth; wife of Ernest, 130 Murphy St. in 1942.

(Q)

Quinn, Mary Alice; 2nd grade Bernard H.S. in 1945. Married J. L. Reedy.

Quinn, Allean

Quinn, Fanny

Quinn, Huse

Quinn, Jerry Wayne; DD214, Vietnam Vet. Born; Feb. 24, 1955. Lived on 111 Congo St. in 1974.

Quinn, Lawson

Quinn, Patty

(Rai-Ran)

Rainer, Daniel

Rains, Sonja

Ramsey, Agness (Ramsey); 1968 75 yrs. old.

Ramsey, Alex W. 'Tick'; DD214,Vet. Young Men United organizer. Son of Joe and Mary (Savage).

Ramsey, Alfred Donald; Korean Vet. Son of Edd W. and Annie Mae.

Ramsey, Allie; wife of Ivy Joe, Maid, lived on 115 Warren St. in 1942.

Ramsey, Alpha

Ramsey, Annie B.; wife of Morton, 413 Beersheba St. in 1942,

Ramsey, Annie Mae (Stokes); 1900-May 4, 1993, daughter of William & Phronie (Gardner) Ramsey.

Ramsey, Annie Ruth; 'Corky' 1946 BHS student.

Ramsey, Barber 'Slick'; 1890, Baseball player.

Ramsey, Bertina

Ramsey, Bessie Louise (Blue); Cook, 321 S. High St. in 1942[story]

Ramsey, Betty Jean (Locke); husband of Kenneth Ramsey. [story]

Ramsey, Bill; Retired A. F. Vet. Moved back to McMinnville in 2011.

Ramsey, Billy

Ramsey, Billy Howard; 3rd grade BHS 1945.

Ramsey, Brown; wife of Tommie L., 108 Etter St. in 1942.

Ramsey, Charles Wesley; 1862-1943.

Ramsey, Clarence Spite; WW1, Vet.

Ramsey, Clyde; DD214, WW2, Vet. Born; Dec. 15, 1924. Lived on 115 East End Drive in 1934.

Ramsey, Carl William; Navy Veteran. Son of Sarah Jean & Clyde.

Ramsey, Charles Wesley; 1862-1943.

Ramsey, Curtis Ledale; 3rd grade BHS 1945.

Ramsey, Darren Alan; Son of Jimmy Ramsey

Ramsey, David R.; lived on 534 Beersheba St. in 1942, WW2 Vet.

Ramsey, Doris; husband of Sallie M., Body man at Up Church Repair Shop, lived on Yankeetown St. in 1942.

Ramsey, Dorothy E.

Ramsey, Dorothy Mae; 3rd grade Bernard H.S. in 1945.

Ramsey, Douglas; Vet. Air Force, Son of Sarah Jean & Clyde Ramsey.

Ramsey, Edd W.; Husband of Annie Mae (Stokes)

Ramsey, Edward Lee; 3rd grade BHS 1945.

Ramsey, Elizabeth; widow of William, lived on 109 Etter St. in1942.

Ramsey, Ernest; DD214, Vet. Born; Mar. 30 in McMinnville.

Ramsey, Fannie; lived on 326 S. High St in 1942.

Ramsey, Florine; 'Sis' 1946 BHS student 7th grade.

Ramsey, Francis

Ramsey, Franklin; 1946 BHS 6th grade student.

Ramsey, Frederick D.; son of Edd W. and Annie Mae (Stokes) Ramsey.

Ramsey, Gail Lois (Battles); wife of Nelson O. Ramsey.

Ramsey, George

Ramsey, Ginny Frances (Savage); Wife of Joe Ramsey.

Ramsey, Helen; 4th grade BHS 1945.

Ramsey, Horace Nelson; 1876-1955.

Ramsey, Herbert; (1911-1994) husband of Roberta (Winton). [story]

Ramsey, Herbert; husband of Carrie V., Porter at Exchange Furniture Co., lived on 418 Beersheba St. in 1942.

Ramsey, Hubert; 1956-1982.

Ramsey, Ida M.; Cook, lived on 116 Murphy St. in 1942.

Ramsey, Ivy Joe; husband of Allie, Cook, at C & O Sandwich Shop, lived on 115 East End Drive in 1942, Father of Joe Edward Ramsey.

Ramsey, James 'Blue'; lived on Egypt Alley in 1942.

Ramsey, James Clarence; DD214, Korean War Vet.1946 BHS football Right End. Born; Dec. 9, 1930.

Ramsey, James F. 'Boomer'; 2012

Ramsey, James Louis; Jan. 13, 1939-Feb. 13, 2011. DD214, Vet. Retired from Nat. Guard, Husband of Peggy (Kennerly). Born; Jan. 13, 1939.

Ramsey, James Monroe. C.; DD214, WW2 Vet. Born; Apr. 17, 1910. husband of Bessie, Driver, lived on 113 East End Drive in 1942.

Ramsey, James Michael Jr.; Son of James, also a store owner, Wife, Linda.

Ramsey, James Michael Sr.; Korean Vet. Store owner (Eastern Star)

Ramsey, James Russell Jr.

Ramsey, James Russell Sr.; Semi-Pro Baseball player 'Rockets', member of East End Church of Christ. [story]

Ramsey, James III: 2000 WCHS Sr., Army Vet. in 2002.

Ramsey, James Stroke; 1902-1978.

Ramsey, Jane (Smartt)

Ramsey, Jennie F. (Smartt)

Ramsey, Jiggs; husband of Vinetta.

Ramsey, Jimmie

Ramsey, Jimmy; Brother of Alfred Ramsey.

Ramsey, Joe Edward; Porter at Sedberry Hotel, [story]

Ramsey, Joe Edward Chiz Sr. [story]

Ramsey, Joe Jr.

Ramsey, Joe Thomas; DD214, WW2, Vet. Born; Aug. 11, 1923. Lived on 115 E. Main Street in 1942.

Ramsey, Johnnie Blevens

Ramsey, Joseph C. Jr.; lived on 326 S. High St. in 1942, Vet. 1912-2001.

Ramsey, Karl William; Vietnam Vet., Navy.

Ramsey, Kathrine

Ramsey, Laura (Miller)

Ramsey, Laura M. (Webb); (1911-1999) wife of William 'Son' Ramsey. 1946 BHS 7th grade student [story]

Ramsey, Leonard Grace (Hammond)

Ramsey, Leroy; Korean Vet. 1946 BHS student, the Bernard High School Gym was named after him.

Ramsey, Lewis; 4th grade BHS 1945.

Ramsey, Linda(); Wife of Michael, Mother of Dwayne and Chelsea.

Ramsey, Lizzie; 1940's.

Ramsey, Louie

Ramsey, Lucy Dean (Ramsey); (Dec. 31, 1916-Aug. 4, 1970), Daughter of Will & Saphronia (Gardner) Ramsey. Maid, lived on Cedar St. in 1942, 'Punch.'

Ramsey, Morton; husband of Annie B., 413 Beersheba St. in 1942.

Ramsey, M. K.

Ramsey, Marsha (Marshbanks); daughter of Louis.

Ramsey, Martha ()

Ramsey, Mary; 2nd grade BHS 1945.

Ramsey, Mary C.

Ramsey, Mary Elizabeth: (Savage): Joe Edward's wife. Mother of Alex and Nelson.

Ramsey, Mary Francis

Ramsey, Mary Roberta (Winton); 1929-1973.

Ramsey, Matthew; WCHS Freshman 2001.

Ramsey, Michael; Husband of Linda () Song Leader at East End Drive Church of Christ, Owner of several Clothes business.

Ramsey, Mya: 2000 WCHS Soph.

Ramsey, Nancy Louise

Ramsey, Nelson O.; Husband of Gail () Ramsey. [story]

Ramsey, Nick; WCHS Soph. 2001.

Ramsey, Nora Francis: 'Polly' Died in Jan. 2002, Sister to Willa B. Tillman (Ramsey), 1946 BHS 6th grade student.

Ramsey, Oceania ()

Ramsey, Paul Herbert; DD214, Vet. Born; Oct. 23, 1949. Lived on 115 Cope St. in 1972.

Ramsey, Paul Lawrence; 1946 BHS 5th grade student.

Ramsey, Peggy

Ramsey, Perline; 2012

Ramsey, Phronie (Sophrona)? (Gardner); May 11, 1876-Dec. 22, 1938. Daughter of Matt & Mary (___) Gardner, wife of (1) John McReynolds, Married Jan. 21, 1893. (2) Bill Ramsey, married Sep. 4, 1905.

Ramsey, Polly (Hancock)

Ramsey, Queen (Winton)

Ramsey, Randolph; Vet. 1946 BHS football player Full back, Semi-Pro baseball player in the 1940's.

Ramsey, Rita Marie; Daughter of Clyde & Sarah, Vice president of Union Planters, Bank at Walmart, Woman of the Year by The Jaycees 2003.

Ramsey, Robert; Husband of Roberta (Winton).

Ramsey, Roberta (Winton); Wife of Robert Ramsey.

Ramsey, Sallie (King); wife of Doris, Yankeetown St. in 1942.

Ramsey, Sarah E.; daughter of Fannie Smith. [story]

Ramsey, Shirley Jean (Smith); 1st grade BHS 1945.

Ramsey, Son; Husband of Laura (Webb).

Ramsey, Tommie L.; widow of Brown, lived on 108 Etter St. in 1942.

Ramsey, Torrell Andre: Rita Ramsey's son, 2000 WCHS Sr.

Ramsey, Tyler; Son of Nelson & Vickie ().

Ramsey, Vermont; BHS football team 1959.

Ramsey, Vickie Lynn: Daughter of Sarah Jean & Clyde Ramsey.

Ramsey, Vinetta; widow of Jiggs, Housekeeper, 534 Beersheba St. in 1942.

Ramsey, Virginia; 'Jinny' 1946 BHS student, Cook, lived on 418 E. Main St. in 1942.

Ramsey, William; husband of Elizabeth.

Ramsey, William 'Bill'; Son of Edd W. & Annie Mae. Retired Vet. Air Force Captain.

Ramsey, William 'Bill Tate'; 1862-1953, husband of Sophrona, 1905, Porter at McMinnville Hardware & Furniture Co., lived on 26 Murphy St. in1942.

Ramsey, William 'Son'; WW2 Vet., 1908-1978. Original member of Post 208, lived on 120 Edgefield Street in 1945. Later in Bolden Green. Husband of Laura (Webb).

Ramsey, Willie Bell; 4th grade BHS 1945.

Ramsey, Willie P.; 1902-1925.

Ramsey, Willie; lived on 120 Edgefield in 1942.

Ramsey, Willis

Randals, Stephen

(Re-Rz)

Redman, Thurman

Reedy, Barry

Reedy, Bill

Reedy, George

Reddy, J. L. Sr.; (1935-2001) Husband of Mary Alice (Quinn). [story]

Reedy, J. L. Jr. 'JR'; Son of J. L. & Mary Alice (Quinn).

Reedy, Jamie; Son of J. L. & Mary Alice (Quinn).

Reedy, Jasmine; Daughter of Kandice

Reedy, Kandice; Daughter of J. L. & Mary Alice (Quinn).

Reedy, Mary Alice (Quinn); Wife of J. L. Reedy.

Reddy, Mary Ann

Reedy, Jerry

Reedy, Omar

Reedy, Ronnie Ronafal; Son of J. L. & Mary Alice (Quinn).

Reedy, Roxie 'Roxanne'; Daughter of J. L. & Mary Alice (Quinn).

Reedy, Terry Allen; Vet. Son of J. L. & Mary Alice (Quinn).

Reedy, Treetar; Daughter of J. L. & Mary Alice (Quinn).

Reedy, Wileen Frenada; Daughter of J. L. & Mary Alice (Quinn).

Reynolds, Brittany; WCHS Freshman, 2001.

Rhodes, Edna; wife of James R., Educator of the 3rd & 4th grades, B H S, lived on 106 East End Drive in 1942.

Rhodes, James

Rhodes, James R.; husband of Edna, Porter at The First Nat. Bank, lived on 106 E. End Drive in 1942, WW2, Vet., Navy, 1935 BHS Grad.

Rice, Henry; ?-1937 Veteran.

Richardson, Ada; widow of Henry, lived on Congo St. in 1942.

Richardson, Henry; husband of Ada.

Richie, William; Porter for N. C. & St. Louis Rail Road in 1942.

Riddle, Susej; 2003 WCHS Soph. lived in Bolden Green.

Ridley, Napoleon; 2nd grade BHS 1945.

Rivers, Ada' wife of Ferman, E. End Drive in 1942.

Rivers, Fermon; husband of Ada, Janitor of Church of Christ on East Main St. in 1942, WW2 Vet., 1935 BHS Grad.

Roach, Bill

Roach, Binnie

Roberson, Candace; WCHS Freshman 2001.

Roberson, Della Ludean

Roberta, Joan; 3rd grade BHS 1945.

Roberts, Gene Allen; 1946 BHS student.

Roberts, Jeffery; Son of 'Kind' Cowan.

Roberts, Joan Ann

Roberts, Cowan; Resturant owner in downtown McMinnville in the 1960's and 70's.

Roberts, Lois Novella; 'Babe' 1946 BHS student.

Roberts, May; lived on Burton's Lane in 1942.

Roberts, Rebecca; Daughter of Sadie () Roberts, YMU Treasurer.

Roberts, Sadie Louise; (single) [story]

Roberts, Scipio 'Jip'; Furniture Repairer, lived on 116 Edgefield St. in 1942.

Roberts, Steve; Son of Cowan.

Robertson, Annette (Williams); Educator at Bobby Ray School, Daughter of J. C. & Jeannette (Strode). [story]

Robertson, April; Daughter of Annette & Randall. Mother of Star.

Robertson, Donald; 1937-Jan. 27, 1994. Son of Lee & Lillie (Patterson) Robertson.

Robertson, Marie (Handcock); Wife of Robert.

Robertson, Martha

Robertson, Matthew; Son of Annette & Randall.

Robertson, Randall; Husband of Annette (Williams).

Robertson, Robert; retired Public Service Worker for 26 yrs. Husband of Marie Hancock.

Robinson, Bettie; wife of Peter, 532 Beersheba St. in 1942.

Robinson, Mattie (Smith); (1890-1958) [story]

Robinson, Peter; husband of Bettie, lived on 532 Beersheba St. in 1942.

Robinson, Sir John; Master Barber, owner of 'Ahead of Times' Shop on Main Street in McMinnville 1990's-2003.

Roderts, Jeffery

Rouse, Annie; widow of Lessie, 501 Beersheba St. in 1942.

Rouse, Lessie; husband of Annie.

Rowan, Bobby; Sister of Carl T. Lives in Sac. Ca. 2003. Was in the 4th grade at Bernard H.S. 1945.

Rowan, Carl Thomas; Korean Vet. [story]

Rowan, Carrie; lived on Egypt Alley in 1942.

Rowan, Charles Edward 'Ched'; Korean Vet., 1946 BHS football, Left Tackle. [story]

Rowan, Edward; Barber.

Rowan, Edward D.; husband of Sarah, Janitor at BHS, lived on 118 E. End Drive in 1942.

Rowan, Ella Mae; 1946 BHS student.

Rowan, Flora; lived on 524 Beersheba St. in 1942.

Rowan, James; (1880-1957), lived on 108 E. Colville St. in 1942. [story]

Rowan, Johnnie (Bradford); Wife of William.

Rowan, Leroy; DD214, Korean War Vet. 1946 BHS student. Lived on 407 E. Main St. in 1952. Born; Jan. 19, 1932.

Rowan, Middleton; worked in the Mills for many years during 1890.

Rowan, Peter; Stone Mason early 1900's.

Rowan, Robert H.; DD214, WW2 Vet. Lived on 108 E. Colville St. in 1942.

Rowan, Sadie; lived in Bolden Green in the 1950's.

Rowan, Sarah; wife of Edward D., 118 E. End Drive in 1942.

Rowan, Sue Tigg (Kell); she lived in Columbia, Tenn. The first cousin to Carl T. Rowan, wife of Dr. Hawthorne. [Story]

Rowan, Thomas Davis; WW1 Vet. Buried in San Antonio, Tx.

Rowan, William M.; DD214, WW1 Vet., Husband of Johnnie (Bradford). Age; 24 in 1918. Original member of Post 208, lived on Rural Route 6 in 1945.

Rucker, Hattie (Wisher)

Rucker, Henry

Rust, William; Shoemaker (Cobbler) in the early 1900's.

Rutledge, Ardella

Rutledge, Billy Sr.; Tn. Dept. of Transportation Supervisor.

Rutledge, Billy Jr.; Pro football player, Arena Football with the Nashville 'Kats' in the 1990's.

Rutledge, Bobby

Rutledge, Christy Ann: 2000 WCHS Sr.

Rutledge, Frank

Rutledge, Jeffrey

Rutledge, Jerry

Rutledge, Kendall; Son of Billy Jr. WCHS Jr. in 2012. Played Football and Basketball.

Rutledge, Larry

Rutledge, Ollie Mai (Wilkerson)
Rutledge, Pearlie (Mount)
Rutledge, Phyllis
Rutledge, Robert B.; (1928-1973).
Rutledge, Ruth C. (Southern); 1929-NA
Rutledge, Suzie
Rutledge, Zada Mae
Ryan, Louis, husband of Maggie.
Ryan, Maggie; widow of Louis, lived on Edgefield St. in 1942.
Ryan, Robert
Ryan, Johnnie; wife of Thomas, lived on Cotter Row in 1942.
Ryan, Thomas; husband of Johnnie, Laborer, lived on Cotter Row in 1942.

(Sa-Si)

Safely, Earl; 108 East End Drive in 1942.

Sanders, Amanda

Sanders, Courtney Cherisse

Sanders, Jimmie

Sanders, Joseph

Sanders, Kenny Denard: 1998 WCHS Sr., 2002 student at TSU, son of Mary Sanders, Mary (Biles); Community Leader, accountant at McMinnville school system.

Sandridge, Hula

Savage, Agnes (Page or Paige)

Savage, Alice; widow of Sam, Maid at Brown Hotel, lived on Congo St. in 1942.

Savage, Alice; wife of Robert, 108 E. End Drive in 1942.

Savage, America (Finger); (1855-1914), wife of Wash Savage.

Savage, Alonzo; husband of Mary E., Clerk at Yager Grocery, lived on Congo St. in 1942.

Savage, Arthur; son of James & Jennie (Edge).

Savage, Beatrice (Grayson); [story]

Savage, Belle (Locke); wife of Hillis Sr., lived on Edgefield in 1942, mother of Marcellus. Later lived in Bolden Green community.

Savage, Bellie (Morford)

Savage, Bill; husband of Jennie (Edge) Savage

Savage, Burks A.; lived on African Street in 1942.

Savage, Clara Elizabeth (Northcutt); (Feb. 1, 1930-Aug. 1956), [story]

Savage, Clara Lee (Bean); wife of Haskell Savage. [story]

Savage, Cornelius; husband of May, lived on 405 Beersheba St. in 1942.

Savage, Dallas 'Squirrel'; Korean Vet. DD214. Born: Feb. 19, 1930. 1946 BHS 5th grade student. Son of James & Jennie. Lived on 108 Edgefield Street in 1950.

Savage, David

Savage, Edward; 1st grade Bernard H.S. in 1945.

Savage, Emerson; WW2 Vet. DD214. Lived on 102 Congo Street in 1946. Born; Jan. 23 1918.

Savage, Emmett

Savage, Eva (Brown); Owner of Hair Dresser business, Wife of Fred Savage.

Savage, Eva (Smith); 2nd of wife of James.

Savage, Frances; lived on 108 Edgefield St. in 1942.

Savage, Fred 'Duck'; Husband of Eva (Brown).

Savage, Fred Donald; Veteran, 3rd grade BHS 1945.

Savage, Gary

Savage, George; WW1 Veteran.

Savage, Glen

Savage, Haskell; husband of Clara Lee, lived on 506 Beersheba St. in 1942, WW2, Vet. DD214, Original member of Post 208 in 1945.

Savage, Hattielene or Hattie Lee

Savage, Henry B.; DD214, WW2, Vet. Born; May 7, 1915.

Savage, Hillis; Son of James & Jennie (Edge)

Savage, Hillis Jr.; (Jun. 23, 1918-2000), Bellman at Brown Hotel in 1942, DD214, WW2 Vet. Lived on 108 Edgefield St. in 1942. Son of Hillis Sr. & Belle (Locke) [story].

Savage, Hillis Sr.; husband of Belle (Locke), Concrete Worker for W. C. Marble & Granite Works, lived on Edgefield in 1942.

Savage, James E.; lived on 405 Beersheba St. in 1942.

Savage, James; son of Bill and Jennie (Edge) 80 years old, died in 1956. [story]

Savage, Jennie (Edge); wife of Bill Savage.

Savage, Lucian; WW1 Veteran.

Savage, Marcellus; Husband of Mary Lou (Martin). 3rd grade BHS 1945. [story]

Savage, Mareda E.; lived on 405 Beersheba St. in 1942.

Savage, Marier

Savage, Mary Arden; 4th grade BHS 1945.

Savage, Mary E.; wife of Alonzo, lived on Congo Street in 1942.

Savage, Mary Lou (Martin); Wife of Marcellus.

Savage, May; wife of Cornelius, 405 Beersheba St. in 1942.

Savage, Robert; husband of Alice, lived on 108 E. End Drive in 1942.

Savage, Sam; husband of Alice.

Savage, Sherman, lived on Nashville RR1 in 1942.

Savage, Sondra L.; [story] Author of 'Words of the Heart' Daughter of Eva.

Savage, Thomas; lived on Nashville Rural Route 1 in 1942.

Savage, Vonso; lived on Yankeetown St. on the North side of McMinnville. [story]

Savage, Walter Lee; son of James & Eva (Smith) Savage.

Savage, Wash; Husband of America (Finger) married in 1806.

Savage, Wesley Lee; Nov. 16, 1908-1979, DD214, WW2, Vet.

Savage, William; Caretaker for Cowan Oldham, lived on Nashville RR1 in 1942.

Scott, Alex; Helper for Lewis & Gilley, Deaf and Dumb (disable), lived on Egypt Alley in 1942.

Scott, Antonia 'Tony'; Army Veteran. [story]

Scott, Author Jr.; 2nd grade Bernard H.S. 1945.

Scott, Eddie

Scott, Eugene M. Rev.; WW2 Vet., Pastor in Brown Town, Golf Pro. [story]

Scott, George Edward; BHS Sr. 1959, [story]

Scott, Grady Frank; 1946 BHS 5th grade student.

Scott, Hester (Mount); Wife of Eugene M.

Scott, Irby; DD214, WW2, Vet. Husband of Maude (Martin), lived on 327 S. High St. in 1942. Born; Sept. 11, 1918.

Scott, Jim; husband of Mary.

Scott, Mary; widow of Jim, lived on Egypt Alley in 1942.

Scott, Mary E., lived on Egypt Alley in 1942.

Scott, Maude Marie (Martin); Wife of Irby. [story]

Scott, Minnie Lee; lived on Egypt Alley in 1942.

Scott, Nellie; housekeeper at High's Funeral Home.

Settles, Ada, or Ida L. (); wife of Booker, lived on 305 S. High St. in 1942, Sarah Jean Ramsey's grandmother.

Settles, Akeem

Settles, Anthony

Settles, Betty (Walling); wife of Hackett, lived on 123 Edgefield St. in 1942.

Settles, Booker; husband of Ida L., Helper for Upchurch Repair Shop, lived on 305 S. High St. in 1942.

Settles, Charles Hackett 'Hack'; husband of Betty (Walling)

Settles, Charles Edward; 1937-1957, son of Hackett & Betty (Walling) 3rd grade BHS 1945. [story]

Settles, Charlie

Settles, Delecia Cauley

Settles, Doris

Settles, Dorothy; 1946 BHS 5th grade student.

Settles, Hackett; husband of Bettie, lived on 123 Edgefield in 1942.

Settles, Jaleasa

Settles, Jamaal

Settles, James

Settles, Jimmy Frank; 5th grade BHS 1945.

Settles, Jimmie; son of Hackett & Betty (Walling)

Settles, Joe; son of Hackett & Betty (Walling)

Settles, Kenneth

Settles, LaDonna

Settles, Lena

Settles, Leonard

Settles, Malika

Settles, Myrtle (Duncan)

Settles, Reese; Maid for Frank Davenport, lived on Egypt Alley in 1942, (1905-1989), died at the age 83.

Settles, Robert

Settles, Rollie; son of Hackett & Betty (Walling), 1st Blacks to attend Voc-Tech Wood Work Class and Graduated May 30, 1963.

Settles, Vera; Wife of Zollie. [story]

Settles, Zollie; son of Hackett & Betty (Walling), Husband of Vera. 1st Blacks to attend Voc-Tech Wood Work class and Graduated May 30, 1963.

Shannon, John; member of East End Drive Church of Christ 2012.

Shell, Clarence; DD214, WW2, Vet. Born; Jun. 6, 1909.

Shelton, Herman; WW2 Veteran DD214. Born: April 15, 1920.

Shelton, Sallie L.; 1946, 44 yrs. of age.

Shelton, Virgina (Blue)

Shockley, Adge (Josephine); Laborer, lived on 104 Edgefield St. in 1942.

Shockley, Bertha (Martin); Wife of Herman.

Shockley, Bobby

Shockley, Carl

Shockley, Casto; 1888-1976.

Shockley, Charles; 1940's Semi-Pro baseball player. 1st grade BHS 1945.

Shockley, Clinton Dewitt; 1st grade BHS 1945.

Shockley, D.C.; 1934-1954.

Shockley, Dorothy Lee (Crockett)

Shockley, Edward; husband of Enzy, lived on Egypt Alley in 1942.

Shockley, Enzy; lived on Egypt Alley in 1942.

Shockley, Ethel; Dish Washer at Brown Hotel Café, lived on 422 Beersheba St. in 1942.

Shockley, Fred; husband of Sarah B., Laborer, lived on 104 Edgefield St. in 1942.

Shockley, Harvey Lee; 1938-1954.

Shockley, Henrietta

Shockley, Herman L.; DD214, WW2 Vet. Born; Jul. 27, 1906. Husband of Bertha (Martin), 1946 BHS 5th grade student.

Shockley, Herman Lee; Vet. DD214, Born: Jan. 17, 1935. Lived on 109 Bernard School Drive in 1954.

Shockley, Horace Edwin; Vet. DD214, 1st grade BHS 1945. Born; Mar. 21, 1937. Lived on 109 Bernard School Drive in 1956.

Shockley, Howard; 1st grade BHS 1945.

Shockley, Howard F.; 1935-1977.

Shockley, Joe; 1st grade Bernard H.S. in 1945.

Shockley, Lillian; wife of Neil, lived on 114 Murphy St. in 1942.

Shockley, Margie; 1946 BHS 6th grade student.

Shockley, Marion

Shockley, Mattie (Brewington)

Shockley, May; 1906-1951.

Shockley, Minnie (Herd)

Shockley, Neil; husband of Lillian, Porter, lived on 114 Murphy St. in 1942.

Shockley, Sarah B.; wife of Fred L., lived on 104 Edgefield St. in 1942.

Shockley, Shirley; (male) WW2, Officer Veteran.

Shockley, Thurman; 1969 member of Clark Church.

Short, Jimmy

Short, Sally J.; died in 1982.

Simpson, Bettye 'Grandma'; Owner of Children's Daycare Center.

Simpson, Chris; Grandson of Bettye.

Simpson, Kayla

Simpson, Lakesha; WCHS JR 2001, Grand daughter of Bettye.

Simpson, Melissa; Warren Co. H.S. Junior 2001.

Simpson, Rafael; Grandson of Bettye.

Sims, Ernie; widow of Joseph, Maid, lived on 118 Edgefield St. In 1942.

Sims, Josie (Hunter)

Sims, Sam C.

Sims, Sam Jr.

Sisk, Ozell; Maid; lived on 418 Beersheba St. in 1942.

(Sma-Smi)

Smartt, Ben

Smartt, Beulah; widow of Polk, lived on 502 Beersheba St. in 1942.

Smartt, Dianah (Pleasant)

Smartt, Doley; 1916, 83 yrs. old.

Smart, Estelle

Smartt, Fern

Smartt, George; Blacksmith in 1870.

Smartt, George Wesley; 1876-1934.

Smartt, Huston; 1888, 18, years old.

Smartt, Izell

Smartt, Jim; 1885-1914.

Smartt, Johnson

Smartt, Kate Lee; 1886-1961.

Smartt, Kate Y.

Smartt, Laura (Wilson)

Smartt, Lethy

Smartt, Margie Ann; 'Tootie,' lived on 502 Beersheba St. in 1942, 1946 BHS student 7th grade. Died Jan. 2012. Taught at Tenn. State University. Lived in Ft. Lauderdale, Fl.

Smartt, Maria (Smartt)

Smartt, Polk; husband of Beulah, lived on 502 Beersheba St. in 1942.

Smartt, Rhonda (Locke)

Smartt, S. V.

Smartt, Sindie B.; 1879-1888.

Smartt, Thola; Maid, lived on 502 Beersheba St. In 1942.

Smartt, Vance; lived on 502 Beersheba St. In 1942.

Smartt, Velma

Smartt, William Mack; 1840-1930.

Smith, Ada; widow of Frank, lived on 109 Edgefield St. in 1942.

Smith, Ann; 1st grade BHS 1945.

Smith, Arthur Jr.; son of W. F. & Era Tennie (Locke), lived on Church St. in 1942.

Smith, Bernice Waldman

Smith, Beverly; [story]

Smith, Bill

Smith, Billie; WW2, Vet. DD214, Born: Feb. 26, 1922. [story]

Smith, Billy; Son of Ruby & Phillip.

Smith, Calvin; Owner of Grass cutting business, Y.M.U. member.

Smith, Charles Davis

Smith, Clark Davis; 1946 BHS 5th grade student.

Smith, Danny Jr.; Son of Dan & Lucile (Carr)

Smith, Danny Sr.; 'Rocket' baseball player, Husband of Lucile (Carr).

Smith, Edward; husband of Mary A.

Smith, Era Tennie (Locke); 71 yrs. wife of W. F. Locke, (1884-1955). [story]

Smith Fannie M. (single); lived on 109 Edgefield St. in 1942, Sarah Jean Ramsey's Mother.

Smith, Floyd 'Knuck'; Son of 'Sugar Bee' & Frank Sr.

Smith, Frank; Husband of Ada.

Smith, Frank Jr.; DD214, WW2 Vet. Born; Mar. 15, 1910. Husband of 'Sugar Bee,' Lived on 109 Edgefield St. in 1942.

Smith, Frank; Husband of Sally Jane (Biles). Vietnam, Desert Storm, DD214,Vet., Born; Mar. 19, 1948. Lived on Route # 3 in 1968.

Smith, Georgia Lucile; 4th grade BHS 1945.

Smith, Georgie Wesley; 1876-1934.

Smith, Glenda J. (Martin)

Smith, Gwendolyn (Martin)

Smith, Hattie Belle (Tucker); (1908-1997) [story]

Smith, Helen (Woodard); 2nd wife of Willie 'Bama'

Smith, J. L. James Lester; Vet. DD214. Navy, Born; Mar. 28, 1942.

Smith, Jack; husband of Leathey.

Smith, James Edward Jr. 'Pooky'

Smith, Joan; 1946 BHS 6th grade student.

Smith, Katheline

Smith, Kenneth; Son of 'Sugar Bee' & Frank Sr.

Smith, Kenny; Son of Frank Jr. & Sally Jane (Biles).

Smith, Kevin

Smith, Lafayette; son of W. F. & Era (Locke)

Smith, Leathey; widow of Jack, lived on 107 E. Colville St. in 1942.

Smith, Lewis; 4th grade BHS 1945.

Smith, Lillie Ann

Smith, Linus; lived on Church St. in 1942.

Smith, Lloyd Dr.; son of W. F. & Era (Locke)

Smith, Lorena; widow of William, lived on Church St. in 1942.

Smith, Louis

Smith, Lucile (Carr); Wife of Danny Sr.

Smith, Maggie (Madison)

Smith, Mary A.; widow of Edward, Cook at Sedberry Hotel, lived on 114 Etter St. in 1942.

Smith, Nita

Smith, Ora; widow of Samuel, lived on 504 Beersheba St. in 1942.

Smith, Paul

Smith, Phillip; husband of Ruby, DD214, WW1 Vet. Lived on 217 East End Drive in 1945.

Smith, Phillip Jr.; Korean Vet. DD214. 'Buddy' 1946 BHS 6th grade student. Born: Dec. 22, 1938. Lived on 125 E. End Drive in 1953. Pastor of East End Drive Church of Christ.

Smith, Roberta; 1946 BHS 6th grade student.

Smith, Ruby; wife of Phillip Sr., lived on 217 E. End Drive St. in 1942.

Smith, Sally Jane (Biles); Wife of Frank Jr.

Smith, Samuel; husband of Ora.

Smith, Sarah Jean

Smith, Sharon Denise (Pleasant)

Smith, 'Sugar Bee'; Wife of Frank Sr.

Smith, Suzie Locke (McReynolds); Lives in the Bolden Green Community.

Smith, Theodose

Smith, Theresa

Smith, W. F.; Husband of Era, he died on Feb. 15, 1954.

Smith, William; husband of Lorena.

Smith, Willie 'Bama'; Husband of Helen (Woodard). [story]

(So-Sz)

Snelling, Hattie; wife of Tom, 119 Edgefield in 1942.

Snelling, Tom; husband of Hattie, lived on 119 Edgefield St. in 1942.

Solomon, Brandon; Warren Co. H.S. 2001 Freshman.

Solomon, Dorothy

Solomon, Edward; son of Sherman & Sadie (Starkey)

Solomon, Elzie; son of Sherman William Solomon.

Solomon, Floyd; WW1 Veteran.

Solomon, Harold; Husband of Magnolia, son of Sherman Sr.

Solomon, Ida (Page or Paige)

Solomon, Jake; Korean Vet, American Legion Sgt. Post 208.

Solomon, Joe

Solomon, Jolene; Daughter of Sherman & Sadie (Starkey)

Solomon, Katherine; Daughter of Molly Mary, 1943-2002 [story].

Solomon, Magnolia (Grayson); Wife of Harold Solomon.

Solomon, Mary Katherine: (1943-2002) Daughter of Sherman & Sadie (Starkey). [story]

Solomon, Molly (Mitchell); Wife of Jake, Mother of Elzie.

Solomon, Richard E.; DD214, WW2 Vet. Born; Aug. 4, 1912.

Solomon, Rosie

Solomon, Roy; Son of Sherman & Sadie (Starkey)

Solomon, Sadie (Starkey); wife of Sherman

Solomon, Sherman William Jr.

Solomon, Sherman William; son of Jake & Molly (Mitchell), husband of Sadie, died in April 2001 at 90 yrs. old. [story]

Solomon, Shirley

Solomon, Sylvia

Solomon, Troy; son of Sherman William Solomon Sr.

Southern, Matthew

Southern, Sarah (Miller); 1849-1930.

Speaks, Joseph; Pastor of First Baptist Church, lived on African St, in 1942.

Spencer, Agnes; wife of Thomas T. in 1942.

Spencer, Annie Carol

Spencer, Delores A.

Spencer, Eunous Dillon; WW2 Veteran DD214. 1946 BHS football Quarter back. Born: Jan. 7, 1928.

Spencer, Eunous Dillon; DD214, WW2 Vet. Navy, lived on 530 East Main St. in 1946.

Spencer, Everett Lee; DD214, WW2 Vet. Born; Aug. 22, 1926. Lived on 530 East Main St. in 1944.

Spencer, Furmon Reams; husband of Bessie, Porter at Brown Hotel, lived on 106 East End Drive in 1942, WW2 Vet DD214. Born; Apr. 15, 1920.

Spencer, Gladys E. (Paige); widow of Russell, lived on 103 East End Drive in 1942, BHS Educator, sister of Mollie (Paige) Lusk.

Spencer, Harrison L. Jr.; WW2 Vet. DD214. Born: June 3, 1922. Lived on 503 Beersheba St. in 1942.

Spencer, James; Porter at Park Barber Shop in 1942.

Spencer, Jerry

Spencer, John Wesley; 1st grade BHS 1945.

Spencer, Karen

Spencer, Mildred; wife of Roy S. in 1942.

Spencer, Oweda; lived on 530 'B' Beersheba St. in 1942.

Spencer, Ronald

Spencer, Roy S.; husband of Mildred, lived on 511 Beersheba St. in 1942, WW2 Vet. DD214. BHS Principal [story].

Spencer, Sarah Elizabeth; 'Little Bit' 1946 BHS 6th grade student.

Spencer, Thomas T.; husband of Agnes, Chauffer at Medical Clinic & Hospital, lived on 105 East End Drive in 1942.

Spencer, Wayne

Spurlock, Billie; husband of Mary, lived on West Locust in 1942.

Spurlock, Bob; Brother of Charles.

Spurlock, Charles; Brother of Bob.

Spurlock, Frank; husband of Tessie, Janitor at Central HS, lived on RR1 in 1942.

Spurlock, George; Cook, lived on Cedar Street in 1942, WW2 Veteran, DD214. Born; Oct. 12, 1912.

Spurlock, Jessie Sarah

Spurlock, Johnny

Spurlock, Maria; widow of Richard, Cook at Myers Place, lived on Burton's Lane in 1942.

Spurlock, Mary; wife of Billie, lived on West Locust in 1942.

Spurlock, Nannie (Scott)

Spurlock, Nedie; wife of Oscar lived on River St. in 1942.

Spurlock, Oscar, husband of Nedie, lived on River St. in 1942.

Spurlock, Pete

Spurlock, Richard; husband of Maria.

Spurlock, Robert; husband of Sallie, Laborer, lived on Cedar St. in 1942.

Spurlock, Sadie

Spurlock, Sallie; wife of Robert, lived on Cedar St. in 1942.

Spurlock, Sammie; Cook, lived on 106 Etter St. in 1942.

Spurlock, Tessie, wife of Frank in 1942.

Spurlock, Tom

Spurlock, Walter; lived on West Locust St. in 1942.

Spurlock, Will; WW1 Vet.

Stallworth, Megan (Borum); daughter of Carolyn (Crabtree) Borum, Middle Tn. State University student in 2001.

Stamps, Nina (Dobbins); wife of Prof. S.M. Sr., first grade teacher at Bernard H.S.

Stamps, S. Davis Jr.; Son of Nina & S. M., Grad 1955 BHS. [story]

Stamps, S. M. Sr. Prof.; Principal of Bernard H.S., Educator [story].

Staples, Anne

Staples, George

Staples, Georgie

Starley, Andrew

Starkey, Emma

Staten, James

Staten, Kristin Ashlie; Abe Thomas Great grand daughter, WCHS 2002.

Staten, Ron Sr.

Staten, Sarah (Darrine)

Stephen, Randals; Barber in 1870.

Stephmason, Ida T.; 1937 48 yrs. old.

Stewart, Robert; lived on Egypt Alley in 1942.

Stokes, Elsie; 1950's.

Stokes, Hobert Vernon; Pastor in the 1950's & 1960's, husband of Jennie, lived on 202 Etter St. in 1942.

Stokes, Jennie; wife of Hobert Vernon Stokes, lived on 202 Etter St. in 1942.

Stokes, Mable Louise; wife of A. J. Guearard Sr., 1935 BHS Grad.

Strode, Benton; Son of Cliffton & Mary. Army Veteran.

Strode, Birdie (Curtis); Daughter of Roy & Mary Curtis.

Strode, Cliffton; Husband of Mary (Shockley). Logger, Farmer, Hauled gravel all over Cannon Co. lived in Bolden Green community.

Strode, C. J.; Son of Lisa & Curtis.

Strode, Curtis; Desert Storm, Retired Veteran, Nat. Guard, Son of Clinton & Jeannette. Father of Markus and C. J. [story]

Strode, Debbie (Grayson); Daughter of Dorothy (Womack)

Strode, Dennis 'Dink'; Son of Clinton & Jeannette.

Strode, Estie Jack; Korean Vet. Son of Cliffton & Mary (Shockley), Mule Legend, husband of Jean Hilma [story].

Strode, James Clinton; Korean Vet. DD214, Husband of Jeannette (Ford), Born; Feb. 13, 1933. Lived on 106 E. End Drive in 1953. [story]

Strode, James Lester; This left hander pitched for coach Leo Davis at the McMinnville City High School. He started with the Kansas City organization. The fastball and slider were his best pitches. He later became pitching Director for the Chicago Cubs. Son of Jeannette & Clinton. Bull Pen coach for the Chicago 'Cubs' Baseball team. [story]

Strode, Jean Hilma (Roberts) Johnson; wife of Estie Strode.

Strode, Jeannette (Ford); wife of James Clinton.

Strode, Jonathan; son of Sheila Hicks

Strode, Katherine; wife of Ralph.

Strode, Lisa (Smith); wife of Curtis, daughter of Lillian (Henny)

Strode, Mary (Shockley); wife of Cliffton.

Strode, Ralph; Son of Mary & Cliffton.

Strode, Ronnie; Husband of Debbie (Grayson).

Strode, Ronieshia; Daughter of Debbie & Ronnie.

Strode, Stephen; WCHS 2000 Senior.

Stroud, Lewis; Barber.

Stubblefield, Charles; lived on Egypt Alley in 1942.

Stubblefield, Edith; wife of Phillip, lived on 107 Edgefield St. in 1942.

Stubblefield, Marquerite

Stubblefield, Norma Lee; 1946 BHS 5th grade student.

Stubblefield, Lettie; lived on Egypt Alley in 1942.

Stubblefield, Marguerite; 1st grade BHS 1945.

Stubblefield, Phillip; husband of Edith, Porter at Cowan Oldham, lived on 107 Edgefield St. in 1942.

Stubblefield, Wilma Jean; 4th grade BHS in 1945.

Sutton, Amy daughter of Marcellus & Elsie.

Sutton, Bertha M.; wife of Frank S., lived on Congo St. in 1942.

Sutton, Elsie; wife of Marcellus Sutton.

Sutton, Eloise; Daughter of Marcellus.

Sutton, Frank S.; husband of Bertha M., Pastor of A. M. E. Church, lived on Congo St. in 1942.

Sutton, Glenn; son of Marcellus & Elsie.

Sutton, Marcellus; 1921-2002, 81 years old, husband of Elsie, Carpenter, Masonry. 'Rocket' baseball Umpire. [story]

Sutton, Robert Lee; son of Marcellus & Elsie.

Sutton, Rosalyn Lee; daughter of Marcellus & Elsie.

Sutton, Veleria Martin; daughter of Marcellus & Elsie.

Swafford, Helen; Maid, lived on RR3 in 1942.

(T)

Talley, Beauford; DD214, WW2 Vet. Born; Sept. 12, 1906.

Talley, Ray

Talley, Vickey (Grayson); Daughter of Dorothy, died in 2001.

Taylor, Dwight

Taylor, Harry

Taylor, Hattie; Owner of two Hair Salons. Husband of Henry Wood.

Taylor, Howard; Vietnam Vet. Brother of Hattie.

Taylor, Isiah

Taylor, James Howard; Vietnam Vet.

Taylor, James III (Toot); 2012

Taylor, Mattie Louise: Wife of William Hayes. 2nd grade BHS 1945.

Taylor, Trace; son of Jalane (Perkins) Grayson.

Terry, Bell; Cook at Farless Place Café, lived on Edgefield in 1924.

Terry, Brenda

Terry, Brian Cole; WCHS 2003 SR., Son of Homer Terry. President of WCHS Black History Club.

Terry, Gladys; Grandmother of Deanna Grayson.

Terry, Homer Louis; DD214, Vietnam Vet. Born; Jan. 21, 1949. Lived on 108 Edgefield St. in 1969. Father of Brian.

Terry, James E.; lived on Egypt Alley in 1942.

Terry, Joann (Coonrod); Wife of Homer.

Terry John Walter 'Snake'; DD214, WW2 Vet., lived on 104 Edgefield St. in 1941. Born; Jul. 30, 1921.

Terry, Johnnie: Daughter of John Walter.

Terry, Joyce (Marshbanks); wife of Homer.

Terry, Jualia

Terry, Nathaniel; DD214, WW2 Vet. lived on Congo St. in 1942. He was 18 in 1942.

Terry, Remus; Semi-Pro Baseball Player, 'Rockets,' lived on Congo St. in 1942.

Terry, Ricky; Son of John Walter, Semi-Pro Baseball, Rockets.

Terry, Sandra Denise

Terry, Shell

Terry, Stacy

Terry, Tim

Terry, Walter J.; husband of Velma, Mortar Mixer, lived on Congo St. in 1942.

Thacker, Marjorie Lillian Wolford (Bolden); Grandmother of Wayne Wolford Sr. [story]

Thacker, Ramey; WW1 Vet, Grandfather of Wayne Wolford Sr.

Thaxton, Perry

Thomas, (Spurlock), Evie or Elvie

Thomas, Annie Marie (Bonner) 1985, 57 yrs. old.

Thomas, Carolyn (Martin); Wife of Harold, daughter of Elmer Sr. & Marjorie (Savage)

Thomas, Christy; Daughter of Carol & Harold.

Thomas, Clopia Elizabeth (Northcutt).

Thomas, Edward, husband of Mary.

Thomas, Elvin; (single) 1911-1977, Daughter of John 'Abe'.

Thomas, Evie

Thomas, Fred Morford; Son of John Abe. Died in April 2003.

Thomas, Freeman 'Skin'

Thomas, George; 1915-1962.

Thomas, George 'Boots'; Father of Freeman.

Thomas, Gracie (Smartt)

Thomas, H. C.; 1939-1978, Son of George 'Boots'.

Thomas, Harold 'Lefty'; Semi-Pro Baseball Player & Coach, [story]

Thomas, Howard; Vet., Son of Harold & Carol (Martin).

Thomas, Hence

Thomas, Hennreitta: daughter of John 'Abe' Thomas. Wife of James Flint Lusk.

Thomas, Howard

Thomas, Ina Pauline (Northcutt)

Thomas, J. W.; 1934-1957, son of 'Abe' & Ina, husband of Louetta (Ikeard) [story]

Thomas, James A. 'Pete'

Thomas James W.; Vietnam Vet.

Thomas, John; 1959

Thomas, John; 1873-1929.

Thomas, John Leonard 'Abe' Sr.; Semi-Pro baseball legend. [story]

Thomas, John Leonard Jr.

Thomas, L.V.; Son of 'Abe'

Thomas, Lawson; husband of Mary, lived on African St. in 1942.

Thomas, Lela (Northcutt); Wife of 'Abe.'

Thomas, Lola

Thomas, Leonard Jr.; 1930-1971.

Thomas, Lorretta (Ikeard)

Thomas, Marshall; 1921-1966.

Thomas, Mary; widow of Edward, lived on 101 E. Colville St. in 1942.

Thomas, Mary; widow of Lawson, lived on African Street in 1942.

Thomas, Mattie; 1st wife of James Elam, Married to Thomas Woods 2nd.

Thomas, Maybelle (Northcutt)

Thomas, Morford; Son of 'Abe'

Thomas, Ray

Thomas, Ray Donald; 'Donald Duck' 1946 BHS 6th grade student.

Thomas, Rodney; Son of Hennreitta.

Thomas, Steve; Son of Harold & Carol (Martin)

Thomas, Sue Carol

Thomas, Terri; Daughter of Harold & Carol (Martin)

Thomas, Wanda Belle;1946 BHS 5th grade student.

Thomas, Wanda S. ()

Thomas, William; Vet, Army 4 yrs., son of Harold & Carol (Martin)

Thomas, Willie; 1904-1929.

Tidwell, Mattie; wife of John G., lived on African St. in 1942.

Tidwell, John G.; husband of Mattie, lived on African St. in 1942.

Tilley, Isaac James; [story]

Tillman, Willa B. (Ramsey): sister to Nora Ramsey

Tipton, Rachel

Tipton, Stephen B.

Toney, Norman; DD214, WW2, Vet. Born; Nov. 25, 1923.

Trim, Al; 2001 Warren Co. H.S. Senior.

Trim, Tyson; 2001 WCHS Sophomore.

Truman, Shelby (Looper); Daughter of Myrena (Womack) & Herman.

Tubb, Ruby Mercer; 1898-1934.

Tubbs, Ashley; Freshman WCHS 2001.

Tubbs, Erica; WCHS 2000 Junior.

Tubbs, Everett

Tubbs, Jack

Tubbs, Jeannie

Tucker, Elias A.; Husband of Mollie (Bolden), 1876-1955. [story]

Tucker, Mollie Agness (Bolden); Daughter of Sarah & George Bolden.

Turner, J. E.; Professor, Principal, Math, Physical Science, at Bernard H.S.

(U-V)

Vannoy, Joan

Vaughn, Antwan; Member of East End Drive Church of Christ.

Vaughn, Clyde William; 3rd grade BHS 1945.

Vaughn, Elzie Louis; DD214, Vet. Born; May 13, 1938. Lived on 202 Yankee St. in 1957. Husband of Muriel (Ramsey).

Vaughn, Fannie

Vaughn, Francis Loleeta; 1946 BHS 6th grade student.

Vaughn, Jennie Belle

Vaughn, John; husband of Lurlene (Allred), lived on Yankeetown St. in 1942, (1891-1974), WW1, Vet Army, DD214. 24 Yrs. old in 1918.

Vaughn, Johnnie Belle

Vaughn, Justin; WCHS 2001 Freshman.

Vaughn, Lee Dean

Vaughn, Lela Evan

Vaughn, Lurlene (Allred); wife of John, lived on Yankeetown St. in 1942, (1907-1968).

Vaughn, Mary ()

Vaughn, Muriel (Ramsey); Wife of Elzie.

Vaughn, Nettie (Cummings)

Vaughn, Tisha

Vaughn, Tom

(Wa-Wi)

Wade, Cecil; 1955 BHS football player.

Wade, Ruth

Waldern, Hallie (McReynolds); Sep. 14, 1881-Mar. 21, 1934. Daughter of Anderson & Percilla (Lamb) McReynolds.

Walker, Allen

Walker, Carrie M.; wife of Eugene, lived on 513 Beersheba St. in 1942.

Walker, Ellen ()

Walker, Eugene Jr.; husband of Carrie M., Cook at Ross Grill, lived on 513 Beersheba St. in 1942.

Walker, Jack; Husband of Ora (Martin).

Walker, John 'Jack'

Walker, Ora 'Sally Ora' (Martin)

Walling, Alfred

Walling, Altie; Daughter of Joe.

Walling, Betty (Patterson); Mother of Zollie & Rollie.

Walling, Betty Lou; 1933-1959 (Single).

Walling, Debra

Walling, Edna; Sister to Betty.

Walling, Elizabeth 'Bettie' (Patterson)

Walling, Joe; (1870-1954). Grandfather of Zollie & Rollie.

Walling, Josephine (McKinley); 65 yrs. old died in 1976.

Walling, Hawthone

Walling, Leatrice (Noble)

Walling, Marcus Willis; DD214, Korean Vet. Born; Jul. 29, 1931. Lived on Rte. 2 Box 262 in 1950.

Walling Marsha; Daughter of Sadie (Roberts). Sadie is Cowan's Roberts sister.

Walling, Oshia (Coppinger); 1883-1911.

Walling, Raymond H.; Sept. 6, 1927-1965, DD214, WW 2 Vet. Navy.

Walling, Smith; died in 1970. Rollie & Zollie's uncle.

Watkins, Jason; WCHS 1998 Senior.

Watson, Minnie (Ms.)

Webb, Beatrice; wife of Ottaway, lived on 109 E. End Drive St. in 1942.

Webb, Dovie; 1897-1963. Daughter of Richard & Susie.

Webb, George; Son of Tyree & Richard Sr.

Webb, Georgia (Williams); Wife of Roy Webb.

Webb, Hazel; Wife of 'Buddy' Young. Daughter of Tyree & Richard Sr.

Webb, John; Mar. 20, 1883-Dec. 17, 1938. Son of Richard & Susie (Faulkner).

Webb, Laura; Daughter of Roy & Georgia.

Webb, Mary; Daughter of Richard & Susie.

Webb, Maude; Daughter of Roy & Georgia.

Webb, Ottaway; husband of Beatrice, Laborer for City Street Dept., lived on 109 East End Drive St. in 1942.

Webb, Richard Sr.; Father of Roy Webb. Slave of Asa Faulkner.

Webb, Richard Jr. 'Dick'; 1884-1962 son of Richard & Susie (Faulkner)

Webb, Robert; Son of Richard & Susie.

Webb, Roy; Husband of Georgia (Williams). Son of Richard Sr. & Susie.

Webb, Sarah; Wife of Rev. George T. Bolden. Daughter of Tyree & Richard Sr.

Webb, Susie 'Queen' (Faulkner); 1856-Aug. 16, 1916, 59 yrs. Old. Daughter of Lane & Patha Faulkner.

Webb, Tyree; Slave, 2nd Wife of Richard Webb Sr.

Webb, Thomas

Webb, Willis M.; DD214, WW2, Vet. Born; Jun. 8, 1923. Lived on 109 East Main St. in 1941.

Weeden, Maxine; Wife of Tom. First Black to work at front desk at Main Post Office in McMinnville. Retired.

Weeden, Tom; Husband of Maxine (). Owned a construction Company.

Weir, Christopher

Weir, Danielle; WCHS Soph. 2001.

Weir, Donta

Weir, Rita

Whitaker, David E.; Husband of Mary E. () of Morrison.

Whitaker, Elzie; 2002 Church of Christ member.

Whitaker, Gloria; Farmers Market Merchant. Mother of Greg. Teacher.

Whitaker, Greg; works at Technology Center. Owns a farm in Morrison.

Whitaker, Leon; Husband of Mandy ().

Whitaker, Mandy (); Wife of Leon.

Whitaker, Mary E. (); Wife of David E.

Whitaker, Robert Aaron 'Bob'; 1932-2002, Worked at Dr. Pepper Co.

White, Charles Jr.; DD214, Korean War Vet. Born; Jan. 9, 1930. 1946 BHS 6th grade student.

White, Charles Sr.; Butcher, lived on N. Ford St. in 1942.Korean Vet.

White, Hallie W.; widow of Jim, lived on African St. in 1942.

White, James

White, Jim; Husband of Hallie W.

White, Julia; Photo 1930.

White, Ke-Yonna; WCHS Junior 2001.

White, Olivia; lived on African St. in 1942.

White, Phillip; Blacksmith in Viola during 1870.

White, Richard; Vet.

White, Susie (McReynolds); lives in the Bolden Green Community.

Whitman, Carrie; wife of Jerry, lived on 108 Etter St. in 1942.

Whitman, Jerry; husband of Carrie, lived on 108 Etter St. in 1942.

Whitman, Margaret L.; lived on 108 Etter St. in 1942.

Wiley, Chea; Daughter of Shanna (Locke)

Wiley, Cory; Son of Bernita & Gregory Sr.

Wiley, Brittany; Daughter of Bernita & Gregory Sr.

Wiley, Brandon; Son of Bernita & Gregory Sr.

Wiley, Gregory Jr.; Son of Bernita & Gregory Sr.

Wiley, Gregory Sr.; Doctor, Husband of Shanna (Locke)

Wiley, Javier; Son of Shanna (Locke)

Wiley, Shanna; wife of Doctor Gregory Sr.

Wilkerson, Clara; 1932-1951.

Wilkerson, Dave; 1928-2001, Farmer.

Wilkerson, Eugene; Pastor, Church of Christ. Husband of Joyce (Locke).

Wilkerson, Jimmy

Wilkerson, Joyce (Locke); Wife of Eugene.

Wilkerson, Kimberly Denise

Wilkerson, Linda Sue (Leftrict)

Wilkerson, Nancy

Wilkerson, Terrell

Wilkerson, Tydale

Williams, Arthur; lived on Egypt Alley in 1942.

Williams, Bartow; Cooked for V. F. W., Country Club.

Williams, Bessie M.; wife of James B., lived on 132 Murphy St. in 1942.

Williams, Bob; Son of Rube.

Williams, Elizabeth; 1897-1926.

Williams, Ester May; Sister to Bob.

Williams, Florence; Cook at Ross Grill, lived on N. Ford St. in 1942.

Williams, Georgia; Educator at BHS 1940's.

Williams, J.C.; Son of Edna, former husband of Jeannette 'Flirt' (Strode).

Williams, James B.; husband of Bessie M., Mill Handyman, lived on 132 Murphy St. in 1942.

Williams, James Clarence

Williams, Jade; WCHS Freshman 2001.

Williams, Jeanette (Strode); former wife 1 of J. C. and wife 2 of Horace Arnold. Mother of Annette.

Williams, Jomeica Adah; WCHS 1998 SR.

Williams, Lynn

Williams, Rube; J. C.'s Grandfather.

Williams, Tia; WCHS Freshman, 2001.

Wilson, Espie; WCHS 1998 Sr.

Winton, Beulah Irene (Thomas); 1934-1965.

Winton, Bobbie M.; BHS 1956 Grad.

Winton, Clara P. (Grayson); 1925-1987, daughter of Willie Lee & Rebecca Sue (Foster) Grayson, wife 1 of McKinley & wife 2 of Hollis Winton.

Winton, Charles J.; DD214, WW2 Vet. Born; Aug. 12, 1918.

Winton, D. L.; 1897-1928.

Winton, Ernest Eugene; 1920-1953.

Winton, Evie (Spurlock); 1959-95 yrs. Old.

Winton Fannie; Wife of George Winton

Winton, Fred 'Mousie'; 1921-1991.

Winton, George; 1873-1951.

Winton, George; Husband of Fannie (Donahue).

Winton, Henry B.; Aug. 19, 1922-1966. DD214, WW2 Vet. Lived in Viola in 1943.

Winton, Hollis

Winton, Hugh; 1888-1967.

Winton, Jessie Mae; Class of 1949, BHS.

Winton, John Henry; 1875-1943.
Winton, Martin
Winton, Mary (McGregor)
Winton, Mary Ellen (Wooton)
Winton; Mary Ellen (Brown); 1919-1943.
Winton, Rosetta (Wilkerson)
Winton, Sadie; 1917-1941.
Winton, Sarah (Duncan)
Winton, Virginia (Elam)
Winton, Walsie (Mercer)

(Wo-Wz)

Wolford, Brittany; Daughter of Matthew Wolford & Lisa Lucious.

Wolford, Erin Marissa; Daughter of Mary & Wayne Sr.

Wolford, Mary Virginia (Espenschied); Wife of Wayne Sr. [Story]

Wolford, Matthew Graves; Son of Wayne Sr. & Norma (Looper).

Wolford, Norma Dale (Looper); Former wife of Wayne Sr.

Wolford, Ruby Emerald; (Single), Mother of Wayne Sr., Daughter of Robert

Wolford & Marjorie (Bolden) Wolford Thacker.

Wolford, Wayne Richard Graves Jr.; Son of Wayne Sr. & Norma (Looper).

Wolford, Wayne Richard G. Sr.; Retired Army, Son of Ruby (single) & Clarence Graves. [Story] DD214

Womack, Albert

Womack, Alonzo; husband of Maria, lived on 121 Edgefield St. in 1942.

Womack, Anna Ruth; Daughter of James & Odie Kay.

Womack, Charles; Son of Lucile (Smith) & Ernest.

Womack, Charles; 1st grade BHS 1945.

Womack, Clarence E.; 5th grade BHS 1945.

Womack, Ernestine; Wife of Brewster Bonner.

Womack, Ernest Jr.; Died in July 1935.

Womack, Ernest Sr.; WW1 Vet., Husband of Lucile (Smith).

Womack, Francis; Daughter of James M. & Odie Kay (Fuston).

Womack, Franklin; Son of Ernest & Lucile (Smith).

Womack, Franklin Roosevelt

Womack, Ida or Ada (Duncan)

Womack, Isaac; Husband of Lottie (Webb)

Womack, James Edward; Son of James M. & Odie Kay (Fuston).

Womack, James M.; WW2 Vet, died 1987, 79 yrs. old. Born; Feb. 6, 1908.

Womack, Lottie (Webb); Wife of Isaac.

Womack, Loretta (Ikeard); Thomas was 1st Marriage.

Womack, Lucile (Smith), Wife of Ernest Womack Sr.

Womack, Mance

Womack, Maria; wife of Alonzo, lived on 121 Edgefield St. in 1942.

Womack, Mariah (Womack)

Womack, Martha Jane; Daughter of James M. & Odie Kay (Fuston).

Womack, Mary (Webb)

Womack, Octavian Lamar Jr.; WCHS SR, 2003

Womack, Octavian Lamar Sr.

Womack, Odie Kay (Fuston); Wife of James M.

Womack, Odie Mae; Daughter of James M. & Odie Kay (Fuston).

Womack, Rufus; Father of Ernest Sr.

Womack, Virginia; 'Jenny' 1946 BHS 6th grade student, Daughter of Ernest Sr. & Lucile (Smith) Womack, wife of Paul Alexander.

Womack, Vivian; Daughter of Ernestine (Womack) Bonner and Richard Borum.

Womack, William; died in 1953-85 yrs. Old.

Wood, Algoma Perry.; 1956 BHS Grad. Army Vet 23years of service. [Story]

Wood, Calvin

Wood, Carlos 'Finance'; Son of Carrie & Malcolm.

Wood, Carrie M. (Phinager); Wife of Malcolm. [story]

Wood, Charles

Wood, Clarence

Wood, Connie L. (Savage)

Wood, Curtis

Wood, Dorothy L.

Wood Effie E.; wife of J. Edward, Educator at Bernard H. S., lived on 520 Beersheba St. in 1942.

Wood, Eugene Franklin; DD214, Vet. Born; Jun. 27, 1933.

Wood, Eva

Wood, Evon

Wood, Ferrell; 1884-1940.

Wood, George Raleigh; Born July 10, 1859, Husband of Maggie. Died 1954.

Wood, Gertrude (Rucker); 1897-1987. Wife of Spurgeon.

Wood, Harold J.; 1956 BHS Grad.

Wood, Hattie (Taylor); Wife of Henry, Self-employed Hair dresser-two business.

Wood, Helen

Wood, Henry; Husband of Hattie (Taylor).

Wood, Henry—Husband of Mary 1800's.

Wood, J. Edward; husband of Effie E., Principal of Bernard H.S., lived on 520 Beersheba St in 1942.

Wood, James E. Vet., Died 1937, 42 yrs. old.

Wood, Jeffrey

Wood, John R.; 1871-1918.

Wood, Jurrel Dean

Wood, Lawrence; Died 1940, 59 yrs.

Wood, Lena

Wood, Lucille

Wood, Luther

Wood, Maggie Belle (Martin); Wife of George R.

Wood, Malcolm Raleigh; WW1 Vet., June 16, 1897-Mar. 9, 1997, DD214. 21 yrs. of age in 1918. Husband of Carrie (Phinegar)

Wood, Mary

Wood, Mary (Rains) Born In 1855.

Wood, Michael

Wood, Sarah; 1969 Member of Clark Church.

Wood, Spurgeon Hadder; 1893-1978.

Wood, Sue; wife of Orbin Wood

Wood, Theresa M.; 'Roddy' 1946 BHS 7th grade student.

Wood, Thomas 'Tom Lee'; Vietnam Vet.

Wood, Tommy

Wood, William T.; WW2 Vet., 1907-1952.

Woodard, Adabell; wife of John, lived on 116 Edgefield St. in 1942.

Woodard, Charles 'PeeWee'; Son of Charles &Virginia (Ramsey).

Woodard, Charles Henry; Korean Vet., Husband of Virginia (Ramsey).

Woodard, Cynthia 'Cindy'; Daughter of Charles & Virginia (Ramsey).

Woodard, Etta M.; lived on 116 Edgefield in 1942.

Woodard, JoAnn (Martin); Husband of Tommy.

Woodard, John; husband of Adabell, Laborer, lived on 116 Edgefield St. in 1942.

Woodard, John Edd; lived on 116 Edgefield St. in 1942, operated a Black funeral home, 1950's.

Woodard, Kay Francis; Sister to Charles Henry. 4th grade BHS 1945.

Woodard, Linda; lives in Detroit, married to Butt.

Woodard, Paul Allen; WW2 & Korean Vet.

Woodard, Tommy; Son of Charles & Virginia.

Woodard, Virginia Louise 'Jennie' (Ramsey): April 4, 1927-Nov. 5, 2012 Wife of Charles. East End Drive Church of Christ in 2012. Daughter of Doris and Sally (Locke).

Woodruff, Dane; Husband of Kim. Works at Bridgestone Tire Plant.

Woodruff, Kim; Wife of Dane.

Woodlee Deborah 'Debo,' Daughter of Franklin J.

Woodlee, David Frank; husband of Mary L., Owned a Pool Room on S. Spring, lived on Cedar St. in 1942, East Main St. in WW1, DD214.

Woodlee, Eli; Blacksmith in Irving College in 1870.

Woodlee, Franklin J.; DD214, Vet., Rocket baseball player. Original member of Post 208 in 1945. [story] DD214, Born; Oct. 26, 1925. Lived on 117 Barnes St. in 1943

Woodlee, Jess Edward

Woodlee, Mary L.; wife of David Frank, lived on Cedar St. in 1942.

Woodlee, Nina; Daughter of Franklin J.

Woodley, Ely; died Sep. 7, 1912, (83 yrs. old).

Woods, Charles; WW1 Vet.

Woods, Eden; 1891-1946, WW I Vet.

Woods, Edmond

Woods, Emma (Crutcher); 1865-1943. Wife of Jordan Woods.

Woods, James; DD214, WW2 Vet. Lived on 116 Edgefield St. in 1945. 2nd Grade at Bernard H. S. 1945. Born; Sept. 17, 1926.

Woods, Jennie

Woods, Jim

Woods, John Benjamin; 1955 BHS Grad.

Woods, Johnnie (Cain)

Woods, Jordan; 1875-1953. Husband of Emma (Crutcher)

Woods, Larry 'Button'

Woods, Lee; WW1 Vet.

Woods, Liza (Crutcher)

Woods, Lucius

Woods, Lucius Long

Woods, Melvin; WCHS SR. 2000.

Woods, Michael

Woods, Morles; WW1 Vet.

Woods, Paul

Woods, Thomas Lee; Vet. Born Dec. 18, 1935.

Woods, Thomas 'Tom'
Woods, William T.; 1907-1952, DD214, WW2, Vet.
Woods, Yolanda; WCHS Soph. 2001.
Worthington, Buford
Worthington, Charlie; 1895-1983.
Worthington, Clarence 'Bo'; Husband of Edna, (1911-1987)
Worthington, Edna (Annie Edna); Wife of Clarence. 1914-
Worthington, Etta (Lusk)
Worthington, George M.; 1898-1941.
Worthington, James; 2nd grade BHS 1945.
Worthington, Laura
Worthington, Monroe
Wright, Ben
Wright, Dwight; WCHS Senior 2000.
Wright, Hattie
Wright, Nettie (Martin)
Wright, Shake
Wright, Vanisha Lanae; 1999 WCHS SR.

(X)

(Y)

York, Albert; Died in 1953.

York, Daisy L.; lived on Egypt Alley St. in 1942.

York, Harriet

York, Huel

York, Hugh L.

York, Jim; WW1 Vet.

York, Josephine; lived on Beersheba St. in 1942.

York, Martha

York, Mary; lived on 305 S. High St. in 1942.

York, Monroe; Head waiter at the Sedberry Hotel in 1942.

York, Veola

York, Wiley 1872-1935

York, Willie

Young, Alford S. 'Buddy'; husband of Hazel (Womack), Son of Hattie (Leftrict) Concrete Worker, lived on 417 Beersheba St. in 1942.

Young, Alfred Bernard; Vet., Son of Mack & Lillian. DD214, Born; Apr. 16, 1947. Lived on 110 Beersheba St. in 1970.

Young, Alma I.; Educator at Bernard H. S., lived on Beersheba St. in 1942.

Young, Alpha Omega; Father of Mack and 'Buddy'. Husband of Hattie (Leftrict). Lived on 419 Beersheba St. in 1942. Helped finance the Waters and Old Walling School house for Black students in the late 1880's.

Young, Bill

Young, Dorothy (Womack); 1st husband was Grayson, Daughter of Ernest & Lucile (Smith).

Young, Harold; Vet., 2nd husband of Dorothy (Womack)

Young, Hattie (Leftrict); widow of Alfred O., lived on 419 Beersheba St. in 1942. Mother of Mack & 'Buddy'.

Young, Hazel (Webb) (Womack); wife of 'Buddy,' Maid, lived on 417 Beersheba St. in 1942.

Young, Irene; (single), Educator at BHS, organist in 1969 at Clark Church.

Young, Lillian (Young); Wife of Mack. Community Leader.

Young, Mack; Educator at BHS and Coach, Husband of Lillian. Stone Mason, Carpenter. Son of Alfred O. & Hattie (Leftrict).

Young, Sammy; Owner of Construction Co. in Ark., Son of Mack & Lillian.

Young, Theta (Bates); Benjamin's Bates daughter.

(Z)

Chapter 8

Organizations & Clubs

Part 1
'The Black Foxes'

Members:

Peggy Henny—President
Mary Curtis—Vice President
Marcia Ramsey—Treasure
Georgia Etter Huggins—Secretary
Peggy Nowlin
Ann Martin
Valerie 'Tootsie' Martin
Joyce Nowlin
Francis Brown
Betty Simpson
Betty Jean Ramsey
James Edward Womack
Willie Mae Hudgins
Peggy Martin
Vicky Sutton

Top L-R; Mary Curtis Betty Ramsey, Peggy Nowlin,
Valerie Martin, James Womack, Peggy Henny
Bottom L-R; Georgia Huggins, Marcia Ramsey,
Ann Martin, Peggy Martin

The Black Foxes was a club consisting of women that had social status in the greater Warren County area. These ladies wanted to be known as people with dignity and pride, brains and good looks, social and communitive skills. One male was included in this prestigious organization, and he was James Edward Womack. (Black Foxes and the 'Wolf') James was very vocal and involved in events such as was done with the Black Foxes.

It all got started by these women attending other women's parties in places such as Manchester, Winchester, Murfreesboro, Shelbyville, Tullahoma, Murfreesboro and Nashville Tennessee. They decided to form their own much needed place to socialize. This was started in about 1977. The first meeting to form the club was at Elmer Martin Sr.'s home in the Leesburg community. The first party was held at 'Dooney's Den' (Howard Henny Jr.) once a month. The building still stands in the Leesburg Community on Higginbotham road today. Some know of this place as the 'Moonlite Club'.

Some of the club's functions were to have the biggest and best Christmas party, and work in the community to help people. They furnished food and fruit baskets for families in need during Christmas. The Black Foxes worked with other organizations such as 'The Shriners, and The Elks Lodge' to raise funds for victims of fires, cancer and in need. This was not done only in McMinnville but surrounding counties. The Black Foxes would extend their services as hostess and escorts for fund raisers.

There was one period were as the Black Foxes held dances for the youth under 18 years of age at the "Rocket Ball Park" on Friday Nights. This was a plan to teach the kids to learn to socialize in a controlled environment.

Once a month a check was given to a deserving family to help with medical bills and other needs.

They were very instrumental in helping the families that lost a loved one by preparing and delivering breakfast for the deceased family. (Orange juice, bacon, biscuits, coffee etc . . .)

Some of the members friends would attend the Christmas parties and came as for as Detroit, Chicago, Cleveland and other cities.

They would have parties that sometimes accompany a live band. The admission was $10.00 a couple starting out, but later reached $15.00 a couple. The organization grew bigger and better then some of the member anticipated.

The Foxes would organize fish fries in order to raise money to have parties.

People from McMinnville and surrounding counties were fascinated by the level of preparedness of this organization. They were the talk of the town. The Black Foxes had out grown 'Dooney's Den' so they ended up having their parties at the civic center. The members would invite whomever they wanted to their own table at some of these events.

This was a time in McMinnville history were women wanted to make a difference, and show their children and loved ones that they had some positive statue in the community.

The Black Foxes were especially thrilled when a group out of Tullahoma called the 'Shrine's' escorted them into the event and sat them at their respected tables, this was truly high class.

In a time were it seemed like every dance or social event that there was a disturbance elsewhere, the Black Foxes can truly say they did not encounter any violence during their tenure.

In the 1980's the members of the club started breaking up, and the Black Foxes discontinued this tradition when some of the members moved out of town.

All of the members agreed that this was an enjoyable time in their lives. Some of the events held were attended by other races, so this was an open minded group.

The treasure Marcia Ramsey says; "I regret that we did not pass on this tradition to our kids."

The Black foxes in 1980

Some members of the Black Fox's organization are honored by the WCHC Black History Club in 2006. L-R; Joyce Nowlin, Maggie Locke, Martin Peggy Henny, Francis Brown, and Marcia Ramsey

Part 2

The Warren County High School Black History Club

The Warren County High School Black History Club was established and founded in 1994 by **Mr. Jeffery Martin** the Assistant Principal.

Mr. Martin thought that it would be good for the students to have an organization at the High School. He was a member of the N.A.A.C.P. youth organization during his high school days at Bernard High School.

This Warren County High School club gives the students a wealth of cultural experience and knowledge and a sense of pride and being who they are and what black history means to them. Everyone and anyone are very welcome to join this interesting club. There is a lot to be learned and gained by joining. Adults and alumni are also welcome to be mentors, and volunteers.

The club has had exchange students from all over the world to participate in activities and events.

Mr. Jeff Martin's dream is coming true; he is planning to venture out to other places as time goes by. Many students would not have had the chance to visit these places if Mr. Martin hadn't made this club his goal.

The BHC club has been involved in the Doctor Martin Luther King's march in Nashville since 1999. So many students of all races took the historic trips even when the Warren County school system did not recognize this day as a holiday. Three (3) years later, Dr. King's Day was considered a holiday in the Warren County school system. This was done in the year 2002. There are still approximately fifty (50) students a year that make the trip to the Nashville march along with several adults, and children.

History was made when the club traveled to Nashville to march in Dr. King's celebration when school was being held in Warren County. This was the year that Dr. Kings Day was recognized in the school system. This was a major accomplishment for the **High School Black History club**.

The club has several fundraisers during the school year; such as fish fries, car washes, pizza sales, hat day, fashion show and a school talent show. The talent show is one event that no one seems to have any questions about, its either you've got it are you don't. The Black History Club and the rest of the school come closer together for this event than at any other time during the school year. Students of all backgrounds get a chance to display their God given gifts, whether it is playing an instrument, dancing or singing a song.

The funds are for field trips and other social and educational events such as trips to Atlanta, GA., Birmingham, AL., Nashville, TN., Louisville, KY., and Memphis, Tennessee. Some of the main sponsors are Dr. Pepper Bottling Co., American Legion Post 208, C&C Trucking, Southern Standard Newspaper, United Steelworkers Union Local 1155 of America, Young Men United and more.

The club consists of a President, Vice-President, Secretary, Treasurer, Reporter, Historian and Public Affairs.

1996-1997
Tracey Johnson—President
Jason Smith—Vice-President
Vanisha Wright—Secretary
Channell Manier—Treasurer
Danielle Cabell—Reporter

1997-1998
Portica Marchbanks—President
Sedrick Cummings—Vice-President
Denica Martin—Secretary
Channell Manier—Treasurer
Danielle Cabell—Reporter

1998-1999
Rashad Thomas—President
Brandy Pinegar—Vice-President
Denica Martin—Secretary

Christy Guerard—Treasurer
Danielle Cabell—Reporter
Sandy Terry—Historian
Keesha Henny—Public Affairs

1999-2000
Keesha Henny / Ernest Gibson—Presidents
Brandy Patton—Vice-President
Leona Tate—Secretary
Kristin Staten—Treasurer
Brittany Martin—Reporter

2000-2001
Keesha Henny / Ernest Gibson—Presidents
Deanna Grayson—Vice-President
Courtney Sanders—Secretary
Kristin Staten—Treasurer
Brittany Martin—Reporter

2001-2002
Kristin Staten—President
Deanna Grayson—Vice-President
Courtney Sanders—Secretary
Brian Terry—Treasurer
Brittany Martin—Reporter

2002-2003
Brian Terry—President
Octavian Womack—Vice-President
Ashley Tubbs—Secretary
Tashius Pleasant—Treasurer
Courtney Martin—Reporter

2003-2004
Courtney Martin—President
Tashius Pleasant—Vice-President
Ashley Tubbs—Secretary
Trista Dillard—Treasurer
Tonia Davis—Reporter

2004-2005
Tonia Davis—President
Krista Dillard / Erin Wolford—Vice President
Whitney Henny—Secretary
Tyler Ramsey—Treasurer
Jonathan Strode—Reporter
Brittany Wiley / Ashton Ramsey—Special Events Coordinators

2005-2006
Whitney Henny—President
Krista Dillard—Vice President
Ashton Ramsey—Secretary
C. J. Strode—Treasurer
Adreama Dennison—Reporter
Trista Dillard / Dahynelia Grayson—Special Event Coordinators

2006-2007
Tyler Ramsey—President
Stephen Whitaker—Vice President
Amanda Bain—Secretary
Sasha Drake—Treasurer
Adreama Dennison—Reporter
Denzell Robinson/ Ariel Drake—Special Event Coordinators

2007-2008
Denzell Robinson—President
Tony Farris—Vice President
Chelsea Ramsey—Secretary
Kyrstal Richmond—Treasurer
Adreama Dennison—Reporter

2008-2009
President—Ashley Grayson
Vice President—Chelsea Whitaker
Secretary—Lyntasia Harris
Treasurer—Shariti Whitaker
Reporter—Damran McKinley

2009-2010
President—Helen Mrema
Vice President—Dominique Harris
Secretary—Nayomi Beason
Treasurer—Ashley Grayson
Reporter—Damran McKinley

2010-2011
President—Ashley Grayson
Vice President—Dominique Harris
Secretary—Tee Smith
Treasurer—Karen Portillo
Reporter—Alyssa Millraney

2012-2013
President—Allyiah Tate
Vice President—Chassity Johnson
Secretary—Jordan Chadwell
Treasurer—She'nce Ramsey
Reporters—Precious Ramsey / Danielle Ramsey

The Warren County High School Black History Club has entertained the Senior Citizens Center, Autumn Street Fair, Nursing Homes and several elementary schools in this area. The Middle school is a regular. There are luncheons that are given to recognize individuals and groups that are doing something good for the community. Educators, Semi-Pro baseball players, past Club members, N H C Nursing home, American Legion Post #208, and others have been recognized in the past at the luncheons. There are many people in the community that are recognized for their support of the high school black history club.

In the year 2008 Warren County High School Black History Club was sanctioned as a Warren County 200th year (Bicentennial) recipient. A luncheon was given for over 25 Black influential people that made a great impact on Warren County and its history. The club participated in getting 25 new voters for the presidential election, in which Barack Obama won, by promoting their interest in front of Wal-Mart Super center as a school project that involves the community. (2008)

Black History Month is always celebrated, and also a Christmas party is given every year.

Reports on famous African Americans local and abroad are assignments given and presented to the students to enhance the quality of the club. Shirts and Hoodies are made with a famous American's photo on the front, and the club's motto on the back. This shows unity within the club.

The club has dedicated its time to promote black history awareness, and any, and everyone are invited to join the club, to get an understanding of black history. Exchange students from around the world have joined and traveled with the club to different locations in the USA.

The Warren County Black History club members have seen places like the Dr. Martin Luther / Cloretta King's tomb, Dr. King's childhood home, the church in which he started preaching, the MLK Museum, Loraine Motel were Dr. King last stayed, Amusement Park in Kentucky, Jazz great, 'W. C. Handy' 'Father of the Blues' house on Beale Street, Historic Churches, Jazz and Sports, and historical Museums in Birmingham, Alabama, Alex Haley's childhood place in Memphis, cable cars in Memphis, the students have eaten in nice restaurants. Some of the trips require a three day, two over night stay in some of the better hotels.

Founder of Warren County High School Black History Club
Mr. Jeffery Martin

Black History Class 2007-2008

Class of 2004

BHC doing the African Dance 2009

BHC in Nashville MLK March 2009

BHC Class of 2006

BHC Performing for WCHS 2009

Leaders of Black History Club as of 2011
Tina Ramsey and Jalane Grayson

Part 3

Young Men United
'Building Character for Life'

The Young Men United organization was established November 1, 1998. Today the membership stands at 13 strong. The ages vary from the twenties to the fifties. Dues are paid to help keep the financial side steady. Donations are accepted, and fundraisers are held on periodic bases.

The Young Men United is a non-profit organization committed to help others in the community and any individual or family who needs help due to health, disaster or financial reasons.

L-R; Wayne, Phyllis, Paul, Rebecca, Steve, Charles, Nelson and Jon.

Founder; Nelson Ramsey

The motto for Y.M.U. is: "Building Character for life." The definition for character is: a special quality or appearance that makes one different from others, distinctive qualities, and a symbol. Young Men United is showing what character is all about. Many of the youth today don't have the understanding of character building.

The Young Men United organization knows the meaning, and the value that comes from being a mentor, and wants to pass its values on to the following generations.

There were approximately 200 kids that attended the first Mini-Fest sponsored by Young Men United. Everyone seemed to enjoy the day. The annual Mini-Fest will be held every August.

The Young Men United took a bunch of children to the civic center to watch the HARLEM GLOBETROTTERS play basketball.

On January 15, 2001 the Young Men United traveled with the Warren County High School Black History Club to join and celebrate in the marching at the Dr. Martin Luther King ceremony in a Nashville Tennessee. Over 60 people went on the bus trip to Nashville Tn. 2001

Young Men United
"Building Character for Life"

The group's main focus is to help the children of Warren County. They feel that they are losing many of the youths to crime, such as: drugs and criminal mischief. Many people have heard of the expression "An idle mind is the devils workshop." YMU believes this is what is going on with the younger generation. The group is trying to take their idle time and make it productive.

YMU believes that it takes a village, and order to raise a child.

This organization has accomplished many goals during the several years. It is the goal to strive to make this a better community for kids to work, get a better education, to play and to live.

YMU has had several annual Mini-fests, which are a carnival atmosphere. This takes up quite a bit of the funds, which have been accumulated throughout the year and it is put back into the community at this time.

A Christmas dinner and party, is given every year in order to show the meaning of this special season. There's also a Christmas float that is entered into the Christmas parade filled with the youth to enjoy.

When there are problems and the YMU are trusted with these problems, and sit down with the people (kids or grown-up alike) and try to help them work the problem(s) out.

This organization is steadily continuing to strive to be the best that they can be as; role models, mentors, responsible adults, friends, teachers and leaders.

YMU meets two to three times a month. This helps the communication run a lot smoother, and the contact with the community is much more effective.

Thank you or your time and any assistance that you may have given, or will give in the future.

Chapter 9

Schools

Corinth School in Viola, Tennessee

'Abe' John Leonard Thomas attended Viola school in the 1920s. There were a couple of teachers that taught at this tiny school during this time. One teacher was Mrs. Hattie Page, and the other was Mrs. Lula Hunter. This happened to be a one-room schoolhouse; during Harold Thomas' time at school, attendance was at 25 to 30 students. The grades were from One which is first-grade to 12th grade. Abe Thomas was one of the earlier students that left from this school that was alive to tell about it. The Viola school is no longer standing.

When you're heading into Viola Tennessee, there is a ball field located on the left-hand side of the road, the old Viola schoolhouse is torn down now, but used to be located on the far side after you pass the ball field. One student remembers attending the school, his name was, Harold Thomas. Thomas remembers his teachers; Bertha Shockley, Jay Cope, and Henrietta Bates.

Transportation to school was easy because school was within walking distance. There was an old stove at the schoolhouse, the stove was used for heating and heating up your lunch. All of the students brought their lunch to school. Water was gotten from the spring that was nearby, and if you had to use the restroom, never fear the outhouse was near.

Viola School 1950

Hiwassee School

Hiwassee school was established in the 1940's and closed about 1957 or 1958. Most kids walked to school because the school was a local establishment.

The School was located on Highway 55, in the Morrison area. The building that student attended is still standing, but has been redone and turned into a factory across from the Hiwassee Church of Christ.

Students; Joleen Solomon, George King, Gloria Whitaker and Louis Battles are just a few that attended this school.

Some of the teachers noted; were, Jessie Flynt, Jessie Crabtree, Bertha Shockley, Gladys Spencer Locke, Edna Etter and Sydna Batey.

Pleasant Hill

Pleasant Hill School (Community Center in 2011)

For most Warren Countians whose memories stretch, a few years back, Pleasant Hill Community which is located off Sparta Highway five miles from McMinnville, is significant to local African-American History for a couple of reasons: The school and the annual fair held there years ago for Blacks.

Again this was a mostly Black populated area with a few whites as well. The community was your typical rural neighborhood. The communities throughout Warren County were as a rule pretty open minded. The blacks didn't have to worry about going to the back door of a white friend's house.

Pleasant Hill was originally called Martin Charge because of the large number of Martins who lived in the community. Later changed to the Pleasant Hill Community, it became home for a United Methodist and Baptist Church; activities and community picnics were centered around church affairs.

There were many activities and functions at the school house. Every August the entire Black communities threw their weight behind the Pleasant Hill Fair, which was primarily organized as an event for Blacks. Blacks weren't barred from attending the Warren County Fair, but in those days, before the 1970's segregation was the norm, the County extension agents worked just as hard to help set up the Pleasant Hill Fair as they did on the main one. This fair was altogether different from the main fair.

Pleasant Hill fair leaders; Carrie Woods, Sadie Martin, Howard Martin, Ora Walker and Mrs. Worthington

1940's - 1950's
PLEASANT HILL SCHOOL

Old photo of Pleasant Hill School Class

L-R; Prof. Howard, Chiquita Martin, Sadie Martin, John Walker

THURSDAY OCTOBER 6, 1955

The largest number of baked goods in history was entered in competition at the Warren County Pleasant Hill Black Fair; Professor S.M. Stamps was fair chairman. Three of the top winners in the bakery department are: Ernestine King, Ernie Shockley and Hattie Barnes.

In the canned goods competition: Irene Jackson and Hattie Wright took first place ribbons. Teens: Margie Ruth Biles and Kathline Woods received blue ribbons for their fair displays.

This is Warren County's seventh year for the Black Fair.

THURSDAY OCTOBER 13, 1955

The Black citizens threaten to integrate the Warren County School System unless a school building is constructed.

The county court ok'd money for a new school in October 1954.

Magistrates of the Warren County Quarterly court, Monday, urged the Board of School Commissioners to rush completion of a Black school center at Pleasant Hill when citizens of the community said they would seek to integrate with nearby white schools if their run-down building is not replaced.

The county court voted funds for construction of a new and modern school at the location at the October 1954 term, and the money has been in the hands of the school commissioners for almost one year.

A large delegation of the communities of Blacks were present for the court session. Marvin Lusk Sr. acted as spokesman for the group, and told the court, "The delay was apparently started as an effort to bring our children into town. Well we're not coming!" "There are plenty of schools around us and we will invoke the segregation law before we'll come to town!" Lusk explained that about 50 students are enrolled at the school "All we ask is a two-room school with a basement or something that will serve as an auditorium and a place for the kids to eat. We're a small group out there, but we're happy and we want to stay," he concluded.

Howard Prater, 11th district magistrate rose to the defense of the Black citizens. "These people have been mistreated," he said. "They're a different color, but their hearts are just as big. A horse wouldn't use their present building for a stall. The building is old and falling apart and there's not even drinking water on the grounds. Unless immediate action is taken, the children will not be able to go to school this winter, and if they do go, they'll freeze," he added. Prater was a member of the committee that investigated the condition of all county schools about a year ago.

He asked the court to go on record as urging immediate action on the building program. The resolution was worded by Squire Lowell and McGee and passed unanimously.

PART II Thursday November 10, 1955: School at Pleasant Hill vetoed; the state asks for consolidation.

The Black citizens of the Pleasant Hill Community were notified late

Tuesday that the State Board had vetoed plans for construction of the school and recommended consolidation Bernard School in town.

Funds for the school were vetoed at the October 1954 term of circuit court; however construction of a plant had been delayed pending recommendation. A letter from the state advised: "The delay in replying to your request to construct a two-teacher Black school in the Pleasant Hill Community has been due to our desire to study the situation in your county. Two people have visited this particular school and the community, and it is our recommendation that the children who are now attending the Pleasant Hill School, as well as those who would attend it in the future, can be adequately educated by attending Bernard School in McMinnville." Six reasons were listed: (1) The city Board of Education has agreed to accept the Pleasant Hill children as well as any other Black student at the Bernard School without cost to the county. (2) County school buses now pick up the older brothers and sisters of these students and haul them to the Bernard High School. These same buses, together with the one now used exclusively for Pleasant Hill School could transport all the children to Bernard at very little additional cost. The distance from the Pleasant Hill Community to Bernard is only about five miles. (3) It is entirely probable that within three of four years The Pleasant Hill School would have to be abandoned. Since most parents will want better educational opportunities than can be provided in a two-teacher school. (4) The Bernard School already has facilities available, such as lunch room, gymnasium, auditorium, and the likes, which could never be made available in a small school. Parents naturally want their children to attend the school which offers most advantages to them. We believe the Bernard School can meet this obligation when two additional rooms have been constructed. It is understood that the City Board of Education is willing to provide these rooms now. (5) Since the children of the Pleasant Hill Community will attend high school at Bernard, it seems reasonable to assume that if they completed their elementary school work at Bernard, they would be more inclined to remain in school until they finish the twelfth grade than they would if they attend a small country school. (6) There was a suggestion that the Pleasant Hill children could not dress as well as the city children and therefore they would not want to come to McMinnville. It was my impression, after visiting both schools that there is practically no distinction between the two groups as to their dress and personal habits at the present time. (7) Finally, your attention should be directed to the fact that a small school with an enrollment of fifty or fewer pupils can never operate a satisfactory lunch program. The feeding of a larger number of children will bring about certain economies in over head costs that can be applied toward better food services in the larger center. More over, there are always some children who may require free lunches, and wherever this is true, the free lunches can be provided more satisfactorily in schools where a large number of children patronize the school lunch room than in small centers.

Professor Howard Martin and student John Hudgins

Bernard High School History

The Schools prior to Bernard High School were in August 1890 a fire destroyed a portion of the old Waters and Walling College Building, then being used as a school for Blacks, located at the end of Church Street in the eastern part of McMinnville. After the fire the town disposed of its interest in the property and erected a frame building on Egypt Street as a school for Blacks. This building also was destroyed by fire a few years later. Bernard was also destroyed by fire in 1945. When this happened the students were allowed to complete their education at East End Drive Church of Christ and Saint Mary's Baptist Church, both on East Main Street.

In the summer of 1921, Professor J. E. Wood, principal of the City School for Negroes, having investigated the Rosenwald Building Program, invited the Committee to McMinnville in interest of building an adequate plant for his people. Mr. Robert E. Clay of the State Department of Education with some other representatives came to the city where they met Mr. J. D. Elkins, Mr. Joe Morford and Mr. Harold Evans. During the meeting, they planned a campaign for building funds. Mr. Elkins, the main speaker, expressed very forcefully, the need of an adequate school building for the Negroes of McMinnville. Mr. Morford and Mr. Evans argued the same good purpose. Then Mr. Robert E. Clay opened the Rosenwald fund to the building purpose of a Negro high school at McMinnville.

In the fall of 1921 the Building Committee composed of Mr. J. D. Elkins, Who was the Mayor of McMinnville; Mr. Arthur Wrightsman, Secretary; Mr. Harry Stubblefield, Chairman; Messrs. Charley Womack, W. H. Reeder, J. A. Seaman and Dr. M. D. Meadows purchased the present site and a seven teacher school building was erected.

Among the Negro citizens who contributed money and labor were: Messrs. Alpha Young, Peter Robinson, Tom Spencer, Press Malone, Sam Leftrict, Steve Speers, Oney Brown, George Huggins, Joe Huggins and Tom Snelling.

In January 1922, Professor J. E. Wood, with the cooperation of his efficient staff of teachers entered the new building amidst the applause and well wishes of the community. A few months later the school was named in honor of O. H. Bernard, The Rosenwald agent who gave so unstintingly his time and money to make this school a success.

Bernard High school as we know it has been in existence for forty seven (47) years, 1921 to 1968. It was used for K-5th Grades during the 1964-1965 year. Segregation started during the 1964 and 1965 year of school, so the school system decided to make use of the building. The area of black teachers in the classroom was over. Even though some of the Black teachers and principal moved to other schools throughout the county, they retired soon after, and there were no other Black teachers to join in.

School Song

Written by A. L. Guerard Sr.

Hail Dear Old Bernard
Thee We Cherish And Adore
And As The Years Pass
We Will Love Thee More

In The Wild World Yonder
Are Your Sons And Daughters Too
They Will Crave Your Percepts
They Will Ee'r Be True

Bernard Dear Old Bernard
May You Ee'r Defend The Light
Bernard Dear Old Bernard
Dear Old Green And White

School Colors

Purple & Gold—1921-1949
Green & White—1949-1965

Principals

Professor J. E. Wood   **Mr. Roy S. Spencer**
Professor J. E. Turner   **Professor Kelly**
Professor Andrew M. Gilbert   Professor Pitts
Professor Charles Dixion   Professor S. M. Stamps Sr.

Teachers

Mrs. Gladys Spencer Locke
Mrs. Mai B. Locust
Mr. Mack L. Young
Mrs. Jessie Crabtree
Mrs. Sadie Martin
Mrs. Jessie M. Flynt
Mrs. Henrietta Bates Curtis
Mrs. Sydna R. Batey
Mr. Ivy Malberry
Mr. Harold Flynt
Miss Irene Young
Miss Clara L. Young
Mrs. Easter Williams Mays
Ms. Lizzie Burton
Ms. Ellen Howell
Ms. Lula Garrett
Ms. Virginia Durley

Ms. Jessica Greene
Miss Edna E. Etter
Mr. Charles A. Dalton
Mrs. Bertha Shockley
Mrs. Mollie Lusk
Mrs. Lula Maynard
Ms. Edith Bates
Mrs. Bessie T. Gwynn
Mrs. Nina Stamps
Mr. Howard Martin
Mrs. Georgia Williams Watkins
Ms. Gladys Wood
Ms. Mae Bell Davidson
Mrs. Effie Wood
Mr. Milton Malone
Ms. Jessie Gwynn
Ms. Livy D. Hall

PTA Presidents

Mrs. Mary Isabell
Mrs. Pearl Bates

Mrs. Frances Bonner
Ms. Juanita Martin

Cooks

Mrs. Vanley Rowan
Mrs. Oweter Spencer
Mrs. Kenzie Mae Myers
Mrs. Lottie Head

Mrs. Shula B. Smith
Mrs. Margaret Leftwich
Mrs. Viola Lowe

Custodians

Mr. Eulous Martin
Mr. Robert Bonner 'Bub'
Mr. Herbert Brown
Mr. Grant Ervin
Mr. Thomas Rowan
Mr. Jay Martin

Mr. Moffit Page
Mr. Miner Gardner
Mr. Jim Greene
Mr. Willie Greene
Mr. James Greene
Mr. Clarence Worthington

Largest Class

1958-22 Members

Smallest Class

1932-3 Members

Teachers with Longest Service

Mrs. Sydna Batey—62 Years
Mrs. Bessie T. Gwynn—44 Years
Mrs. Edna E. Etter—43 Years
Mrs. Mai Locust—40 Years
Mrs. Gladys Spencer Locke—40 Years

Built around the theme, "Build and Educate for a Better World," the program included several choral numbers by various musical organizations of the school. The Bernard choral groups were noted for being outstanding in their field, back in 1949.

1949 — 1965

BERNARD SCHOOL

Bernard To Play Five Home Games (Sept. 1958)

Local fans of the Bernard Tigers are in for a treat this year with five of the teams' nine gridiron contests being scheduled at the home stadium, S. M. Stamps Sr., principal revealed this week.

Stamps and Coach Charles Dalton attended the Middle Tennessee Conference, at which the playing schedule for mid state colored teams was formed, last week at Centerville. Both Dalton and Stamps stated that they were well pleased with the schedule set up for the Tigers.

The Tigers will open play with Tullahoma, there, on September 10. Their first home game is with Lebanon, and will be played on September 25. Winchester will furnish the opposition for Bernard's homecoming game on October 16. Dalton said it is hoped that a post-season game can be scheduled, either here or away, on November 14.

The Complete Tiger schedule of play is as follows:

Sept. 10 . . . . Tullahoma . . . . There
Sept. 18 . . . . Carthage . . . . There
Sept. 25 . . . . Lebanon . . . . Here
Oct. 2 . . . . Lewisburg . . . . Here
Oct. 6 . . . . South Pittsburg . . . There
Oct. 16 . . . . Winchester* . . . Here
Oct. 23 . . . . Fayetteville . . . . Here
Oct. 31 . . . . Gallatin . . . . There
Nov. 6 . . . . Shelbyville . . . . Here
Nov. 14 . . . . Open . . . .

* Homecoming

In the 1950's BHS would hold their football games at Memorial Stadium, because there was no place to call their own.

Veterans' Day Is Observed At Bernard (1958)

"The Horrors of War" as related by three Korean War veterans who actually experienced action on the field of battle highlighted the observance of Veterans Day at Bernard School on Tuesday.

S. M. Stamps, Sr., The school principal, said that a large number of local colored residents filled the auditorium for the program, which opened at 8 a. m.

The three veterans taking part in the program were Charles Peppers, Wilson Martin and Leroy Rowan. Rowan holds the Purple Heart for wounds received in action. Each of the three veterans, who are currently taking veterans training at the school, related their experiences in 10-minute talks, Stamps stated.

Opening with the presentation of prepared papers on "The Horrors of War" by the freshman class, the one-hour program was concluded with a talk on world peace and a prayer by the principal.

Sturgis Monroe Stamps Sr.

Principal: S. M. Stamps, Born in Winchester, Tennessee: reared in Sallisaw, Oklahoma. Professor Stamps was married to a teacher by the name of Nina Dobbins. In 1948 the Superintendent of (Black) education in Tennessee contacted Professor Stamps. Stamps was appointed Principal of the segregated Bernard High School, where he remained until school integration got under way at McMinnville City High School, and Central High School. Stamps served two years as Assistant Principal at City High before he retired in 1966. Professor was the first black person to become assistant Principal in Warren County after schools were integrated.

In the early 1950's Professor Stamps and Eulous Martin were instrumental in starting the Pleasant Hill Fair. Howard Martin was the Principal of the Pleasant Hill School.

The (Leroy Ramsey Gym) was erected in 1951 and the site was used for Bernard's very first basketball team. Football had already been a part of the students few extra curricular activities. In the summer months, students in the community around Bernard swam in the Collins River, and there was a history of drownings. In the 1950's a swimming pool was put on the school property, so the gymnasium opened all summer to provide recreation for the black children.

Professor S. M. Stamps was the driving force behind the success of Bernard High School, during his reign.

We don't remember anytime when he was out of uniform; a suit, white shirt, bow tie and dress shoes.

Mrs. Sydna Ruth Cope Batey (Martin)

Born in McMinnville, Tennessee in 1906, Sydna went to Bernard High School were she graduated with two other students. Later she went to College the summer after High School.

She was sixteen years old when she attended (A & I), now Tennessee State University and received her teaching certificate. She taught for the first time at an East Tennessee school for one year. Then she returned home to Warren County to teach. After settling down and sinking roots she met and married Livingston "Livy" Cope. She would later Marry Sam Batey around the 1950's.

Her first few years teaching were at Smartt Station School then at Cummings Chapel. The schoolhouse for blacks was one room. The Copes lived a quarter of a mile away in a country home during the week, and on the weekends they'd return to their house in McMinnville. This went on for about six or seven years. Underprivileged black children were taught at this school also.

Mrs. Sydna later joined the Bernard teaching staff. She taught fifth and sixth grades until the school closed because of school integration.

Mrs. Sydna Batey at this time taught at West Elementary School from 1968 until 1971. She could have retired in 1968 but choose to continue on. She began teaching at home with Adult Students, after leaving West Elementary.

Mrs. Sydna sang in the church choir and played piano, fished when having the chance and enjoyed life to the fullest. This woman taught up until her untimely death in 1987. She lived to be eighty-one years old. "She was another influence on my life," says Wayne Wolford "I was one of her students in 1960 in the sixth grade before moving back to Saint Louis." She was a warm caring individual, and when she spoke, you listened. It was pretty hard to teach a group of youngsters when just a few feet away stood a playground where football, basketball or softball were being played. There were times when someone would climb the fences in order to retrieve a ball off the roof of the school. Mrs. Sydna accomplished a feat that is hard to reckon with. She taught in Warren County for sixty-four of the sixty-five years as a teacher. There are a lot of her students living here today. She has made a wonderful impact on us all. Mrs. Sydna was definitely a teacher's teacher.

Mrs. Sydna Batey

Top—Prof. Stamps, B. Starkey, Robert Blevins, Charles Settles,
M. Lusk, J. Settles, T. Weeden, and Mack Young.
Middle row—H. Lusk, Franklin Womack, Harold Thomas,
H Shockley, Elzie Vaughn, C. Shockley.
Bottom-Charles Crabtree, Jimmy Ramsey, Charles Womack,
J. McGee, Vernon Ramsey, Tommy Reynolds, Sammy Young.

Bessie Taylor Gwynn (1895-1980)

Bessie was born in Athens, Alabama on February 17, 1895. Born into poverty only thirty-two years after the emancipation proclamation freed her ancestors. Gwynn like most other blacks of her time, had little hope of an education or advancement beyond some form of menial labor.

Her father was a tenant farmer whose yearly income barely provided the necessities to survive, but somehow her parents saw fit that she would obtain a basic education by sending her to Trinity School, a private institution for blacks run by the American Missionary Association. While she attained a basic elementary education, the experience also whetted her appetite for more learning. She moved to Nashville in 1911 and graduated from a normal school in 1915, which was actually the High school of Fisk University.

Her Warren County ties came when she was contacted by Professor Spears from McMinnville in regard to a teaching job at the black high school. Gwynn accepted at once, realizing the need to repay her school debts, thus starting her on a life long career.

The teaching conditions facing a female teacher in Warren County in 1915 were bleak at best. The school building was a small frame structure located on the south side of Egypt Alley an area now owned by Burroughs-Ross and Colville Company. The building had no electricity and contained approximately 250students, when everyone attended, which was rare, because most kids had to help at home in order to survive. From all indications, she accepted the conditions with optimism and enthusiasm. It was a difficult task to inspire her students to obtain a good education. Some of the parents of those attending could neither read nor write, and had never had employment requiring those skills. With little urging or inspiration from parents, students were not likely to have a great desire to get an education.

Motivation required a unique person to instill the students with a desire to better their role in life. Bessie Gywnn was just that person. Former United States Ambassador to Finland and former student, Carl T. Rowan, had this to say about Mrs. Gwynn: "Among the things that I did not have was electricity in the little frame house that my father built. It was her inspiration, that inspired me to spend many hours squinting beside a kerosene lamp reading Shakespeare and Thoreau".

Mrs. Gwynn seemed to have complete control of any situation she endeavored. I remember as a child admiring this thin-framed lady, (and I do mean lady). The way she talked, smiled, and walked. It was almost impossible to keep up; with the rapid pace she maintained. If

I had stayed in McMINNVILLE instead of returning to St. Louis I would have had the honor of being taught by this extraordinary human being. Such is life" (Wayne Wolford). Bessie T. Gwynn, teacher of Home Economics and English plus Music, married Roy Gwynn and was buried by his side in 1980.

Charles A. 'Coach' Dalton

Sept. 1936-June 1998

Charles Allen Dalton, son of Ella Lyles and Melvin Dalton was born September 30, 1936 in Sumner County, TN.

'Coach' Dalton could have been a Harlem Globetrotters if he had chosen, but stayed home, preferring to spend his life helping others.

Dalton began his career in Warren County at the age of twenty-two, when fresh out of college, he took the job of teacher/coach at Bernard High School in 1957, then an all Black school. This was the start of a lustrous career.

He was a standout athlete at Mississippi Valley State, where he excelled in Basketball and Track. He was inducted into the Mississippi Valley State Sports Hall of Fame. Dalton was named to the All-State Basketball Team in Mississippi during his four years of college eligibility, and most importantly an Honor Student. Dalton was part of the school's first graduating class in 1957.

His accomplishments on the baseball diamond caught the eye of Big League scouts, who offered him a job with the Chicago Cubs. He turned the offer down.

A little known team of traveling basketball players then approached 'Coach'. The Harlem Clowns offered him a lucrative contract to play with the team, but he turned that down to continue his education. The team would later become known as the world famous Harlem Globetrotters.

Sometimes during a basketball practice at Bernard, 'Coach' Dalton would show one of his many skills, such as dunking two basketballs at the same time.

Dalton served as coach for thirty-nine years in the Warren County school system before he retired in 1994. During his career, he taught and coached at Bernard High School, Southside Elementary, Warren County Middle School and Warren County High Schools.

His coaching spanned several sports including basketball, track, softball and football. He also taught Industrial Arts and Physical Education.

'Coach' Dalton did show McMinnville his baseball talents with the McMinnville 'Rocket' Semi-Pro Baseball team for two years in 1972 and 1973, playing the outfield and first base.

A good friend in sports was Lester Caldwell, the retired Vice President of First National Bank in McMinnville. Lester remembers when 'Coach' started playing fast pitch softball over at the fairgrounds. "He thought it would be easy to hit this kind of pitch, says Lester, compared to a regular baseball, but he found out different. I watched him in the first game we played and he was so frustrated, because he struck out all three times at bat." Charlie was a competitor, and there was no way this was going to get the best of him, so he started to bunt his way on base and found out he was almost unstoppable. Charlie was a left handed batter, and had exceptional speed, so by the time he laid down a bunt he was already at first base before a play was made on him, because of his long strides."

'Coach' was a kid person. If a kid needed help in any way 'Coach' was there. During the 1950's and 60's, kids would eagerly wait by the swimming pool for a late model 'Beetle' (Volkswagen) to turn the corner so they could enjoy the water activities for the day. They knew the moment they saw the 'Beetle,' 'Coach' was in it. This was just like someone waiting for Christmas everyday. There weren't many activities for young Blacks in Warren County during these years, but 'Coach' always opened the Bernard Pool and the Leroy Ramsey Gym so that the kids would have something to do. There was basketball, inside the gym when it wasn't too hot, and when the weather permitted the courts were use outside. Swimming was a good pass time. There was also time for boxing, and dancing the latest dance craze to the 'Juke Box.' Mr. Dalton was a very good role model, and person. We thought the world of 'Coach' Dalton.

He knew his sports, but was not listened to by his peers in the school system. He could have easily been a head coach at the High school, but was not given the opportunity. Instead he was always called upon to be an assistant at City High. Warren County wasn't ready for a Black head coach.

This man could stand flat-footed under the basket and jump straight up and dunk a basketball. The most amazing thing I'd ever seen was this man could dunk two (2) basketballs at one time. He would put on a show for us sometimes. This was an attention getter. Just seeing, talking to, and having the privilege to know this great man was a dream come true for many who felt his presence. He was our Michael Jordan, or at that time 'Dr. J' (Julius Ervin).

'Coach' did some volunteer coaching after he retired from the school system. He was always helping out the junior league teams.

In addition to his school coaching and teaching duties, Dalton officiated and directed various sports leagues around the county and was involved in youth basketball camps.

In light of his devotion to athletics in Warren County, The Warren County High School Gymnasium was named in Dalton's honor. This showed that he did what he said while he was alive—earned respect. The gym is one of the few known public buildings named after a Black American in Warren County, one of the first being Huddleston-Jennings American Legion Post #208. (Noted as a large establishment). A photo and short story in plaque form are mounted on the wall in front of the gymnasium lobby.

Dalton married Frankie Mae (Biles) Dalton, they had two sons, Allen & Charles Dalton Jr.; three daughters, Liesa, Terri, and Debra.

'Coach' died in the summer of 1998 from a bout with cancer. He was sixty-three years old. With his passing, he leaves behind a legacy of public service and an indelible mark on Warren County Sports. Helping others and attain respect were his main goals in life. He loved kids, and because of his influence over them, their lives were changed for the better.

He was a member of East End Drive Church of Christ. Charles A. Dalton died at River Park Hospital following a bout with cancer. He was 63 years old. 'Coach' Charles Allen Dalton rests in peace at Gardens of Memorial Cemetery.

'Coach' Charlie A. Dalton believed that respect was most important; respect is something that had to be earned. He was well respected in Warren County.

Black (Colored) Schools in Warren County

Warren County, Leesburg, Oak Grove, Bibey, Pleasant Hill, Cope's Chapel, Hopewell, Corinth, Hiawassee, Finger's Chapel, Martin's Chapel, Allizona, Cummings Chapel, Walker House, Viola, Burks and Bolden Green.

Bernard High School

Mrs. Edna Etter

Mrs. Mollie Monroe Lusk

Bernard High School field trip at the Coca-Cola plant.

1946 Bernard High School football team.

Students of Bernard High School; Henrietta Thomas—
Elois Sutton-Anna Mae Perkins

Chapter 10

Photos

1960 Boy Scouts; Karl Ramsey and Jerry Martin.
Club scout leader James Moody Evans.

Boy Scouts; L-R Pee Wee, Tommy, Mark, Arbury,
Jerry, Larry, and Ralph

Black funeral home before High's funeral home would take
Blacks into their main facility.

Mrs. Sue Wood

Phillip Smith, Mary Sanders, E.B. Malone

Mark is the director of Tennessee federal Bureau Investigation for the state of Tennessee pictured with his sister Kathy, and his mother Thelma Gwyn.

Doctor Terry Etter—Dentist

Ella Richmond Store Manager for Districts

Mrs. C's clothing store owners are Roy and Mary Curtis 2010

Warren County First Black Head coaches from left to right
Coach Jackson, basketball coach for Boyd school,
Coach Malcolm Montgomery—basketball coach for
Warren County high school, Coach Johnson—football coach
for Warren County high school.

Rob Wood Auto detail owner

Rev. Jerry Martin and Rainbow Coalition leader Rev. Jesse Jackson

Baby Freddy Nowlin and Mother Lera (Curtis) Nowlin

Christine (Strode) Grayson

Angellette Gerard, E.B. Malone and Marjorie Thacker
presenting a NAACP award.

Cowan Roberts; restaurant business owner on spring street.
1950s through 1960s.

'T. C.'
Terry Cope; internationally known comedian.

Danny Smith
Vice President of Security Federal Bank and community leader.

CPSIA information can be obtained at www.ICGtesting.com
Printed in the USA
LVOW080707220213

321143LV00002B/7/P